WINE REGIONS OF
THE SOUTHERN HEMISPHERE

Wine Regions of the Southern Hemisphere

HARM JAN DE BLIJ

Rowman & Allanheld
PUBLISHERS

ROWMAN & ALLANHELD

Published in the United States of America in 1985
by Rowman & Allanheld, Publishers
(A division of Littlefield, Adams & Company)
81 Adams Drive, Totowa, New Jersey 07512

Library of Congress Cataloging in Publication Data
de Blij, Harm J.
  Wine regions of the southern hemisphere.
  Bibliography: p.
  Includes index.
  1. Wine and wine making—Southern Hemisphere.
I. Title.
TP559.S645D4 1984   641.22′2′091814   84-17949
ISBN 0-8476-7390-1

85 86 87 / 10 9 8 7 6 5 4 3 2 1

Printed in the United States of America

CONTENTS

Cartography
by
Florida Resources and Environmental
Analysis Center
Florida State University

James Anderson
Cartographic Director

ILLUSTRATIONS

Plates

FOREWORD

This is a book about viticultural frontiers. The overwhelming majority of the world's wine consumers, and the great majority of producers, are located in the Northern Hemisphere. All the most familiar wine regions lie in Europe and North America. Bordeaux, Beaujolais, Chablis, the Mosel-Rhine, Rioja, Napa and Sonoma are commonplace in the northern consumer's mental atlas. But when it comes to the Southern Hemisphere, the geographic reference is generally much less precise. Southern Hemisphere wines tend still to be identified mainly as "Australian" or "Chilean."

And yet the regional diversity of Southern Hemisphere viticulture is enormous. From Andean slopes to Australian plains, from Argentinian piedmonts to South African shores, the regional geography of Southern Hemisphere winegrowing is varied and full of contrasts. The regional names may not be as well known on world markets as their northern counterparts, but their wines evince the strength of regional identities. To be somewhat familiar with the Southern Hemisphere's wine regions is to greatly enhance one's appreciation for the southern wines.

Toward this modest objective *Wine Regions of the Southern Hemisphere* is directed: to contribute to the familiarity and visibility of Southern Hemisphere wine regions, and to describe appreciatively a sampling of the wines these regions produce. The story of viticulture's diffusion into southern South America, South Africa, Australia, and New Zealand is a fabulous saga, a history of pioneering, of desperate failure, and of glorious success. Religion and commerce, altruism and greed, disease and disaster, luck and misfortune all played their parts. Out of the frontier era arose six major national wine industries, each displaying, today, substantial regional differentiation, a sign of maturity. Two of Australia's major wine regions, the historic

Hunter Valley and the declining Barossa Valley, probably are the hemisphere's best known (or rather, least obscure) overseas. But Australia's Coonawarra and Margaret River districts (to name just two) are as worthy of international attention, if not more so. New Zealand's Auckland hinterland and Hawke's Bay district, South Africa's Stellenbosch and Paarl, Argentina's Rio Negro-Neuquén (in addition to Mendoza), and Chile's Maipo and Rapel districts are among wine regions of similar interest, their wines often distinctive and regionally representative. The wine industry of Brazil is not well known—the southern state of Rio Grande do Sul produces some noted wines—and Zimbabwe's wine areas are not on many mental maps of Southern Hemisphere viticulture. Such are the topics of this volume.

One of the singular pleasures accruing from a serious interest in viniculture lies in the discovery not only of interesting wines, but also of people who share this avocation. After I wrote *Wine: A Geographic Appreciation* (Rowman & Allanheld, 1983) I came to know a circle of colleagues, geographers and others, whose enthusiasm and support proved that wine lovers have a special bond. That circle has grown even larger as the present book progressed, and no mere formal acknowledgment could adequately express my gratitude.

In the United States, at the University of Miami, I was assisted by Mr. Donald Rallis, whose enthusiasm for the Geography Department's viticulture course led to his field trip to the Cape wine country and the collection of valuable data for the South Africa chapter, and by Ms. Sharon Phillipps. Mr. John W. Ladd, a graduate of the Colorado School of Mines (where we met during my assignment as Visiting Professor), took an interest in viticulture and sent me first-hand field notes from Argentina, where he was based at Mendoza City. Mrs. Nancy Muller translated a manuscript on Chilean winegrowing. Dr. Robert Hosmon, Professor of English at the University of Miami and noted wine columnist, alerted me numerous times to wine-related developments in the Southern Hemisphere and gave me much of the benefit of his own tour to Stellenbosch and Paarl. Mr. and Mrs. Marc Rudolph of New York City, who represent a major Brazilian wine firm, secured historical data, photographs, and vintage information from Rio Grande do Sul. Dr. James W. King of the University of Utah sent me useful material on several Southern Hemisphere wine regions, as did Dr. Harold A. Winters of Michigan State University, Dr. John J. Baxevanis of East Stroudsburg State College, Professor W. S. Barnard of the University of Stellenbosch, and Dr. Edwin W. Snider of the National Geographic Society. I am grateful to Dr. John P. Dickenson of the University of Liverpool, United Kingdom, whose own writing on Brazil (cited in the bibliography) was among the first in English to focus on that country's wine indusry, and who shared much additional information with me. I also thank Dr. Henry Wright of the University of Michigan, who gave me the opportunity to taste two Madagascar wines.

In Chile, Mr. Pablo Guilisasti Gana responded with great efficiency to my queries relating to wine classification issues, and forwarded to me the government's new legal code relating to viticulture. I also thank Ms. Andriana Nieto of Viña Undurraga, Mr. Jorge Prieto Correa of ProChile, Mr. Miguel Rafael Fuenzalida of the Cooperativa Agricola Vitivinicola de Talca, Mr. Juan Manuel Ortiz Lizarralde of Viña Linderos, and Ms. Elizabeth Diaz Retamal of the Asociacion de Exportadores y Embotelladores de Vinos of Chile. In Argentina, Lic. Gustavo A. Pescatori of the Instituto Nacional de Vitivinicultura provided me with cartographic, photographic, and legal documentation in response to my questions about geographic organization of the industry. In Brazil, Dr. Juan L. Carrau of the Instituto de Biotecnologia sent me relevant items in connection with the institute's vinicultural work, and Mr. Giuseppe Nahaissi, General Manager of Almadén (Brazil) provided information on National Distillers' Brazilian venture and alerted me to the recent work of José Oswaldo Albano do Amarante.

In South Africa, I acknowledge with gratitude the hospitality of the Stellenbosch Farmers' Winery and the Cooperative Winegrowers' Association (K.W.V.), and especially the assistance of Mr. David Hughes, Mr. Frans Malan, and Ms. Lucille van der Wiele. The chapter dealing with South Africa was reviewed in detail by Mr. John Platter, whose comments and suggestions were invariably relevant and useful. In Australia, Dr. Bryce Rankine, Dean of the Faculty of Oenology at Roseworthy Agricultural College, commented incisively on Chapter 8, and I deeply appreciate his productive and helpful annotations. In New Zealand, Mr. Peter Saunders, Editor of the *New Zealand Wineglass*, has been in some way involved in this effort almost from the beginning.

Over several years this pleasant excursion has been shared with my wife, Bonnie, and together we spent many hours in sunny vineyards and fragrant cellars. She has much the better palate, and I owe to her many an observation printed in these pages. To her go the greatest thanks of all, not least for her patience as the notes so pleasantly taken in the field were slowly committed to paper in the study.

The cartography for this volume was prepared by the staff of the Florida Resources and Environmental Analysis Center, Florida State University, under the direction of Mr. Jim Anderson. The cartographers were Mr. Peter Krafft, Mr. Ken White, and Ms. Wendy Wotring. The work of Ms. Kathy Kelleher and Ms. Patty Wilson, both of the University of Miami, also is gratefully acknowledged. I recognize with appreciation the assistance so freely and frequently given by my friend and colleague, Dr. Peter O. Muller, Chairman of the Department of Geography at the University of Miami. I am deeply appreciative of the assistance given by the National Geographic Society, where I presently serve as editor.

I also thank the staff of Rowman & Allanheld, who transformed my pages of manuscript, sets of labels, and stacks of maps into this handsome book. Again Mrs. Janet Johnston did the expert editing, Mrs. Linda Holzman was responsible for handling the art work and assembling the book, and Mrs. Tobi Krutt saw it through the production stages. My peripatetic editor, Mr. Paul A. Lee, shares my enthusiasm for the subject of this book and supervised its transition accordingly.

As readers will perceive, a geographic viewpoint prevails in *Wine Regions of the Southern Hemisphere*. I take this opportunity to acknowledge my extraordinarily good fortune in having been able to pursue a career in this fascinating, versatile, and endlessly stimulating field. One of geography's principal dimensions lies in the study of the relationships between human societies and natural environments. Certainly wine is an appropriate geographic topic, because it results from a series of processes that begin with soil and climate and turn on culture and tradition. Wine, at its best, has been described as the summation of a region, a distinctive representation of the place and the people creating it. Hence the focus in this book is on the Southern Hemisphere's wine *regions* and the wines they produce. A joyous geography it is.

1

SOUTHERN CLIMES FOR NORTHERN VINES

Centuries ago the unknown lands of the Southern Hemisphere fired the imagination of explorers and drew the first European settlers. Southward along the west and east coasts of South America they came, over Atlantic waters to southern Africa, across the Indian Ocean to Australia, and thence to New Zealand. In the wake of these pioneers followed migrations that would transform the geographies of those distant regions. As the European imprint strengthened, the modern map took shape. In southern South America, scattered Indian populations were engulfed by the rising human tide from Iberian and other Mediterranean shores. South Africa became black Africa's most "Europeanized" country. In Australia, the indigenous peoples, never numerous, were no match for the invading settlers. New Zealand's Maori lost their primacy in the Land of the Long White Cloud.

Pervasive as the European diffusion was, the southernmost countries of the Southern Hemisphere never grew as populous as their European sources. Only Argentina, with a population approaching 30 million, and South Africa, also with nearly 30 million (4.5 million European) have substantial populations by European standards. Chile has just 12 million inhabitants, continent-sized Australia some 15 million, and New Zealand about 3 million (0.3 million Maori).[1] During five centuries of European emigration, distance proved a powerful intervention.

With the European settlers came European cultures, and the lands of the Southern Hemisphere set out in contrasting social directions. In Chile, southernmost outpost on South America's west coast route, a complex cultural mosaic evolved in which Spanish legacies are strongest, but Italian and other sources are influential. South Africa's European origins are chiefly Dutch and British, but with an important French infusion. Australians speak English, although one-fifth of the population has mainland European ancestors. New Zealand has often been described as the most English country outside England.

Although the settlers came from diverse European sources, they did share certain cultural traits. Whether they were British or Spanish, Protestant or Catholic, farmers or miners, and whether they came as free immigrants or in bondage as exiles, most had a taste for spirits. And among them were some who wanted not just alcohol but something superior: wine. In this respect they were like Europeans everywhere in the New World, but the Southern Hemisphere was less amenable to this desire than other realms. Here stood no wild vines bearing grapes with which winemaking experiments could be carried out. When European explorers first reached North America, they found species of both subgenera of *Vitis* growing in profusion. The wines yielded by their grapes were not satisfactory, but in the absence of alternatives they served their purpose. No such options were available south of the equator, where wild vines did not grow. Thus the history of European settlement in the Southern Hemisphere involves the story of the introduction of the grapevine into regions where no vines had ever stood.

The earliest plantings of the vine south of the equator occurred in South America, but not in the regions famed for their wines today. The subjugation of the Inca and other Indian peoples of the Andes channeled the Spanish conquest southward, and of course the church played a key role in the expansion of Spanish hegemony. Religious ceremony required the use of wine, and Catholic priests were among the first to plant the grapevine for this purpose. The initial plantings may have been in the cool Andean highlands near Cuzco, in the Inca heartland, perhaps before 1540. But those vineyards were not to endure. The Andean environment proved unsuitable for viticulture, and the Indian peoples preferred their traditional beer to the Europeans' wine. Since Peru's European population clustered in the lower zone west of the Andes, facing the Pacific Ocean, Lima emerged as the country's capital and largest city. Thus the Jesuit priest who selected the coastal oasis of Ica, south of Lima, for Peru's vineyards had the better judgment.

Peru was not destined to become a major winegrowing country, however. Peruvian wines briefly found their way to European markets early in the present century, prior to World War I, but their novelty soon wore off. Peru's southern neighbor, Chile, was to become one of the Southern Hemisphere's major wine producers—but here, too, viticulture had inauspicious beginnings. Again the vineyards were planted for altar wine; to supply the settler population with table wines was a secondary objective. For three centuries after its timid beginnings the Chilean wine industry was hostage to the church, and developed little.

Winegrowing began in Argentina during the same period (the mid-1500s), and here, too, the vines were introduced in relatively inhospitable areas. Scholars are unsure whether the first vines arrived from Chile or came via Bolivia through the valley of the Humahuaca River, but they agree that the vineyards were in existence by 1560. They probably stood in the northern provinces of Santiago del Estero and Córdoba, far from the country's modern viticultural heartland. The industry remained dormant for centuries, until it was vitalized by the arrival, in the nineteenth century, of a wave of Italian immigrants.

Brazil, too, hosted the vine early, but its wine industry succeeded much later. Spanish Jesuits planted grapevines (probably brought from Argentina) in what is today the southern state of Rio Grande do Sul in the 1620s. More than a century later, Portuguese immigrants introduced new varieties from their homeland. But Brazil did not take its place as a major Southern Hemisphere wine-producing country until the twentieth century.

When Europeans intending to settle in southern Africa, Australia, and New Zealand departed from their home ports during the seventeenth and eighteenth centuries, the absence of wild vines in the southern lands was well known, and sailing ships routinely carried vine shoots as part of their cargoes. When the Dutch East India Company established its base at Cape Town in the 1650s, vines were planted in the shadow of Table Mountain almost immediately, and wine was produced before the decade had ended. The small fleet of boats that carried Australia's first permanent European settlers had grape seeds aboard and stopped at Cape Town to collect vine shoots as well as victuals. These seeds and shoots were not transported for religious purposes. The vines were planted at Cape Town and Sydney Harbor for commercial reasons—sale, not ceremony. While the small vineyards of South America remained the virtual monopoly of the priests, the wine industries of South Africa and Australia prospered.

In South Africa, the settlers were fortunate that Cape Town's environment was suitable for viticulture. Beginning in the 1680s, winegrowing received an additional boost from the arrival of hundreds of French Huguenot refugees. Many of these French families had experience in winemaking and knew how to take advantage of the Cape's favorable climate. In Australia, viticulture's beginnings were more difficult. The vines planted near Sydney Harbor were attacked by disease and fungi, and the first really successful viticulture developed decades later and 100 miles north of the city.

Given the path and direction of European settlement in the Southern Hemisphere, it is not surprising that New Zealand was settled last, and that its wine industry has been the latest to emerge. Although a churchman planted the first vines (about 1820), the commercial possibilities were initially recognized by an Australian winegrower in the 1830s. New Zealand's first wine for public consumption was made in 1840.

Thus the initial diffusion of the grapevine to those regions of the Southern Hemisphere capable of sustaining it occurred during the period from about 1550 to 1820—nearly three centuries of slow expansion, failure, and success. Little was known about the soils or climates of the regions under colonization, and much of this early viticulture was trial and error. Many of the old settings proved inhospitable, but as the settlement frontier grew, new and more favorable areas came into use. Almost everywhere, the surge of European out-migration during the nineteenth century stimulated the wine industries of the immigrant countries, and the modern historical geography of these industries begins about a century ago. Since then, Argentina has become the Southern Hemisphere's largest wine producer (and one of the five leading producers in the world); Chile's wines have gained a wide reputation for quality; Brazil's wine industry has made enormous gains, especially in recent years; South Africa's wines have gained their place among the world's best; Australia's huge potential for quality and volume has been realized; and New Zealand has begun to produce premium wines that are attracting world attention.

Environments for Viticulture

The mid-latitude zones of the Northern Hemisphere are the natural range for the genus *Vitis* and its numerous species, and the plant grew wild for tens of millions of years before people began to domesticate it. If planned winemaking (although in a rudimentary form) began in Armenia some 8000 years ago, the practice remained confined to the northern lands for more than seven millenia. Against this background the presence of the grapevine in the lands of the Southern Hemisphere seems brief indeed.

In very general terms, the grapevine prefers a moderate environment without extremes of heat or cold. In the Northern Hemisphere, the great majority of all vineyards lie in a zone between approximately 30° and 50° latitude and, more specifically, between annual isotherms 10°C (50°F) and 20°C (68°F). This zone includes all of Mediterranean Europe, where viticulture first became an agricultural specialization, much of the contiguous United States and part of southern Canada, and large areas of China and Japan. When the same perimeters are drawn across the lands of the Southern Hemisphere, a strong contrast is immediately apparent. The potential wine regions of the south are much smaller than those of North America and Eurasia. Only Australia lies substantially within the viticulture zone, but its aridity is a limiting factor.

The wine lands of the Southern Hemisphere, as the map underscores, consist of tapering, mountain-dominated South America; truncated, plateau-rimmed southern Africa; drought-dominated Australia; and exposed, insular New Zealand. In the Northern Hemisphere, winegrowing developed in Mediterranean areas where the climatic regime was (and is) characterized by a warm, dry summer that allowed the grapes to ripen. Today this climatic regime is named *Mediterranean*, and it occurs not only in southern Europe, but also in western North America. As the technology of winegrowing has evolved, the most salubrious environments have been found to lie on the margins of these Mediterranean zones: in Bordeaux where the summers are somewhat more moist, in Burgundy where the summer weather is rather cooler, and in the Napa and Sonoma valleys where a transition also prevails.

Analogous conditions are not common in the Southern Hemisphere. Chile's area of Mediterranean conditions is cut off by the Andes Mountains toward the north, and by cold and excessive moisture to the south. At South Africa's Cape, the Mediterranean zone is small (it would be larger if the landmass extended farther to the south) and the favored marginal areas, even smaller. In Australia, a Mediterranean regime prevails in two small areas, one in the general vicinity of Adelaide and the other in the far southwest, in the hinterland of Perth. Adelaide lies at the center of a cluster of important wine regions, and the area around Perth was one of Australia's modern viticultural frontiers. New Zealand's North Island has a small zone of dry-summer climate along its east coast, and here some of the country's best wines are made.

Given these limitations, it is remarkable that so much has been achieved by winegrowers in the Southern Hemisphere. In terms of environment for quality, Argentina probably is least well endowed. Yet Argentinian *vinos finos* have gained increasing recognition on international markets as good wines that can compete with premium wines from more favored regions. Chilean wines also have a deserved reputation, and South Africa's wines were in demand in Europe two centuries ago. Some Australian wines have had stunning success on European tasting circuits, and New Zealand has recently produced wines that would rank second to none.

Southern Climates

The earth's climatic regimes range from torrid equatorial to frigid polar. Climatologists, using temperature and precipitation records, seasonal patterns, and vegetative responses (among other criteria) have identified and mapped five major and a large number of smaller climatic regions. The major regions (equatorial, desert, temperate, cold, and polar) have in turn been subdivided into a total of twelve subregions, of which one is the Mediterranean type previously mentioned. On an idealized, "model" continent extending from equatorial to polar latitudes in either hemisphere, these regions and subregions would develop in predictable locations. The humid equatorial region, also called the *rainforest* for the vegetation it supports, would straddle the equator (as in fact it does in major areas of the world), giving way northward or southward to a zone of less rainy *savanna* with increasingly pronounced dry seasons. A belt of drier *steppe* would adjoin the savanna in either hemisphere, flanked in turn by a dry *desert*. Contrasts between east-coast and west-coast conditions become increasingly pronounced. Continuing poleward, the desert would yield to steppe as moisture increases again, and adjacent to the poleward steppe zone would lie the dry-summer *Mediterranean* climate so important to viticulture historically. In higher latitudes, this regime would yield to the humid *temperate* climes marked by more summer rainfall, or by the moist, cool-summer *marine west coast* climate. (The former prevails over much of the southeastern United States, and the latter dominates in coastal regions of the Northwest.) Still farther poleward, the temperate conditions would yield to the harsher winters and greater extremes of the cold or *continental* climates of the Midwest and much of Canada. Nearest to the poles lie zones of *tundra* and *polar* climate.

A comparison between this model climatic map and the real world yields some valuable insights concerning the factors that influence climatic regimes. Mountain ranges and plateaus, ocean currents warm and cold distort the pattern just described. And yet the overall distributions it represents can be discerned on the actual map of world climates (Fig. 1.1).[2] Not only are humid-equatorial conditions flanked by savanna and steppe (the African continent displays this especially well in mirror-image fashion on both sides of the equator), but Mediterranean conditions occur in both hemispheres, and approximately in the expected latitudes. Elsewhere, it is true, land elevation, irregular coastlines, and other surface features disrupt the global pattern.

The real-world contrasts between the Northern and Southern Hemispheres are especially noteworthy. The Southern Hemisphere has much less land and much more water than the Northern, especially in the higher latitudes. As a result, the entire continental climatic type, which occurs over vast regions of the Northern Hemisphere in both North America and Eurasia, does not occur at all in the Southern Hemisphere. A comparison between the two hemispheres in terms of the total land area between latitudes 30° and 50° emphasizes this contrast.

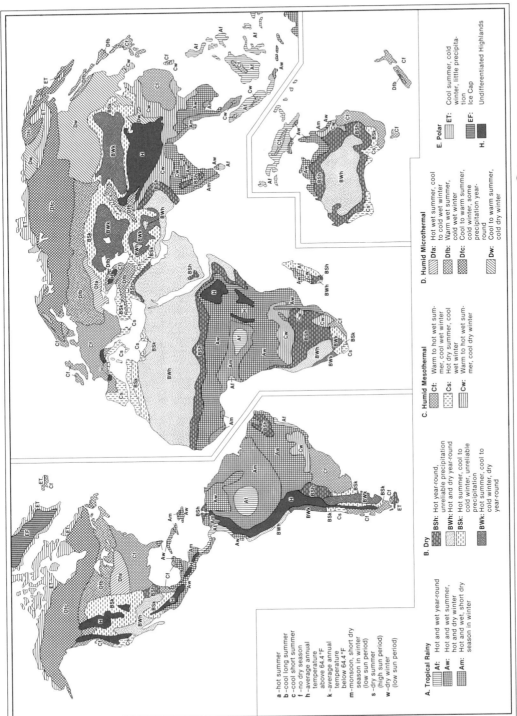

Figure 1.1. *Generalized climatic regions of the world, according to the Köppen-Geiger system of classification and regionalization.*

A. Tropical Rainy
Af: Hot and wet year-round
Aw: Hot and wet summer, hot and dry winter
Am: Hot and wet, short dry season in winter

B. Dry
BSh: Hot year-round, unreliable precipitation
BWh: Hot and dry year-round
BSk: Hot summer, cool to cold winter, unreliable precipitation
BWk: Hot summer, cool to cold winter, dry year-round

C. Humid Mesothermal
Cf: Warm to hot wet summer, cool wet winter
Cs: Hot dry summer, cool wet winter
Cw: Warm to hot wet summer, cool dry winter

D. Humid Microthermal
Dfa: Hot wet summer, cool to cold wet winter
Dfb: Warm wet summer, cold wet winter
Dfc: Cool to warm summer, cold winter, some precipitation year-round
Dw: Cool to warm summer, cold dry winter

E. Polar
ET: Cool summer, cold winter, little precipitation
EF: Ice Cap

H.   Undifferentiated Highlands

a – hot summer
b – cool long summer
c – cool short summer
f – no dry season
h – average annual temperature above 64.4°F
k – average annual temperature below 64.4°F
m – monsoon, short dry season in winter (low sun period)
s – dry summer (high sun period)
w – dry winter (low sun period)

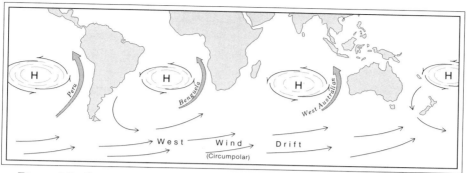

Figure 1.2. Ocean currents and pressure systems in the Southern Hemisphere.

Air masses carry to the land areas the moisture they absorb over the oceans—unless something interferes with this process. They also bring moderating temperatures and cloud cover. On the other hand, air masses can carry frosty polar conditions to lower latitudes, and many a vineyard has seen the promise of a mild spring dashed by an invasion of Arctic air.

At first glance, the peninsular-insular character of the Southern Hemisphere landmasses suggests an openness to maritime influences. But several conditions influence the process that carries moisture inland. The first of these is the temperature of the water offshore. Along the west coasts of the three continental landmasses flow three cold-water currents: the Peru (Humboldt) off South America, the Benguela off Africa, and the West Australian Current off Australia (Fig. 1.2). These currents carry subpolar cold to the shores of the Southern Hemisphere's mid-latitude lands, and they have much to do with the deserts that limit cultivation in northern Chile, South Africa–Namibia, and western Australia.

A second factor contributing to the distribution of precipitation in the wine regions of both hemispheres is the prevalence of persistent pressure systems in which vertical air movement determines whether precipitation will occur and where. The dry ocean-facing littorals of all three Southern Hemisphere landmasses are influenced not only by the cold offshore currents, but also by dominant and durable high-pressure systems centered over the ocean, in which air subsidence occurs. This means that air descends from high to lower altitudes, warming in the process and acquiring, not dropping, its moisture content. Such a stable high-pressure system exists much of the time over the Pacific Ocean, extending to the Andes' western flank; while it stays there, drought will prevail (Fig. 1.3). But the system, and similar systems in the south Atlantic and Indian oceans, does migrate with the swing of the seasons, moving north and south (and expanding and contracting somewhat) with the southern winter and summer. In the summer its control is strongest, and it seems to prevent moisture-carrying air from reaching the wine regions. During the winter it moves away and allows moisture-laden "lows" to approach.

The third spoke in the wheel of mid-latitude climate is the prevailing wind direction. The mid-latitude viticulture zones of the Southern as well as the Northern Hemisphere lie principally in the globe-girdling belt of air movement appropriately called the westerlies. This means that weather systems in this belt tend to move from west to east, and at the surface, winds from westerly quadrants blow more

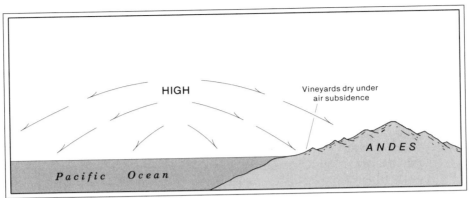

Figure 1.3. *High-pressure conditions off the Andes' western flank contribute to the summer-dry season in Chile's vineyards.*

consistently than from other directions. It explains in part why areas facing the very ocean that is the source of moisture can nevertheless be deserts: as the moisture-laden air mass approaches, it crosses the cold waters of the offshore current. Still over the water, the air is cooled, and precipitation falls—not on land, but over the water (Fig. 1.4). By the time the system reaches the coast, it is much less moist, if not virtually dry. In Chile, the wine country lies in sight of the ocean, but with the exception of some favored areas much viticulture must take place under irrigation, in the valleys of streams coming off the Andes. It is something of an environmental irony.

The westerly movement of air masses across land areas in the viticulture zone also has significance on the eastern side of the continents. Because the prevailing air movement is from inland directions, the coastal and near-coastal areas experience far less maritime influence than they would if weather systems moved in the opposite way. This has crucial consequences for the vineyards. In Australia's New South Wales, for example, the dominantly westerly air flow brings dryness to the vineyards,

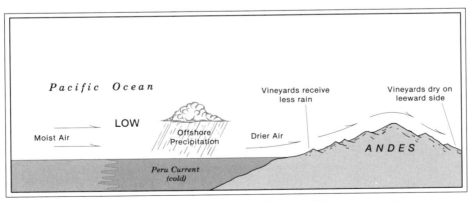

Figure 1.4. *When a moist air mass approaches the Chilean coast, its moisture content is much reduced as it traverses the cooler zone over the Peru Current.*

which is needed during the ripening and can help against diseases brought on by excessive humidity. On the other hand, the prevailing air movement can prevent moisture from reaching the vineyards, causing damaging drought and heat stress. The effect of the regime is well illustrated in the Hunter Valley, 100 miles north of Sydney and just twenty-five miles inland from the Pacific Ocean, where average annual rainfall is a mere 27 inches.

A fourth factor to be considered is the topography of the Southern Hemisphere's landmasses. Southern South America's natural environments are dominated by the towering Andes range, one of the world's great mountain barriers. Air mass movement, precipitation, temperature, and all else are controlled or strongly affected by the Andes which, east of Chile's main wine country, reach elevations above 20,000 feet in a series of parallel ranges. The Andes stand in the path of the westerlies, compensating orographically for the lost moisture over the cold ocean waters in the Peru Current. On the windward side, Chile receives moderate precipitation in its principal viticulture zone (Santiago records an average of 14 inches annually; Concepción to the south has 30 inches), and as they cross the mountain peaks the air masses sustain the Andes' permanent snow cover. (Much of the Andean chain receives moisture for its snow cover via the trade winds from Atlantic Ocean sources, not from the Pacific.) This is critical to Argentina on the lee side, where rainfall is minimal and the natural environment is a near-desert. The Andean snows feed the streams and aquifers that form the mainstays of Argentinian viticulture. What the high Andes take away in one form, they return in another (Fig. 1.5).

The climate of southern Brazil is neither dry-summer Mediterranean (as it is in the Chilean wine country) nor desert-steppe (as prevails in the irrigated Argentinian vineyards). The climatic regime in Rio Grande do Sul, Brazil's southernmost province and its chief viticulture region, is comparable to that of much of the southeastern United States: it is marked by moderate temperatures, warm summers, and year-round precipitation without a well-defined dry season. These are not ideal conditions for viticulture, but interior upland slopes in Rio Grande do Sul, and in neighboring provinces of Santa Catarina and Parana as well, moderate the temperature and humidity and enable the vine to produce.

Southern Africa does not extend nearly as far southward as does South America, nor is its physiography marked by a mountain chain of comparable dimensions. The African continent does not even reach 35° south latitude, and Cape Town, near its southern end, lies at 33° 48′ south, while Santiago, in the middle of the Chilean wine country, lies at 33° 26′S—virtually at the same latitude. Many of Chile's vineyards lie in latitudes southern Africa does not even reach, suggesting that South Africa's viticulture region is indeed truncated (Fig. 1.6). Significantly, this means that South Africa lacks much of that transitional zone between Mediterranean and more humid temperate regions where the world's best vineyards lie.

On the other hand, southern Africa's wine country is not walled off by high mountains. The Cape region is hilly, and even mountainous in places, and some vineyards are situated in spectacular valleys. But the premium regions, notably Stellenbosch and Paarl, lie open to maritime influences that allow nonirrigated vineyards to produce the finest wines.

Northward, the Cape's Mediterranean environment yields to steppe and, quickly,

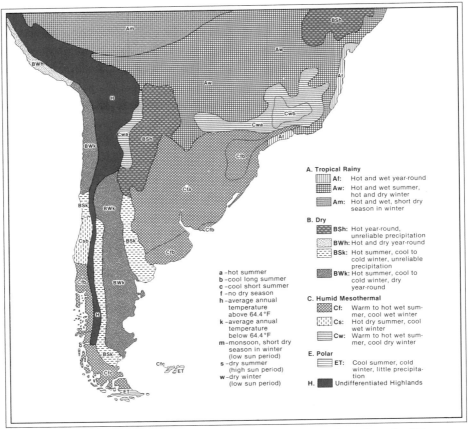

Figure 1.5. Climatic regions of southern South America, based on the Köppen-Geiger System.

to desert conditions. Several of the country's designated wine regions lie in this transitional zone, and their wines are remarkable. Eastward, the summer-dry regime gives way to a more evenly distributed rainfall pattern and, into the Karroo interior, to drier conditions as well. Irrigation makes viticulture possible in these marginal zones.

Wine grapes are grown and wine is produced in two other areas of southern Africa. One of these lies along the Orange River, where vineyards under irrigation produce blending wines. The other area lies in Zimbabwe, South Africa's landlocked neighbor to the north. Here the elevation of the African plateau cools the tropical heat (Zimbabwe lies between approximately 16° and 23° south latitude), but rainfall regimes are not favorable for viticulture. In Zimbabwe, as will be noted later, winegrowing was stimulated not so much by natural environment as by political circumstances.

The map of Australia's climates reveals the extent of drought on the island continent (Fig. 1.7). The heart of Australia, fully half the landmass, classifies as

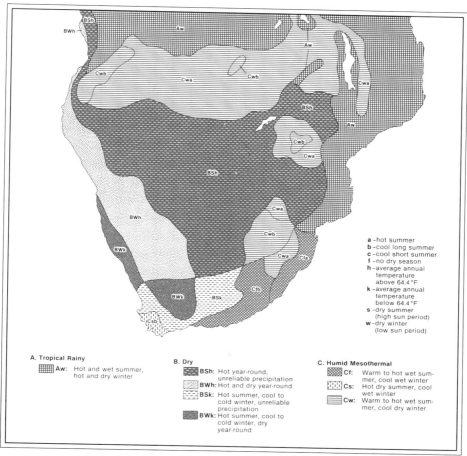

a –hot summer
b –cool long summer
c –cool short summer
f –no dry season
h –average annual
  temperature
  above 64.4°F
k –average annual
  temperature
  below 64.4°F
s –dry summer
  (high sun period)
w –dry winter
  (low sun period)

A. Tropical Rainy

Aw: Hot and wet summer,
     hot and dry winter

B. Dry

BSh: Hot year-round,
      unreliable precipitation

BWh: Hot and dry year-round

BSk: Hot summer, cool to
      cold winter, unreliable
      precipitation

BWk: Hot summer, cool to
     cold winter, dry
     year-round

C. Humid Mesothermal

Cf: Warm to hot wet sum-
     mer, cool wet winter

Cs: Hot dry summer, cool
     wet winter

Cw: Warm to hot wet sum-
     mer, cool dry winter

Figure 1.6. Climatic regions of Southern Africa, based on the Köppen-Geiger System.

desert; surrounding the desert is a wide belt of steppe. The northern savanna zone is unsuitable for viticulture, so that winegrowing is confined to an arcuate region extending from east-central New South Wales through Victoria to South Australia (roughly from north of Sydney to the environs of Adelaide), with pioneer developments in Western Australia and in Tasmania.

Northern Australia is seasonally affected by the southeast trade winds, and classifies climatically as savanna country; southern Australia (and hence the viticulture regions) lies mainly under the influence of the westerlies. Australia, smallest of the continents in area, also is the lowest in overall elevation. The Great Dividing Range, which flanks Australia in the east rather than dividing it, reaches just 7,316 feet at Mount Kosciusko, the highest point on the entire landmass. Thus there is less impediment to latitudinal air movement than in South America, but prevailing pressure systems and air movements severely limit maritime influences over the continent. The precipitation map reflects this: the highest totals are received in a

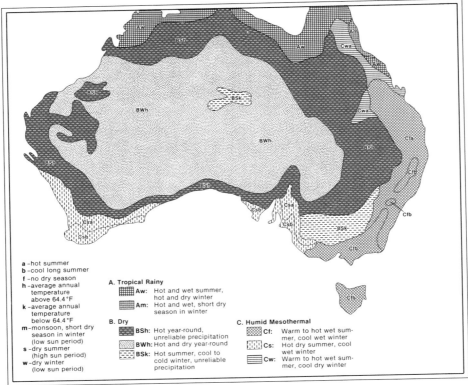

Figure 1.7. Climatic regions of Australia, based on the Köppen-Geiger System.

zone from the Cape York Peninsula around the east coast to the island of Tasmania, the orographic influence of the Great Dividing Range clearly reflected by greater amounts of moisture. Few places in Australia receive as much as 100 inches of annual precipitation; in the wine regions, 30 inches or less is normal.

Mediterranean conditions occur in two comparatively small areas of Australia: the southwestern corner in the hinterland of Perth and in South Australia in the interior behind Adelaide (see Fig. 1.7). In Victoria and Tasmania, old and new vineyards stand under cool-summer temperate conditions, the summers more moist than in true Mediterranean zones. In New South Wales, the summers remain moist but are warmer than they are farther to the south. Thus Australia has vineyards under a wide range of climatic regimes: warm- and cool-summer temperate, Mediterranean, and irrigated steppe and desert. This environmental diversity is reflected in the variety of Australian wines.

New Zealand is by far the smallest of the Southern Hemisphere's wine-producing countries, but it is in many ways the most interesting. On the generalized map of climatic regions, New Zealand is shown as a cool-summer temperate region without a pronounced dry season. But such a generalization conceals the environmental contrasts on the country's two major islands. New Zealand lies 1000 miles from the nearest landmass, so that it is totally exposed to maritime influences. To the north, a stable and persistent oceanic high pressure system prevails. The westerlies lie to the south. During the summer, the high pressure system tends to dominate, while the westerlies have stronger influence during the winter. But New Zealand's exposure permits subtropical and subpolar air to make contact along a front that often affects regional weather. Thus the country's weather is highly variable, and a warm, comparatively dry summer good for grape ripening may be followed a year later by a cloudy, gray, and wet one.

New Zealand, furthermore, is a country of high elevations (especially on South Island) and strong relief. A mountain backbone with elevations up to 12,349 feet, the Southern Alps, extends some 300 miles across the heart of South Island. Its effect on passing air masses is shown by the differences between its wet western side and its drier east and northeast. South Island's vineyards lie in these eastern and northern areas, but the major vineyards of New Zealand lie on North Island, which also—by virtue of its lower latitude—is warmer. Although North Island does not have elevations as high as those farther south, it, too, is marked by climatic contrasts. The central volcanic plateau at the heart of which lies Lake Taupo is flanked in several directions by areas suitable for agriculture, including viticulture. The northern peninsula is warmest, but along the east coast, near the shore behind Hawke's Bay, a climatic regime with a dry-summer period develops. As will be detailed in Chapter 9, New Zealand's environments for viticulture are anything but uniform, climatic generalizations notwithstanding.

If there are strong differences between the natural environments for viticulture in the countries of the Southern Hemisphere, they do share one characteristic of some importance. The Southern Hemisphere's summer arrives a half-year "before" that of the Northern Hemisphere, so that a given year's vintage can be in the bottle and on northern markets before the northern harvest has even begun. Depending on the nature of the vintage, harvesting may begin as early as January, or more commonly in February or March; wines that do not require long development in the winery may be bottled in June or July and reach markets in the Northern Hemisphere in August or September—carrying on their labels a vintage year still anticipated there. One might infer a certain advantage from this, one of very few benefits bestowed by nature on the winelands of the Southern Hemisphere in the competitive world of wine.

2

THE GRAPES AND
THEIR DIFFUSION

The Jesuit, Dominican, and Franciscan fathers who first planted the vine south of the equator at least had this advantage: they had seen the vines succeed in the New World and they knew that their grapevines would eventually take hold. They were well acquainted with the evidence in Mexico, where the vine stood as early as the 1520s and where new missions were quickly adorned with additional plantings. From here they took vine shoots and grape seeds, first to Peru and soon thereafter to what is today Chile. The southern diffusion of *Vitis* had begun.

Those priests and settlers who pioneered viticulture in the Southern Hemisphere secured for themselves a place in history, even if their vineyards did not always prosper. Thus Bartolomeu de Terrazas claims immortality not because of the few vines he planted near the Inca capital of Cuzco started a major industry, but because in 1540 (or perhaps a year earlier) he was the first to grow wine grapes in the southern tropics. Cuzco lies within 14 degrees of the equator, and De Terrazas undoubtedly hoped that the cooling effect of the mountainous Andes would be beneficial. So it was, but Cuzco was not to become a wine center. The subjugated Indian population, preferring its traditional beverages, did not take to wine; and no large European settler population developed here.

Some vines still stand near Cuzco today, and to this extent De Terrazas proved his point. But another pioneer, Francesco de Carabantes, chose a more receptive Peruvian locale. The desert coastal zone of Peru is interrupted by a string of some

SEMI-SECO

FUNDADA EN 1889

TACAMA
ROSÉ

ELABORADO Y EMBOTELLADO POR:
NEGOCIACION INDUSTRIAL VITIVINICOLA TACAMA S.A.

M.R.

NORMA ITINTEC No 210 027
PRODUCTO PERUANO

ICA-PERU

AUT IMP No 019

AMARU TLF 518541

10° GL. m.n
750 cl.
REG IND 11-0623-C

The historic Tacama vineyard at Ica, Peru, long produced mainly fortified wines. Today dry table wines (above) and sparkling wines (below) represent the wider range of styles made here. The Tacama vineyard may be the oldest continuously producing vineyard in the Southern Hemisphere.

40 oases sustained by stream water from the interior mountains. De Carabantes planted vines in one of these, the oasis of Ica about 160 miles by road south of the capital city, Lima. This marked the beginning of Peru's largest and most enduring wine region, the Tacama Vineyard.

Both De Terrazas and De Carabantes participated in the introduction of the vine in the area of what is today Chile. Naturally, the first plantings occurred in the north, probably during the late 1540s, but soon the Spanish conquerors and their missionary companions reached the salubrious region known today as Middle Chile. Here the coastal desert gave way to well-watered, green, undulating countryside. To the east, the snow-capped Andes promised a steady supply of nourishment to the streams in their wide, open valleys. Summer warmth was assured by lengthy periods of blue, cloudless sky. It did not take long for the Spaniards to realize that they had found an ideal environment for grapegrowing.

Soon the settlement at Santiago was surrounded by vineyards, and the first wine was vinted in the late 1550s. Some of the new plantings were destroyed by Indians, who understood the connection between wine and the altar of the merciless invaders' god, but their opposition failed to halt the vine's diffusion. "Chile had become a land rich in vines by 1570, and five years later their number had trebled"; ships plying the western South American coast carried Chilean wines to northern settlements.[1] The vine had found its first home in the Southern Hemisphere.

Settlers and missionaries, soldiers and farmers in Spanish colonial America applauded these developments, but winegrowers in Spain viewed them quite differently. Shipping wine from Iberia to the expanding settlements of Middle and South America was a lucrative business, but the success of viticulture first in Mexico and now in South America as well, endangered that trade. Spanish winegrowers, some of them powerful men, put pressure on the government, urging King Philip II to limit viticulture in Spanish America. In 1595 the king issued a decree to restrict vine planting in Mexico and to prohibit its further expansion in Peru and Chile. But Chile lay far from the source of this edict, and the colonists were not only adventurous but also independence-minded and competitive of spirit. King Philip's decree had some effect in Mexico (it failed to halt the vine's diffusion there as well) but very little in southern South America.

In the meantime, the grapevine crossed the Andes and became established in Argentina (Fig. 2.1). It may, in fact, have come south from Peru, via Bolivia and through the Grande River's Humahuaca Pass into northern Argentina, and thus along, rather than across, the Andes. By whatever route it came, there is no doubt that the vine stood in the northern province of Santiago del Estero in 1557. It may have been planted even earlier around the mission at Córdoba, as some historians suggest, and the Jesuit priest Pablo Cedron may have been the pioneer of Argentinian viticulture. Undoubtedly Juan Jufré, who owned vineyards near Santiago in Chile in the 1550s and who later founded the Argentinian city of San Juan, had a hand in the diffusion of the vine to the Cuyo—the region comprising the three provinces of San Juan, San Luis, and Mendoza. In Mendoza would develop Argentina's greatest wine region. The city of Mendoza, today the country's viticulture headquarters, was founded in 1561, and vines were planted nearby before the end of the decade.

Winegrowing in Argentina did not experience an early surge comparable to Chile's. Control by the missionaries was more stringent, and Spain's restrictive rules

Figure 2.1. Diffusion of the vine in South America.

The wine industry of Brazil began its modern era of development about a century ago, when European (mainly Italian) immigrants revived the nearly dormant viticulture of Rio Grande do Sul. Cooperatives such as Aurora and Garibaldi played a key part in this expansion. Hundreds of winegrower families combined to produce the annual vintage. This historic photograph reflects the early days of Aurora. For a comparison, see the modern facilities of the company, shown in Chapter 6. (Courtesy of Cooperativa Aurora.)

were obeyed more rigidly than in Chile's distant frontier. The settler-owned vineyards soon produced more than enough wine to satisfy local demand, and after proving its ability to prosper east of the Andes the vine diffused but slowly. Not until three centuries later did Argentina take its place among major wine producers.

The diffusion route that carried the vine from Mexico to Peru, to Bolivia, Chile, and Argentina led next to Uruguay and Brazil. It is possible that Spanish seafarers brought vines to Uruguay soon after the first landfall, but no reliable record of it survives. Jesuit missionaries came from Argentina, however, and among them was R. Gonzalez de Santa Cruz, who entered what is today Brazil's southernmost state, Rio Grande do Sul. In 1626 he founded the mission at Santa Cruz do Sul and introduced the vine there. Development of viticulture was very slow, for even the hardy grapevines used by the missionaries had difficulty in southern Brazil's damp, warm summers (and the Jesuits never did find the state's best locales). Portuguese settlers came in growing numbers to southern Brazil during the eighteenth century, bringing with them their own familiar varieties of the vine, but they, too, failed to establish a real wine region. Again the industry had to await the nineteenth century, when European immigration from Italy and Germany brought change and progress.

Grapes of the Missions

Considering the range of environments under which the Spanish invaders planted their vines in Middle and South America, one might well wonder what grape variety, in the sixteenth and seventeenth centuries, turned out to be so adaptable and versatile. The fact is that no one is absolutely certain. The grape the Europeans brought to the Americas was a variety of *Vitis vinifera*—but when viticulturists tried to find its Iberian ancestor, it could not be located. Not unreasonably the grape was given the name *Mission* in the New World, and although it acquired other names as it diffused across the Americas, it is still known as such in many areas, California included.

The Mission may not be one of vinifera's noble varieties, but it would be difficult to exaggerate its importance to American viticulture. It tolerates environments that would discourage most of its relatives, and survives heat, drought, humidity, and other adversities. It develops a strong trunk and can stand by itself, its branches or canes heavily laden with a yield two to three times as large as other vines. Its big, heavy bunches may not appear as tightly packed and well structured as those of other *vinifera*, but the grapes withstand mold and rot even when they are left on the vine after ripening. In the early days of American viticulture, grape picking (not to mention vineyard maintenance) often was a hit-or-miss proposition, with inexperienced labor and poor organization. So the Mission's grapes were often harvested late. Yet they survived to allow the winemaker to produce passable wine. Not many *vinifera* would have done the same.

The ecological relationship between the vine and its natural environment is one of continuous adjustment. Transplanted, the variety changes subtly to adjust to its new circumstances, and develops "clones" in the process. Sometimes the clones are given new names. In the case of the Mission, it became known as the *Criolla* as it spread from its Mexican heartland (or, to give it its full name in Argentina, the *Criolla de Vino*); in Chile it acquired the name *País*. And despite its shortcomings, especially its low acid and weak color, the Mission continues to occupy extensive vineyards in South America, a living legacy of the days when viticulture was in its infancy and wine was a ceremonial necessity rather than an industrial mainstay.

The Mission and its clones are dark-skinned grapes, but its most agreeable wines are whites or rosés (in Argentina, rosé-style wines are referred to as Criollas). It is certain that the early missionary-grapegrowers also tried to cultivate light-skinned grapes, and they had some success with a hardy variety of the Muscats, probably the Muscat of Alexandria. The history and heritage of the Muscat family of grapes are much better known than the Mission's. It stood on slopes facing Mediterranean shores three thousand years ago, and was domesticated and dispersed by the ancient Greeks and perhaps even earlier. Over time, and in its various European locales (Italy, southwest France, Alsace, Greece, Germany) the Muscats developed their own individual character, the results of the ecological interaction among variety, environment, and winegrower. It is a process similar to that observed in the Mission and, in fact, in all cultivated varieties or *cultivars*.

The Muscat of Alexandria may have been planted in North Africa and thus acquired its unusual name. If the first Muscats were taken from Spain to the New

World, as is likely, the variety may have been a close relative then growing in Iberia, or perhaps the very same variety under a different name, the Moscatel Romano. In the Americas it diffused widely as the Muscat d'Alexandrie, and for good reasons. The Muscats do well in warm to hot and dry conditions, and much of Mexico and coastal South America presented just such environments to the Spanish invaders. The Muscat of Alexandria is a white grape (red Muscats also exist) that ripens late and produces a fairly large harvest. It is quite tolerant of inefficient harvesting and slow delivery to the winery but, again like the Mission, it is not a distinguished grape for winemaking. Planted in Peru, Chile, and Argentina, it became the basis for brandy-making. To this day, Peru's *Aguardiente* and Chile's *Pisco* are distilled from wine made from the Muscat of Alexandria. Chile's long-term concern over alcoholism is in a large measure due to the popularity of its high-alcohol Pisco, which has the status of a national drink.

The Mission and the Muscat of Alexandria were not the only varieties with which the pioneer grapegrowers experimented, but for a long time they had no real rivals. They adjusted to local environments and withstood occasional adversities, they produced under the poorest of vineyard care (often they grew not in vineyards but climbed on the walls and fences of the mission buildings), and they produced adequate, if not exceptional, wine. Under the best conditions of Middle Chile and vinted with care, their wines were quite acceptable. There was little incentive to change, and when the first attempts at diversification were made, the wisdom of staying with the known cultivars was quickly confirmed. When southern Brazil's first sizable Portuguese settlement took place, in the early eighteenth century, the new immigrants found only the unfamiliar Criolla grape growing around several missions. They imported other *vinifera* cultivars from Portugal, under the assumption that they knew these home varieties better and would find suitable environments for them. Most of the vines (and others imported later from France and Italy) died; when they survived and bore fruit the grape bunches were attacked by mildew and rot. The Mission had its merits.

Founding Fathers

By the time the nineteenth century was three decades old, the Mission had stood in the Americas for three hundred years, gracing Catholic missions from California to Chile. With the Muscat of Alexandria it had become the basis also for whatever commercial winegrowing there was in western North America and in southern South America—which was, to be sure, not very much. The Mission and Muscat had proved that *vinifera* would grow in the New World, and there were winegrowers who envisaged the introduction of other varieties from Europe, and the emergence of major industries.

Some of these winegrowers actually introduced new European vines, as Joseph Chapman and Louis Vignes did near Los Angeles (California) in the 1820s. But in California as well as in Chile and Argentina, the fledgling industry awaited a founder, someone who saw the opportunities, seized the moment, and set a new course.

In California, of course, it was the famous Agoston Haraszthy who played that role. He arrived in 1849, bought an estate and built it into the largest winery in the state, experimented with European vines, researched and wrote articles on winegrowing, constantly promoted the industry, and eventually persuaded California's governor to send him to Europe to select vine shoots for experimentation. He returned in 1861, having arranged for the transportation of about 100,000 vine shoots representing 1400 European grape varieties (among them, probably, the Zinfandel). From his nursery the vines dispersed throughout California. Haraszthy achieved singlehandedly what others had for decades been hoping for. His innovations marked the beginning of the modern age of California viticulture, and appropriately Haraszthy is remembered today as the "father of California's wine industry," although he appeared on the scene long after the missionaries had planted the first *vinifera* there.

In a remarkable way, events in Chile and Argentina took a similar turn, and at about the same time. Chile's Haraszthy was a remarkable man named Silvestre Ochagavia Echazareta who, in 1851, saw the potential for viticulture on the French model in Chile. Ochagavia realized that areas of Middle Chile exhibited soil distributions, drainage patterns, and climatic regimes very similar to the France with which he was familiar, and yet the País variety dominated viticulture. Ochagavia had the resources to enable him to bring a number of French viticulturists to Chile, and he effected the importation of thousands of vine shoots from France and Germany. Within a short period the Cabernet Sauvignon, Merlot, Malbec (locally called *Cot*), Petit Verdot, and the Pinot Noir among red varieties, and the Chardonnay, Sauvignon Blanc, Riesling, and Sémillon among whites were introduced and planted in accordance with the French advisors' instructions. In addition, the French technicians built a number of *Bodegas de Vendimia y Elaboracion del Vino* (Winecellars for the Development of Fine Vintages), some of which survive to the present day. They taught methods of viticulture and viniculture that elevated Chilean winegrowing to a new level of excellence. Meanwhile, Ochagavia rallied local winegrowers to his cause, and several Chilean names that were to rise to national and international prominence were involved, including Luis Cousiño, Domingo Concha y Toro, Manuel Antonio Tocornal, Luis Pereira, Maximiano Errazuriz, Alejandro Reyes, and Francisco Subercaseux. A consummate politician and negotiator, Ochagavia also persuaded the Chilean government to support the industry. Ochagavia truly deserves his accolade as the "father of Chilean viticulture."

A similar honor has been bestowed upon the Argentinian winegrower Benegas. As the historian Edward Hyams writes,

> The . . . Agoston Haraszthy of Argentina was don Tiburcio Benegas; there are, in fact, curious likenesses between the two men; both took the lead in confused communities where leadership was wanting; both had distinguished careers in local politics on the grand scale; both were men of education, good sense and great energy.[2]

And both saw large vineyards planted with the Mission-Criolla in the knowledge that other *vinifera* would produce far better wines. Benegas settled in Mendoza in 1865, married into a viticulturist's family in 1870, and bought a vineyard estate in 1883. He enlarged his estate by planting thousands of vines imported first from Chile and later from France, built a large and modern *bodega*, and published (again like Haraszthy) a guide for local winegrowers on viticulture and viniculture using the new cultivars.

Benegas was not alone in his labors, nor was winegrowing his only avocation. Miguel Pouget also brought French grapevines to Mendoza, and Justo Castro, another winegrower, planted the new imports in neighboring San Juan. Indeed, Benegas's most significant contribution to Argentina's wine industry may have been his determined support of the plan to extend the railroad from Buenos Aires to the city of Mendoza, thus linking the wine region with the country's expanding rail network. Until the completion of this project, in 1885, wine from the province went to domestic markets on horse-drawn wagons, often on rough roads. Such transit did not serve the wine well, and one result of the railroad's completion was to improve the quality of the marketed wine. The trains also could carry a much larger volume of wine, but most important of all was their impact on population distribution in Argentina. With Mendoza now "opened up," tens of thousands of immigrant farmers, many of Italian ancestry, flooded into the province and into neighboring areas. They supplemented the grape varieties already there—Cabernet Sauvignon, Malbec, Merlot, Pinot Noir, Sémillon—with their own, including the Barbera, Bonardo, Trebbiano, Pedro Ximenez, and various Muscats. Now began the revolution of Argentinian viticulture Benegas had envisaged. Winegrowing not only transformed Mendoza, coloring the irrigated desert green; it diffused also into San Juan, La Rioja, Salta, Jujuy and Catamarca, and southward into Neuquén and Río Negro. Soon the trains carrying wine to Argentina's eastern markets also contained shipments destined for foreign consumers. Argentina was about to take its place as one of the world's largest wine-producing countries.

Brazil experienced neither Chile's qualitative nor Argentina's quantitative revolution. The Portuguese immigrants of the eighteenth century were unable to overcome southern Brazil's environmental obstacles, and not until the 1830s did the industry stir. That moment of revival resulted not from the introduction of suitable *vinifera* varieties from Europe, but from the arrival of quite a different vine: an American variety of the Labrusca known as the Isabella. This grape does not make attractive wine, but it did resist the diseases to which southern Brazil's *vinifera* constantly succumbed. After early experiments with it succeeded, the Isabella became the mainstay of the vineyards of Rio Grande do Sul. Whether this was a step forward from the Criolla is debatable. In any case, when Brazil during the 1870s and the years that followed was settled by Italian immigrants, the Italians found the Isabella unacceptable and began to replace the American vines with *vinifera*. The Italians in southern Brazil (and the German immigrants as well) sought—and found—the country's better locales for viticulture. In the area of Caxias, Bento Gonçalves and Garibaldi, a triangle about 60 miles north of coastal Porto Alegre, lies the heart of Brazil's modern wine industry, a further testimony to the cultural succession that forged the continent's wine regions.

Van Riebeeck's Vines

When the Dutch East India Company appointed Jan van Riebeeck to lead its group of settlers at South Africa's Cape of Good Hope, its judgment was sound. Van Riebeeck had been at the Cape previously, rescuing a group of shipwrecked Europeans in 1648. He was there more than two weeks, and took note of the natural environments. In April 1652 he returned under orders to establish a revictualing station at the foot of Table Mountain, and the settlement that was to become Cape Town was born. Van Riebeeck's men built a fort and dwellings, and they laid out the first farmlands. As the Cape revealed its Mediterranean climatic regime, its summer dry and warm, its winter cold and wet, Van Riebeeck realized that his first impressions had been correct: more than perhaps anything else, the vine would flourish here. He requested, within months of his arrival, that Amsterdam send vine shoots, but usable cuttings did not reach the Cape until mid-1655. Planted on the slopes of Table Mountain, these vines took hold, and in February 1659, Van Riebeeck wrote a now-famous entry in his logbook: "Today, God be praised, wine [was] pressed for the first time from the Cape grapes."

Thus Van Riebeeck was truly the father of South African viticulture. He was so enthused by the success of his first vintage that he set about expanding his acreage, adding vines and lavishing the most meticulous attention on them. When he was transferred by the company to Java, he had laid the groundwork for an industry. His successful vines probably were the same Muscat of Alexandria that had been introduced in South America a century earlier, and they may have come from the same source in Spain; at the Cape this variety was called the Hanepoot, the name it retains to this day. Possibly some French vine shoots also reached the Cape, but historians are not certain about this. In any case Van Riebeeck, the Company Commander, had set the example for the free settlers who were also arriving at the Cape. His vineyard holdings reverted to company control, but new vines were planted, both by company representatives and free *burgers*, throughout the 1660s. Wine from these vineyards was shipped to Dutch settlements in the East Indies, and while not all of it arrived in drinkable condition, the Cape's first foreign wine market had been established.[3]

If Van Riebeeck were to share his role as founder of the South African wine industry, it would be with Governor Simon van der Stel, who took up his appointment at the Cape in 1679. When Van der Stel's term began, he found the Cape winegrowers so successful that they were neglecting other crops in favor of wine; the Company was aiding them in this by purchasing all excess wine the vintners could not sell on the open market. Winemaking practices had degenerated to a deplorable state, as the greedy growers could sell any wine at inflated prices and did not bother much with quality. Van der Stel in 1686 issued a resolution, approved by the company's council, which stipulated that "the inhabitants shall in future not be at liberty to press any wine before the vineyards have been visited by a committee and pronounced by the commander to be of the requisite maturity."[4] Winegrowing at the Cape no longer was an industry struggling to establish itself. The time had come to establish and protect its reputation.

Van der Stel traveled throughout the southwestern Cape, looking for suitable settlement sites (and potential for vineyards). One area that especially impressed him lay about 30 miles east of Cape Town. Here he founded a settlement and etched his name permanently on the map: Stellenbosch. That name has become synonymous with the best of South African wines, as the Stellenbosch district is sometimes referred to as the "Napa Valley of the Cape" (Fig. 2.2).

But Van der Stel put his name on the viticultural map in another way. In 1685 he acquired a large estate in the neck of the Cape Peninsula, behind Table

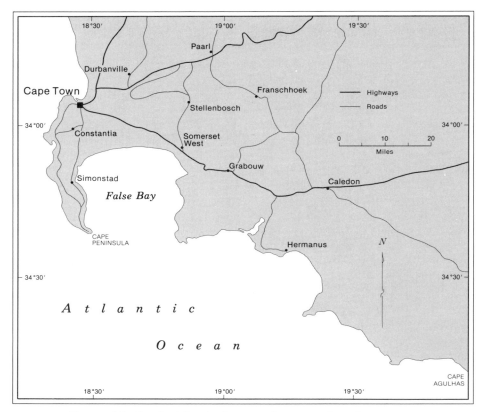

Figure 2.2. South Africa's Cape and its viticultural toponyms.

Mountain. He named it Constantia, and over the next several years planted nearly 100,000 vines on the property. These he tended with great care, setting an example for the winegrowers at the Cape; in his winery Van der Stel assembled the most modern equipment for winemaking then available. Having thus created a model, he urged other winegrowers to press their grapes in a large, clean, modern, cooperative winery, in order to produce better wines. But the local growers resisted this, arguing that Van der Stel was trying to gain control over their livelihood.

Undaunted, the governor developed his Constantia estate, and his wines became known as the Cape's best. It is certain that his vineyards contained both white and red Muscats, and it is possible that he also experimented with Chenin Blanc, Cabernet Sauvignon, Pinot Noir, and Shiraz. From his Muscats, blended with some Frontignan (another Muscat variety) Van der Stel made sweet, strongly scented, soft wines that achieved an international reputation for their excellence. They were in demand from the East Indies to Europe, and were referred to in admiration as "the governor's wines." Van der Stel had proved what the Cape was capable of, and the entire industry benefited.

The governor was a politician and winegrower; he also was a bon vivant, a civilized man who loved the good and beautiful things in life. He built a magnificent

CONSTANTIA WYN VAN OORSPRONG

GROOT CONSTANTIA
LANDGOEDWYN
CABERNET SAUVIGNON

Grown, made and bottled on the Government
Estate Groot Constantia, Constantia, Cape.
Gekweek, berei en gebottel op die Staats-
landgoed Groot Constantia, Constantia, Kaap.

PRODUCE OF SOUTH AFRICA · PRODUK VAN SUID-AFRIKA

C.T.P. LTD.

*Still today, Groot Constantia is one of the Cape's leading
wine estates. The homestead (manor house), now a museum,
graces Constantia's labels.*

homestead in the Cape-Dutch architectural style that has been associated with South
African viticulture ever since, and filled it with the best assemblage of furniture
and art to be found at the Cape. After he retired as governor in 1699, he continued
his work on his beloved Constantia until his death in 1712.

While Van der Stel was governor, the first substantial group of French Huguenot
settlers arrived at Cape Town. By the year 1690 they numbered some 150—seemingly
a small party until it is compared to the free settlers, of whom there were just
300. The French families were given land in the area of Stellenbosch, Paarl (another
district destined to become famous as a wine region), and Franschhoek (French
Corner). Their skill at viticulture and winemaking set an example for the other
settlers, and the French imprint on Cape winegrowing was made. The Huguenots
also introduced additional grape varieties to the Cape, since they were familiar with
Mediterranean environments and saw opportunities at the Cape the Dutch did not.

Van der Stel may, in fact, have acquired his first Chenin Blanc vines from these immigrants. They also may have brought the so-called Green Grape (probably the Sémillon) and the Saint Emilion to South Africa, although the time of arrival of these cultivars during the first fifty years of Cape winemaking is uncertain.

After Van der Stel's death the wine industry went through an unremarkable period. The export trade faltered, and Constantia was subdivided and sold. The largest of the three parcels of land carved from Constantia, which also contained the great residence and winery, was renamed Groot (Great) Constantia. In 1778 Groot Constantia was purchased by the Hendrik Cloete family, and it was to remain under the family's control for more than a century. This was an eventful period, for the Cape passed from Dutch to British control, first temporarily in 1795 and more lastingly in 1806. The wine trade had become better organized, and there were regular consignments of wine to Batavia, capital of the Dutch East Indies, but the wines from Groot Constantia remained the Cape's only truly distinguished wine. The British takeover produced a new economic order, however, and when Anglo-French conflict deprived the English consumers of some of their favorite wines, the Cape provided an alternative. The Cloete family was now making the noblest wines Groot Constantia had ever produced: fortified reds and whites of great intensity, "heavy and luscious, and probably made of a blend of varieties such as Pontac, Muscat de Frontignan and Red Muscadel."[5]

When the British instituted preferential tariffs for Cape wines on the profitable English market, the industry thrived. On the coattails of Constantia, Cape winegrowers shipped more wine to Europe than ever before. Such was Groot Constantia's reputation that King Louis Philippe of France instructed the captain of one of his frigates to buy for him a "considerable quantity" of the *Vin de Constance* when visiting the Cape. Groot Constantia's records of 1833 contain proof of the sale; it was by no means the only shipment destined for Europe's royalty.[6]

But all was not well with viticulture at the Cape. Certainly there were other capable and conscientious winegrowers in South Africa, and their good wines also reached overseas markets. Unfortunately, there also were those who made inferior wine, heavily fortified, rough, and coarse, and their shipments, too, arrived in Europe. Soon the inconsistency of Cape wines began to reduce their acceptance, and when the British government in 1861 abolished the preferential tariff the export trade, already troubled, collapsed.

The industry had one more chance. When Europe's vineyards were being ravaged by *phylloxera*, there was an opportunity to resume large-scale exports, because *phylloxera*'s arrival in South Africa was delayed. But the Cape's wines had become so poorly made that they arrived in Europe in undrinkable condition, and the trade failed. And then Cape winegrowing faced disaster. The dread disease reached South Africa, decimating the vineyards, in the 1880s. Groot Constantia lay waste; its glory faded, the estate was sold to the colonial government for a fraction of its value just decades earlier. Recovery began when the remedy against *phylloxera*—the grafting of European vines on American rootstocks—was introduced. The industry's revival, ironically, was so strong that another threat arose: overproduction and price collapse. This was the situation in 1918 when the Cooperative Winegrowers' Association (KWV) was formed, ushering in the modern era of South African viticulture.

South Africa had proved that its environments favored the vine; the wine

The Steen, South Africa's adaptation of the Chenin Blanc, is bottled as a varietal and used for many other styles and blends ranging from Sherry-type wines to sparkling wines.

industry's fluctuating fortunes had more to do with the winegrowers than with climate or soil. Among the many cultivars introduced from France, Spain, Italy, and elsewhere, some succeeded well at the Cape, while others did not. The Cabernet Sauvignon has yielded superb wines at the Cape, and the Riesling also has produced satisfactorily. Two varieties, however, are of special interest, one white and one red. The white variety is the Steen, the grape whose wine is sometimes bottled under that name or as *Stein*. The red variety is the remarkable Pinotage, a grape as closely associated with the Cape as the Zinfandel is with California.

The Steen has stood in South Africa for centuries, and it may have been one of Van Riebeeck's vines. It was long believed that the Steen was a truly South African cultivar, perhaps the result of a natural *métis* or crossing between introduced *vinifera* varieties. But ampelographic analysis proved that the Steen is in fact France's Chenin Blanc, the Loire Valley grape that was brought to the Cape during Van der Stel's time and perhaps even earlier. In the more than three centuries it has stood in South Africa, the Steen has adapted itself to local environments, to such an extent that even specialists are uncertain about its relationships. "In South Africa, the vine changed so much that it does most things better than its parent does in France . . . it makes wine high in both sugar and acid, it has a rich flavour and a recognisable flowery bouquet."[7] The Steen yields distinctive dry wines and is used for brandy- and sherry-type wines, but it is for its semi-sweet to late-harvest, sweet styles that it has gained its greatest reputation. The Chenin Blanc-to-Steen trans-

The Pinotage has been described as South Africa's Zinfandel. Its use has spread from South Africa to New Zealand, where it produces pleasant, mainly light red wines.

formation is one of the world's best examples of the grapevine's versatility and adaptive capacity.

The Cape's most interesting red cultivar is the Pinotage. Unlike the Steen, this really is a cultivar of South African origin. It was created by a South African oenologist, Abraham Perold, in the 1920s. He crossed the Pinot Noir with the Cinsaut, then still called the Hermitage. Combining these names, he called his new variety the Pinotage, and began experimenting with it. For decades the Pinotage remained an obscure cultivar, but winegrowers planted it in increasing quantities and, in the 1950s, a Pinotage entered in a wine competition was awarded first prize. Now it gained in popularity, and its qualities came to be appreciated: it ripens early, has a high sugar and acid content, is resistant to virtually all diseases, and can withstand excessive sun and even strong winds. It is vinted into styles that range from long-lived, complex, dark wines to fruity, early drinking, lighter wines, and the Pinotage remains one of the Cape's most interesting cultivars.

The Pinotage sometimes is referred to as the Zinfandel of South Africa, and there is some truth in the comparison, even to the question of origin. While the source of California's Zinfandel remains a mystery (repeated "solutions" to the problem notwithstanding), the origin of the Pinotage is beyond doubt—or is it? Perold's work is a matter of record, but Pinotage wines in the tasting betray a slight

Sydney Harbor, where Australian viticulture began. The first vines may have stood in the gardens in the left foreground of this photo, facing the water.

foxiness that has led some specialists to suggest that it may in fact be a hybrid (a cross between a *vinifera* and a non-*vinifera* variety) or that, at the very least, some American parentage came into the mix. So the Pinotage shares with the Zinfandel an ancestral riddle to keep ampelographers working—and tasting.

Arthur Phillip's Legacy

In 1788, when the English Captain Arthur Phillip led his small flotilla of sailing ships to the east coast of Australia, Cape winegrowing prospered. Relations between Holland and England were good, and Phillip called at Cape Town for revictualing, and to add to his collection of vine cuttings and grape seeds. The grapevine would be an important component of agriculture in New South Wales.

The first permanent Australian settlement was founded on the south bank of an estuary now named Port Jackson, mouth of the Parramatta River (Fig. 2.3). The site today is the heart of Australia's largest city, Sydney, and the place where the first vines were probably planted is now the Royal Botanical Garden. It is only four miles to the open ocean, and it lies virtually at sea level. Sydney today is known for its hot and humid summers, and so it was in the late 1770s. The vines grew, but the grape bunches rotted; disease invaded the small vineyard and the first experiment at viticulture failed.

Phillip realized that vine planting should be tried elsewhere, and so he went

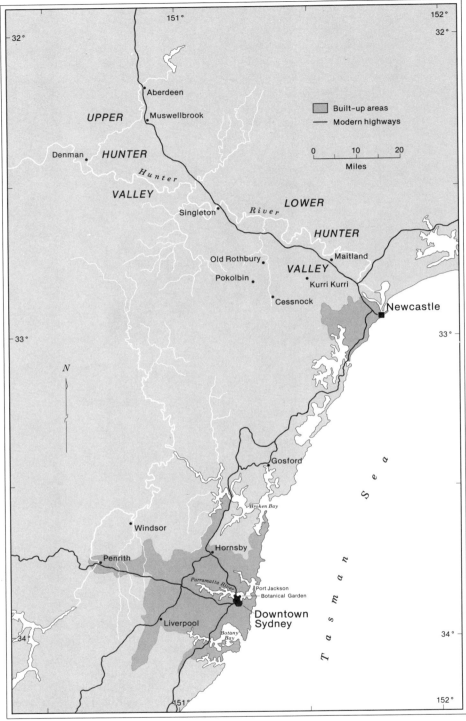

Figure 2.3. Early viticultural locations in New South Wales: Sydney and the Hunter Valley.

inland along the Parramatta to the approximate place where the stream widens into its estuarine valley, about sixteen miles from the coast and more than a hundred feet above sea level. In 1791 he cleared three acres of land and planted vines here, and although conditions were far from ideal these vines did bear grapes good enough to be vinted.

Several farmer-settlers in the Sydney area followed Phillip's lead and planted vineyards in the Parramatta Valley. But the captain never saw his own initiatives succeed, nor those of the settlers to whom he served as an example. His health deteriorated to such a degree that he was forced, in 1792, to return to England. Unlike South Africa more than a century earlier, viticulture in New South Wales barely survived in the two decades following the commander's departure. Small rows of vines grew and then failed, and there was no industry worthy of the term. Winegrowing was a patchy and ephemeral business.

Revival came as a result of the efforts not of one dominant figure, but several. Gregory Blaxland, pioneer and explorer, planted a vineyard in 1817, using Cabernet Sauvignon cuttings brought from the Cape. Like Phillip's vines, Blaxland's vineyard stood in the Parramatta Valley, but Blaxland achieved something unprecedented: in 1822 he sent a sample of his red wine to England, where it was awarded a medal. He repeated this accomplishment several years later, and thus put Australian wine on the map. Another early leader was Captain John MacArthur who, with his sons James and William, experimented with vines and eventually succeeded in establishing Australia's first commercial vineyard, at Penrith (still near the original settlement, about thirty miles west of central Sydney). In the late 1820s, annual production reached 20,000 gallons.[8] Of the three MacArthurs, son William proved to be the most influential winegrower, promoter, and organizer. He, too, saw some of his wines win prizes at English competitions. In 1844 he published a book containing advice on Australian winegrowing. Later he organized Australian winegrowers into the New South Wales Vineyard Association. Certainly William MacArthur's name is among those of the founding fathers of Australia viticulture.

The man who most often is described as the father of Australian winegrowing is the colorful and indefatigable James Busby. Some historians are of the opinion that Busby does not, alone, deserve this accolade, but of his impact on Australian viticulture there can be no doubt. He arrived at Sydney in 1824, a young man (born in 1801) already convinced that winegrowing had a great future in Australia. Wasting no time, he acquired land in the area that was to become one of Australia's premier wine regions, the Hunter Valley about 100 miles north of Sydney. He then took a teaching position with combined responsibilities at an agricultural school, and concentrated his work on viticulture. Next he published his first book on winegrowing. All this he accomplished in the first two years after reaching New South Wales. He was, indeed, a man of boundless energy. In 1831 he left for Europe, traveling through the wine countries of Spain and France and despatching to Australia thousands of vine cuttings representing several hundred European grape varieties. These were planted in the botanical gardens of Sydney and Adelaide, and from the growing vines cuttings were taken to other areas and vineyards. It was, without question, Busby's greatest contribution to Australian viticulture. Singlehandedly he had vastly increased the range of available cultivars with which winegrowers on the advancing settlement frontier could experiment. Among the varieties Busby brought to Australia were the Shiraz (the so-called Red Hermitage of the Rhône Valley), the White Hermitage (really the Ugni Black of France), the Sémillon, and several Muscats. The Shiraz, in some ways, has become to Australia what the Pinotage is to the Cape and the Zinfandel to California: a grape variety that yields characterful and characteristic wines with strong regional qualities.

Busby continued to publish books and articles about viticulture, and his Hunter Valley farm, which he had named Kirkton, was operated by a relative, William Kelman, who produced good wines there. In the meantime, Busby had become interested in New Zealand, and after an exploratory visit he left Australia in 1833 to take up residence in Britain's most remote colony. At Waitangi, near the Bay of Islands on North Island's northern peninsula, he planted the selection of vine cuttings he had brought with him from Australia and, indirectly, from Europe. In New Zealand, too, there are those who regard Busby as the originator of local winegrowing, and as the father of the industry.

Certainly Busby, in Australia as well as New Zealand, made contributions on behalf of viticulture that merit the highest of praise. Busby did not live to enjoy such honors: he always felt that his efforts had gone unappreciated, and eventually he left New Zealand and lived out his life in England. But his place in history is secure. Although he never made wine in the Hunter Valley, his name remains associated with Kirkton, where William Kelman used Busby's European vine cuttings to develop a vineyard that, in the early 1840s, was producing notable wines with the White Hermitage (or Ugni Blanc) and other varieties. This period marks the beginning of winegrowing in the Hunter, and Busby's name remains inextricably connected with this Australian wine region, still perhaps the country's greatest.

New South Wales truly was Australia's pioneer viticulture region, and wine-growing everywhere else followed the eastern example. The first vines in Victoria were planted in 1834, and thus nearly fifty years after Captain Phillip's original plantings in the Sydney area. South Australia's first vineyards date from the late 1830s. The initial winegrowing experiment in the Barossa Valley, thirty miles north-northeast of Adelaide, did not take place until 1847 when Johann Gramp planted some vines not far from where the huge Orlando winery stands today. Another legendary figure in Australian viticulture, Joseph Seppelt, began growing vines in the Barossa in the early 1850s. Many farmers who journeyed overland from the east coast to Victoria and South Australia, or who came in increasing numbers by sea to newly founded Melbourne and Adelaide, started mixed-crop farms and specialized in viticulture after discovering that grapes would grow well in these newly opened areas. Viticulture in Victoria grew explosively, as was the case in South Australia, acreages soon overtaking those in the Hunter Valley. It was all made possible by Busby's vines, which still stood in the Adelaide area and were dispersed all over the southern colonies.

As in Chile and South Africa earlier, Australian viticulture now developed regional specializations. The Southern Vales, Clare Valley, and Coonawarra in South Australia, Great Western and Tahbilk in Victoria, the irrigated regions in the Murray River Valley, and the newer pioneer regions in Western Australia and Tasmania all prove the wisdom of Captain Phillip and his successors.

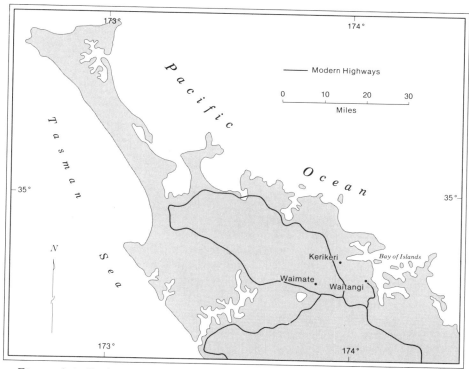

Figure 2.4. Early grape-growing locales on the Northland Peninsula, New Zealand.

Samuel Marsden's Initiative

The history of viticulture in New Zealand goes back even farther than the days of James Busby. As early as 1819 the Reverend Samuel Marsden recorded in his diary that he had planted grape seeds at Keri Keri in North Island, and a few years later he cultivated some vines near Waimate (Fig. 2.4). Some of Marsden's vines were still standing when James Busby first visited New Zealand, although there is no strong evidence that Marsden ever managed to produce a vintage from them.

Hence it is Busby, not Marsden, who is referred to as the father of New Zealand viticulture, the pioneer of the industry. But while Busby brought his European vines from Australia and wrote prescriptions for New Zealand winegrowers as he had for Australians, he too was unable to launch a truly successful, growing industry in New Zealand. Some French settlers on South Island, near the site of the modern city of Christchurch, managed to produce wine from their modest vineyards, but their experiment also failed in the long run. Members of a religious order, the Marist Brothers, established vineyards in the Hawke's Bay area on North Island's eastern coast, and their venture proved more durable; however, production was for sacramental purposes, not (until more recently) for commercial sale.

The northernmost vines in New Zealand today stand not far from the site of Marsden's original vineyard. They belong to the acreage of Continental Wines, near the town of Whangarei.

In fact, Marsden's initiative and Busby's enthusiasm bore fruit so many decades later that their connection with the country's modern wine industry is tenuous indeed. In the interim, an Italian viticulturist, Romeo Bragatto, advised the government on local potentials (in the 1890s); *phylloxera* struck; prohibition prevailed; and the industry barely survived. As recently as 1938 there were fewer than 200 acres of vineyards devoted to wine grapes in the entire country.[9]

Developments over the past two decades (See Chapter 8) have confirmed Marsden's intuition and Busby's wisdom. Bragatto, who reported favorably on viticulture's prospects in New Zealand, was proved correct: in just two decades the country has progressed quantitatively as well as qualitatively at an unprecedented pace. Busby had brought to New Zealand the European vines that did so well in Australia, but New Zealand was hit harder by *phylloxera* than was Australia, where large regions were spared. This led to the introduction of resistant American varieties, but the wines made from *Labrusca* were not acceptable. The industry's modern revival was made possible, as elsewhere, by the introduction of European varieties protected by grafting on disease-resistant American rootstocks. It also was facilitated by research and experimentation, resulting in the identification of suitable locales for particular varieties.

Modern New Zealand viticulture, thus, does not have roots in a past as distant as the Cape or even Australia. The most widely planted cultivar, the Müller-Thurgau, is an artificial cross based on the Riesling; it was developed by a Swiss oenologist in the 1880s and did not even exist in Busby's time. Another successful variety, the Pinotage, was introduced from South Africa in recent years and made New Zealand its second regional base. But New Zealand's winegrowers also succeed with older, venerable varieties such as the Cabernet Sauvignon, Pinot Noir, Chardonnay, and Sauvignon Blanc. New Zealand may come chronologically last, but it is not viniculturally least.

3

ANTIPODAL ATTITUDES

Certainly the wine regions of the Southern Hemisphere share a geographic handicap: their distance from the world's major wine-consuming markets. Apart from the cost of long-distance transportation, which has an effect on the price of every bottle, wine does not always travel well. Excessive heat, cold, or motion can spoil wine, and despite technological advances in both the preparation of wine for such journeys and the conditions of transport, problems still arise. Thus the domestic markets are especially important to the well-being of these distant wine industries, and what has been achieved in the Southern Hemisphere should be seen in the context of cultural traditions. Per capita consumption is highest in Argentina and Chile, and much lower in Australia, New Zealand, and South Africa. Wine industries also are sensitive to government policies, and these policies are of course a part of local culture and tradition. To a greater or lesser degree, wine has religious associations; as an alcohol-containing beverage its consumption must be in some way regulated by government. Production and qualitative classification also become political issues, and as an intoxicant wine constitutes an objective for moralists. The impact of culture and tradition on a wine industry could be no better illustrated than in the United States, where a period of prohibition set the industry back incalculably and where wine continues to be regulated by a government agency that also is responsible for hard liquor, tobacco, and firearms.

One would assume that enlightened and supportive government action would be demonstrated most effectively in the Southern Hemisphere countries peopled from wine-drinking, Mediterranean-Iberian sources, but this is only partially true. Argentina, the hemisphere's largest producer, also has a large domestic market with the highest per-capita consumption. The growth of the industry, especially in the

The headquarters building of the Instituto Nacional de Vitivinicultura, in the city of Mendoza, Argentina. In addition to its headquarters, the INV has a number of field offices in the country's dispersed wine districts. (Courtesy of INV.)

period after 1940, led the Argentine government to create, in 1959, the National Institute of Viti- and Viniculture (*Instituto Nacional de Vitivinicultura* or INV). Headquartered in the city of Mendoza in the heart of the wine country, the INV not only governs grape-growing and winemaking but also assists the industry through research, development aid, and promotional efforts. The INV certifies the quality of wines destined for overseas markets, and it simultaneously represents Argentina's wine industry in international arenas. The institute sometimes is described as a government within a government, and its power reflects the status of Argentina's viticulture as the country's third leading industry. Inevitably it has had its critics, especially when, after a period of vineyard expansion based on tax breaks and low-interest credit to prospective grapegrowers, there was serious overproduction and a price collapse in 1981. There are those who argue that the INV has promoted quantity at the expense of quality. But the global recession and troubled national economy caused much of the crisis of the early 1980s, and Argentina's wine industry simply mirrored these conditions. If it has not been immune to error, the *Instituto* nevertheless gave unity and coherence to the Argentinian wine industry and promoted its cause with the strength of official sanction.

Wine consumption is almost as much a part of Argentinian culture as it is a French and Italian custom. For many years the availability of low-priced Argentinian meats made the steak-and-wine meal an Argentinian tradition, which accounts for the high percentage of red wines consumed in the country (nearly 50 percent, including "criollas" and so-called clarets). But Argentina's home consumers did not press for quality as Europeans and North American wine drinkers did, so that the

Argentina's wine industry constitutes a major element in the national economy. Alone among Southern Hemisphere wine industries, it is quantitatively of world class, ranking among the five largest. The dimensions of the vineyards are enormous, as are the facilities for handling the huge harvest.

most ordinary wines always found ready markets. Then per-capita wine consumption suddenly peaked in 1970 with slightly more than 24 gallons, and a decline began. By the mid-1980s it had dropped to 20 gallons. This contributed further to the problems of the wine industry at home, at a time when other adversities were also being felt.

The varying fortunes of the Argentinian wine industry were not, however, caused by destructive intervention, prohibitionism, or other official obstruction. The nation's political and economic difficulties notwithstanding, the wine industry persisted, since wine's status as an essential element of local tradition was never threatened.

The same cannot be said for the wine industry of Argentina's neighbor, Chile. It is another one of those geographic ironies that Argentina, with a difficult natural environment for premium winemaking, has had a favorable social climate, whereas

Chile, capable of—and known for—quality winegrowing, has been far less hospitable. When Chilean viticulture entered its modern era, in the 1850s, the government encouraged the industry and helped winegrowers make the transition from old grape varieties to better ones from France. During the twentieth century, successive Chilean governments assisted smaller winegrowers by providing low-interest loans for the purpose of creating cooperative wineries. But even before modernization began, alcoholism was a social problem in Chile, and from time to time the specter of prohibition appeared. Government action to control this phenomenon inevitably had a negative impact on the industry, especially when such action took the form of limiting the cultivation of the vine in favor of food crops deemed to be more essential to the nation. Then the industry fell victim, in the early 1970s, to Chile's first serious attempt to redistribute its large landholdings. Old vineyards were pulled up and the land parceled out, and recovery did not begin until still another governmental change occurred.

Several organizations in Chile support and promote the wine industry. Perhaps the most effective of these is the *Federacion de Cooperativas Agricolas Vitivinicolas de Chile,* an association of ten winegrowers' cooperatives that markets as much as 15 percent of the country's annual production and buys grapes from small growers owning some 35,000 acres of vines. Chile's vineyards are highly fragmented, not to say shattered, and thousands of growers own less than two acres of vines. Without the cooperatives, set up with government support, they could not continue to cultivate grapes, having neither the capital nor the space to maintain wineries. Thus the *Federacion* and its members serve a crucial purpose.

Another important organization is the *Asociacion de Exportadores y Embotelladores de Vinos de Chile.* Not only does this association count among its members the most important producers in the country, but it also acts as a liaison between winegrowers and the government. For example the *Asociacion* long pressed the Ministry of Agriculture for the designation of Chilean "denominations of origin," official wine regions and subregions that would resemble classification systems in Europe and elsewhere. As Chapter 4 describes, that effort had significant success in 1979 and 1980.

One can only speculate what Chile's wine industry might have achieved if it had enjoyed consistent government support, but the situation could have been still worse. One positive result of governmental concern over alcoholism has been the tight, and mostly constructive, regulation of winegrowing. The established rules in some ways resemble French *Appellation d'Origine Contrôlée* wine laws, and include controls over yields per unit area, alcohol content of the finished wine, and terminology associated with aging periods. These controls, and Chile's advantageous natural environments, have contributed strongly to the international reputation of the country's fine wines.

The cultural *milieu* for wine in Brazil has improved markedly in recent decades, and especially since the mid-1960s. Brazil's remarkable economic growth enlarged the consumer base, and Brazilians who had been drinking expensive foreign wines as a matter of social standing discovered that the domestic industry also could produce good wines. During the boom period of the 1970s production doubled, and the government supported this expansion by providing technological assistance and credit to winegrowers. The industry received a further boost through the constructive involvement of overseas companies from France and the United States. Almaden, for example, has a joint American-Brazilian enterprise in Rio Grande do Sul, and Moët & Chandon provides assistance with bottling and packaging. These international involvements signal Brazil's entry into the foreign market, where Brazilian wines are yet little known. The economic slowdown in Brazil (as elsewhere) inhibited the growth of consumption of wine at home, so that Brazilian growers have looked for export markets as an alternative.

Brazil has taken its place among the Southern Hemisphere's major wine producers, and it potentially has a larger domestic market than all other southern wine producers combined. But per-capita wine consumption in Brazil is yet low, and despite its dominantly Portuguese heritage, Brazil is not a wine-drinking country in a class with Spain or Argentina. Thus the future of the Brazilian industry will depend upon local education and promotion, and to some extent upon success in foreign markets. Crucial to all this is the role of the government, whose enlightened support has helped Brazil's wine industry progress so far so fast.

South Africa did not have to await a late nineteenth-century surge of Italian immigrants to bring vitality to its wine industry. From the beginning, winemaking was encouraged and aided, and the Dutch-French farming population at the Cape developed a thriving business. When, early in the nineteenth century, the British presence at the Cape grew larger, and English tastes for table wines and fortified wines increased the demand, the winegrowers responded. More important, England's conflict with France had severed trade (and hence wine) connections with the European mainland, so that Cape wines found ready markets in Britain; a preferential tariff made this export trade even more profitable. South Africa's wine industry experienced a half-century-long golden age—which ended abruptly when, in 1861, the British terminated the special market advantage for Cape wines. Many vineyards were uprooted, and those that were not were invaded by the dread disease *phylloxera* in the 1880s. Recovery was followed by disastrous overproduction and price collapse, and in 1918 this situation heralded the beginning of the industry's modern era.

South Africa's KWV, the Cooperative Winegrowers' Association, was established in 1918. Its chief objective was, and remains (in the words of its constitution) to direct, control, and regulate the sale and disposal by its members of their produce, and to secure a continuously adequate return for such produce. Born of the crisis during and after World War I, the KWV rescued the industry and, in the mid-1920s, achieved government recognition as the governing body of South African winegrowing.

The KWV claims a unique status among world winegrowers' associations, and certainly there is nothing quite like it anywhere else. All winegrowers in South Africa must be KWV members and are subject to its rules, although winegrowers also may join other cooperative wineries. Relationships between these other cooperative wineries and the KWV have not always been amiable. Premium estate wineries and quality-oriented cooperatives sometimes found their needs and objectives in conflict with KWV regulations. During a period of overproduction, for example, the KWV can prohibit the planting of new vineyards, even on a prestigious estate that does not market its wine through the KWV or any other cooperative. This may mean that problems at the mass-production level inhibit experimentation and development at the premium level, and it probably has slowed the evolution of

The central administrative offices of the Cooperative Winegrowers' Association (KWV) are located at the association's stately La Concorde, Paarl, South Africa. (Photograph by D. Rallis.)

some areas of great potential. The KWV did rescue the Cape wine industry in the 1920s, but its restrictions have weighed heavily on the country's winegrowing in recent decades.

On the other hand, successive South African governments have generally supported and encouraged the industry, and the commercial tradition that was established at the Cape in the 1650s has been maintained. One manifestation of this support is the Oenological and Viticultural Research Institute of the Directorate of Agricultural Technical Services, located just outside the town of Stellenbosch on a former farm, Nietvoorbij. The Institute was established in 1955, and Nietvoorbij was acquired in 1960, including more than 500 acres of land for experimental viticulture. A large headquarters building and cellar were completed several years later, and additional land parcels for experimental grapegrowing were added in the Cape's outlying districts. The Institute performs its research with the aid of the most modern equipment extant, and the expertise of its large staff ranges from pedology and climatology to ampelography and chemistry. Soil-cultivar relationships, irrigation, fertilizing, disease control, vineyard techniques, and many aspects of wine production are studied, and the results made available to winegrowers who request it. The Institute, furthermore, acts as an independent agency in the supervision of laws and regulations governing South African winegrowing.

The dimensions of the South African wine industry should, however, be viewed in the context of the country's multiracial population. The sector with the strongest wine-consuming tradition, of course, consists of people with European

The Oenological and Viticultural Research Institute at Nietvoorbij, near Stellenbosch, is tangible evidence of the government's support for the wine industry. (Photograph by D. Rallis.)

ancestries; they number fewer than five million. In the vineyards of the Cape, the majority of the workers are of mixed or "Coloured" origin, and while they too consume wine their numbers are under three million. Wine is not a traditional drink among the country's large black majority nor among the Asian minority. Promotion of wine in these potential markets has had some slight effect, but the key to the industry's prosperity continues to lie in the white sector of the home market and in the export of high-priced, quality wines. The United Kingdom long has been a major market, and in the 1980s South African wines appeared in greater quantities in North American wine shops.

Before Australia became a commonwealth, the wine industries of the colonies of New South Wales, Victoria, and South Australia went their own ways, protected from competition by the colonial boundaries. Tariff barriers allowed the Hunter Valley wineries virtually uncontested domination in the large urban area of Sydney; winegrowing in Victoria was oriented toward Melbourne, and South Australia's Barossa Valley had Adelaide as its major urban market. Then, in 1901, the situation changed radically as a result of the customs agreement that was part of the formation of the federal union. Wines could now cross state boundaries unimpeded, and a flood of low-priced South Australian wine displaced the Hunter Valley wines. As a result, the Hunter Valley went into a lengthy decline, and vineyards in South Australia and Victoria thrived.

Australia's wineries did not escape the vicissitudes experienced in other Southern Hemisphere countries, and indeed the world: economic recession, market isolation during World War I, overproduction, price collapse, reorganization, revival. But Australia's wine industry had other, local problems as well. In part these had a cultural origin. The prestigious and productive Barossa Valley had been settled mainly by German immigrants, and during the war years a strong anti-German feeling arose in this, a British commonwealth. So strong was this animosity that the Australian government actually passed legislation to rid the landscape of German names: the famed Kaiser-Stuhl cooperative was renamed Mount Kitchener (many wineries, including Kaiser-Stuhl, regained their original German names in later years).

Another problem for the wine industry was the government's policy of settling returning members of Australia's armed forces. Although the majority were awarded land in irrigated areas of the Murray and Murrumbidgee basins, others were settled on parcels carved out of superior wine regions, even the Hunter Valley. The soldier families, all too often, were unprepared for a life as winegrowers or grapegrowers. When the economic depression struck and the domestic market collapsed, the government in some areas offered the soldier-grapegrowers a bonus if they would uproot their vines and substitute other kinds of farming; many took the offer and some long-established vines were cut down. Not until the renewed isolation of World War II did real recovery occur, because home consumption increased at unprecedented rates during this period. Again the government alloted land to returning soldiers, and the postwar period at first witnessed a decline in vine acreage—until, in the 1960s, the promise of the war period was confirmed, and per-capita consumption began a steady upward trend. More important, Australian tastes changed from sweet and fortified wines to table wines, and public education and promotion bore fruit.

Even during the past twenty-five years of progress and success, Australia's wine industry has not, of course, been without problems, and these illustrate well the crucial role of government in the evolution of this specialized, fragile enterprise. By keeping tariffs on imported wines high, the domestic industry can be effectively protected—at the risk of lowered initiative toward quality because of the lowered threat of competition. By facilitating and supporting wine exports to foreign markets, the government committees must decide what will be sent to represent Australia (and other southern wine countries) in overseas competition. By taxing wines without adequate consideration of the consequences, state- and national governments can endanger the future of entire regions or areas of specialization. In Australia, for example, the government in the late 1970s increased the excise on local brandy by more than 80 percent, whereupon domestic sales of (chiefly South Australian) brandy declined by more than one-third. The Riverland wine region faced a crisis, and did not rebound until the government repealed its ill-advised action.

The Australian wine industry still expands regionally, and improved governmental awareness of its special needs is now among the main reasons. In South Africa, too, a wide range of tax advantages and tax benefits aids the winegrower. In New Zealand, on the other hand, government has found it difficult to strike the necessary balance. This is not surprising in view of the comparative recency of the wine industry's modern expansion there; it is essentially the product of the 1970s.

Winegrowing began in New Zealand more than 150 years ago, but by the beginning of World War II there still were fewer than 200 acres of vineyards devoted

The Viticultural Research Station at Te Kawhata, New Zealand. This research station, with adjacent experimental vineyards, is operated by the Ministry of Agriculture and Fisheries.

to wine grapes in the entire country. New Zealand's real potential began to be realized in the 1960s, and during the 1970s vineyard acreage expanded by as much as 1000 acres annually, reaching 13,000 by the mid-1980s. This was rapid growth indeed, and it was coupled with a far-reaching vinicultural reorientation as well as a qualitative revolution. Small wonder that administrative action did not always keep pace. Commented an Australian Senate Committee in a 1977 report on tax policies:

> [New Zealand's] wine industry is penalized by comparison with other sections of the liquor industry in that beer and spirits pay a specific duty per gallon in lieu of sales tax, whereas wine attracts a sales tax of 20 percent on the wholesale price. Because the wholesale price includes the costs of bottles, packaging, labor and freight, all of which are beyond the wine maker's ability to control, the effect of [New Zealand's] *ad valorem* sales tax grossly inflates the final retail selling price of New Zealand wines.[1]

On the other hand, government support through investments by its Development Finance Corporation, and by the imposition of substantial customs duties on imported wine, had a more positive effect on the domestic wine industry.

New Zealand's domestic market is small, and its per-capita annual wine consumption one of the lowest in the Western world, just slightly more than 3 gallons. This represents, nevertheless, a 50 percent increase over the early 1970s and reflects the growing appreciation of New Zealand wines by the home consumer. Still, there has not been the loyalty to the domestic product seen in Australia. "Whereas New Zealanders tend to believe that anything imported is better, Australians have a much greater faith and loyalty to their . . . wine," writes the editor of a

New Zealand wine magazine.[2] And this, of course, is an important issue, because Australia's larger market is the obvious initial goal for New Zealand wine exports. During the 1980s Australia and New Zealand negotiated a Closer Economic Relationship (CER), under the terms of which the flow of wine across the Tasman Sea will become increasingly free; beginning in 1986, a four-year reduction in tariff barriers will lead to totally open competition for all wines on both markets in 1990 and beyond. It will be the ultimate test for this, the smallest but potentially the best of the Southern Hemisphere's major wine industries.

The Southern Hemisphere presents a wide range of regional climates and microclimates, and a diversity of cultures, traditions, and attitudes in its wine regions. The hemisphere's wine-producing countries have seen their industries develop in different directions, but there are common threads, historic as well as modern. The absence of wild vines precluded anything like the sequence of events in North America. Distances to profitable European markets always were large for all, and intensified the isolation of two world wars. The search for the best and most suitable environments for viticulture continues wherever winegrowing takes place. The story of wine in the Southern Hemisphere is the saga of the ultimate alliance between the human spirit and the civilizing vine.

4

CHILE:

FACING THE PACIFIC

O n the entire world map there is no other country quite like Chile. Its ribbon of land lies wedged between mountain and ocean, 2700 miles long but averaging a mere 110 miles in width. In the north, where Chile borders Peru and Bolivia, the countryside is desert and the heat is tropical. In the far south, where fiordlike bays indent the coast and the strip breaks up into thousands of islands, Chile penetrates the frigid waters of Antarctic seas. Chile is the textbook example of what geographers call an elongated state: a country whose pronounced attenuation has played a significant role in national life. And indeed Chile's historical geography is replete with tales of strife and competition on its northern and southern frontiers.

Standing on Chile's Pacific shore, one is able to see the snow-capped Andes Mountains that form the country's physical as well as political boundary. Travel the rising slopes inland, and at the border as one turns to look westward lies the Pacific Ocean. Viewed from such perspectives, the country's narrowness and confinement are acutely evident. Chile is the Andes' western embankment, a pediment at the foot of one of the world's greatest mountain chains. Behind Santiago, Mount Aconcagua reaches nearly 23,000 feet, the highest mountain in the Western Hemisphere but by no means the only Andean peak to exceed 20,000 feet. The Andes are a formidable barrier indeed.

But the Andes are not the only mountains in Chile. In the middle segment of Chile's elongated zone, the country—narrow though it is—has a coastal range rising directly out of the Pacific, a *cordillera* that exceeds 7000-foot elevations in the north (west of Santiago), declines to little more than 1000 feet near Concepción, where it is interrupted, and then emerges again to exceed 5000 feet south of Valdivia. Farther to the south this coastal range becomes the backbone of the island of Chiloë.

The effect of the coastal *cordillera*, which has the landscape of a series of flat-topped, valley-cut plateaus, is to create an elongated basin between the Andes and these Pacific highlands. This basin, the Central Valley, contains Chile's core area, its *Nucleo Central*. Near its northern end lies Santiago, where many of the first vineyards were planted (Fig. 4.1).

Chile's rivers are short, wild, and crucial to viticulture. They flow off the Andes, fed by melting snow and orographic precipitation, and cut their way directly to the Pacific Ocean. Their strength and volume increase from north to south, and in northern Chile's dry zone the Río Loa is the only stream to reach the sea; the others die out in the Atacama Desert's rock and sand. The Río Copiapó, at about 27° south, also reaches the Pacific, in the process supporting a 100-mile ribbon of settlement and agriculture, including grapegrowing. The Copiapó River is traditionally regarded as the southern end of the Atacama Desert; southward both the volume and the incidence of streams increase, though slowly at first.

In the middle segment of Chile, the rivers flowing off the Andes cross not only the Central Valley but the coastal range as well, there cutting canyonlike valleys through the highlands. In this region, the rivers are vital to agriculture, providing a steady supply of water for irrigation during the growing season. They are important in another way, having for millions of years deposited the sediments that now constitute the deep and fertile soils in their basins.

The Central Valley extends between the approximate latitudes 33° and 42° south, which is within the environmental zone most favorable for viticulture in the hemisphere. In the general latitude of Coquimbo, about 30° south, the desert conditions that dominate northern Chile give way to moister weather, and the zone of Mediterranean regime begins. The winters are mild and wet, the summers generally cool and dry. In Santiago, the coolest winter months (June and July) average 46° F. in temperature. Winter frosts occur in the Central Valley, but more frequently in its southern half than in the north. Snowfall is unusual, although not unknown.

The Mediterranean regime has its strongest and most typical expression in the northern Central Valley. Toward the south, temperatures decline and the characteristic summer-dry season fades as rainfall increases. At Santiago in the north, annual rainfall is only about 14 inches, almost all of it coming during the winter months. Around Concepción, about the midpoint of the Central Valley, annual precipitation is more than 30 inches and rain can come during any month of the year; the summer-dry season has all but disappeared. Now the regime known as marine west coast (see Fig. 1.5) develops, and precipitation and cloud cover intensify. At the latitude of Valdivia the annual precipitation along the coast is well over 100 inches.

Climatic regions usually merge along broad transition zones (as the Mediterranean regime does in yielding to other climes in Europe). But in Chile, the transition from Mediterranean to non-Mediterranean conditions is quite sharply defined. It happens along the valley of the Río Bío-Bío as it crosses the Central Valley: the

Figure 4.1. Chile and its Nucleo Central.

northern slope of the river's basin still carries imprints of Mediterranean conditions, but these are missing to the south. As a result, the Río Bío-Bío is traditionally taken as the dividing line between the northern and southern halves of the Central Valley. It is the northern half that is properly called the country's core, the *Nucleo Central*.

For all intents and purposes, the Bío-Bío region also is the southern limit of winegrowing in Chile. Some farmers have tried to grow grapes even in the former province of Cautin, but cold temperatures and excessive moisture have discouraged this. The combined effect of cold offshore waters, cool winds, the Andean wall, and excessive moisture is to limit viticulture to about 40°S in Chile (and effective viniculture to several degrees north of this). In New Zealand, by contrast, wine grapes are grown as far as nearly 44°S. Chile's winegrowing zone is limited indeed.

This is true in a northward direction also. North of the valley of the Río Aconcagua, the Central Valley closes off, the terrain quickly becomes desertlike, and amid the rock and scrub the only cultivation occurs along the streams. Here the vine stands among other crops, exposed to searing heat and sustained by irrigation. The streams die out at Copiapó; northward they become ephemeral and fail to reach the sea. Thus heat and drought limit viticulture to the north, as do cold and wetness to the south. Grapes can be—and are—grown from latitude 27° south to 40° south, but the premium winegrowing regions lie in a much narrower zone, corresponding approximately to the northern half of the Central Valley, between latitudes 32° and 38° south.

Regions of Chile

Chile's pronounced attenuation has given rise to several kinds of regional subdivision. Every country has what geographers call "perceptual" regions, that is, regions of popular consensus (such as the Midwest in the United States or the Midi of France). In Chile, seven such traditionally recognized regions exist. From north to south, these are the Great North or *Norte Grande* of the vast desert astride the Tropic of Capricorn; the Little North or *Norte Chico* adjacent; the Central Heartland or *Nucleo Central* of Middle Chile; the Bío-Bío region; the Frontier or *La Frontera* south of Bío-Bío; the scenic lake region of the forested south, called *Los Lagos*; and *Canales*, the water-channeled region of Chilean Patagonia overlooking Antarctic waters.

These, however, are impressionistic divisions of Chile. Until recently, the country was divided into provinces that were more specifically defined. As the map shows, these extended from the mountainous Argentinian border to the Pacific Ocean (Fig. 4.2). The provinces were smaller in the populous middle part of the country, and larger in the northern desert and southern frontier regions. Premium wine production may be said to extend from Aconcagua in the north (that is, the valley of the Aconcagua River) to the former province of Bío-Bío in the south, which is essentially the basin of the Río Bío-Bío, another of Chile's major rivers.

The Chilean government has established thirteen administrative divisions of Chile, and these are viticulturally important because they also have been used in the creation of official, designated wine districts. Some of these administrative regions

Figure 4.2. Provinces and regions of Chile.

consist of sets of adjacent provinces, but not in the far north or south. The four large northern provinces (Tarapacá, Antofagasta, Atacama, and Coquimbo) each acquired their own regional status, with the cities of Iquique, Antofagasta, Copiapó, and La Serena as their respective capitals. In the frontier south, the three political regions are De Los Lagos (south of the province of Cautin and centered on Puerto Montt), Aisén del General Carlos Ibañez del Campo (or Aisén for short, with Coihaique the capital), and Magallanes y Antartica Chilena, with Punta Arenas as its administrative headquarters.

Between these large regions of the north and the south lie the six regions of Chile's heartland. Aconcagua, north of the capital, consists of the former provinces of Aconcagua and Valparaiso, and has the city of Valparaiso as its capital. Next comes Santiago (or properly the Metropolitan Region of Santiago) comprising the capital city and its provincial environs. South of Santiago's region lies O'Higgins, consisting of the old provinces of O'Higgins and Colchagua and centered on the city of Rancagua. Still farther south is the region of Maule, encompassing the former provinces of Curicó, Talca, Maule, and Linares and served by the city of Talca. Adjacent lies the Bío-Bío region, formed by the old provinces of Ñuble, Concepción, Bío-Bío, and Arauco and headquartered in the port of Concepción. Finally there is the region of Araucania, consisting of the former provinces of Malleco and Cautin, with the city of Temuco as its capital.

In the shorthand of Chilean administration, these thirteen regions are given numbers for quick identification. Thus Coquimbo is region IV, Aconcagua is V, O'Higgins is VI, Maule is VII, and Bío-Bío is VIII, and so on; agricultural data from government sources sometimes simply refer to a region as "VI" or "VIII."

GENERALIZED WINE REGIONS

In the most general way, Chilean viticulture may be divided regionally into three segments, although some differences of opinion still prevail regarding their boundaries. Few would argue about the location or extent of Chile's northernmost winegrowing region, the Pisquera zone. It lies north of the boundary between the regions of Coquimbo and Aconcagua and extends northward as far as viticulture remains possible in the desert environment (Fig. 4.3). Here the vines stand in stream-fed, ribbon-shaped oases, their juice is distilled, and the chief product is a brandylike wine called Pisco. The alcohol content of Pisco is high, ranging to as much as 45 percent, and it is usually mixed with lemon juice and sugar and consumed as Pisco Sour, regarded as a national drink in Chile. Pisco has been made here for a very long time—it has been popular for centuries and contributed strongly to problems of alcoholism—and it has undeniably had an adverse effect on the national wine industry. Prohibitionism, aimed mainly at the widespread and excessive indulgence in Pisco-based beverages, affected the table-wine producers as well.

South of the Pisquera zone lies the heartland of Chilean viticulture, the Regadío zone. This Central zone extends from Aconcagua in the north to the Maule River in the south, where, according to the simplest regionalization, it gives way to the Secano zone, the southernmost winegrowing region. There is no sharp break along the Río Maule, however. As conditions become moister toward the south,

Figure 4.3. Wine regions of Chile.

irrigation fades out, so that it may be appropriate to recognize a Transition zone between Regadío and Secano. No irrigation of any kind occurs in the "true" Secano zone.

The fourfold regional division of Chile suggested by Figure 4.3 has environmental as well as viticultural justification. In the Pisquera zone, drought dominates and all vineyards are sustained by irrigation. In the Regadío (Central) zone, precipitation increases from north to south; it averages just 10 inches annually in the Aconcagua area, 20 inches in O'Higgins and Colchagua, and about 28 inches in Talca. Virtually all the northern vineyards in the Regadío zone are irrigated, but as precipitation increases toward the south, unirrigated vineyards expand. By the time the Transitional zone develops, about as many vineyards are unirrigated as are irrigated. South of the last of the irrigated vineyards begins the Secano zone, which is limited to the south by excessive moisture and coldness.

The distribution of irrigated vineyards also displays a longitudinal variation. As Figure 4.3 suggests, there is an "unirrigated zone" located on the slopes of the coastal cordillera. Some Chilean viticulturists divide both the Regadío and the northern Secano (or Transition) zones into irrigated and unirrigated subregions, although, as noted, the unwatered vineyards expand beyond the coastal ranges as latitude increases in the Bío-Bío region. Hence the distinction loses much of its significance toward the south. The unirrigated zone is of special interest in the Cauquenes area of the former Maule Province (see Fig. 4.2), where notably favorable microclimates make possible the production of some of Chile's best Rieslings and Sauvignon Blancs.

Thus Chilean winegrowing, even within its comparatively narrow latitudinal range, takes place under a great deal of environmental diversity—and the wines evince this. Within a 400-mile stretch of Chile lie vineyards under desert, steppe, Mediterranean, and even marine west coast conditions. At their best, Chilean environments constitute a powerful ally of viticulture, the climate ranking among the most favorable in the world. Water supply is reliable; soils, especially in the Central Valley, are deep and coarsely textured. But no two latitudes in Chile are exactly the same in terms of environmental conditions, and this too is reflected by the country's wines.

REGIONS OF ORIGIN

Chile's wines have long enjoyed an international reputation for quality and consistency. Truly poor vintage years are rare under Chile's equable climatic regimes, and vinicultural practices and marketing procedures are strictly regulated by government control. It has been suggested that Chilean vintages have varied more as a result of domestic political circumstances than climatic vicissitudes; the Marxist period of the early 1970s was a difficult one for the industry, and quality suffered.

This is not to suggest, however, that Chile's wines, in good years, do not vary in character and style. What has been said about regional variations in precipitation and temperature from the Pisquera to the Secano zone indicates that grapes in various parts of the country will develop differently during the ripening season. Cultivars of the north—the Muscats, the Folle Blanche, the País—are not the same

CONCHA y TORO

ESTATE   BOTTLED

75%
Cabernet Sauvignon/Merlot
25%

RAPEL RED TABLE WINE

The classic blend of many fine Chateaux of Bordeaux.
Cabernet Sauvignon for complexity and longevity,
Merlot for softness and elegance.

1981

PRODUCED AND BOTTLED IN RAPEL CHILE BY VIÑA CONCHA y TORO S.A.
ALCOHOL 12% BY VOL.   CONTENTS 1.5 LITER
IMPORTED BY EXCELSIOR WINE & SPIRITS CORP. NEW YORK, N.Y. 10016

Beginning in 1980, wine region identifications appeared on Chilean wine labels. This Cabernet-Merlot from Concha y Toro was made, as the label states, in the Rapel Region.

as those of the Central Regadío zone, where the noble grapes prevail. But the Cabernet Sauvignon in the Aconcagua area produces a different wine than the same cultivar does on the banks of the Bío-Bío.

Chilean wines are exported to many countries, including the United States and several European markets. The evolution of E.E.C. regulations governing wine classification and commerce stimulated a number of other countries to tighten their own wine laws, especially those with strong trade connections with the Common Market.

Chile was one of these countries. Government control over viniculture practices had long been quite rigorous, but regional designations were traditional and a matter of custom rather than law. In 1979, the Ministry of Agriculture established an initial regionalization of Chilean viticulture, officially recognizing the following seven *Regiones Vitivinicolas:*

1. The Atacama region, for wines produced in Region III, the former Atacama Province.
2. The Coquimbo region, for wines produced in Region IV, the former Coquimbo Province.
3. The Aconcagua region V, for wines produced in the former provinces of Aconcagua and Valparaiso.
4. The Maipo region, for wines produced in the Santiago Metropolitan Region.

The cellars of the famed old firm Undurraga once lay well removed from Santiago's urban area. Today the winery, shown here, is surrounded by urban sprawl.

5. The Rapel region, for wines produced in Region VI: O'Higgins and Colchagua.
6. The Maule region, for wines produced in Region VII: the former Curicó, Talca, Linares, and Maule provinces and, in addition, the wines of Nuble province of Region VIII.
7. The Bío-Bío region, for wines produced in Region VIII: the former Concepción, Arauco, and Bío-Bío provinces, but not including Nuble.[1]

This, of course, represents the most generalized regional subdivision of Chilean viticulture. The system is based on the existing administrative framework, and has the effect of grouping individual and quite distinctive winegrowing districts together under a single designation. In 1980, the government issued a decree establishing subregions for four of the seven wine regions: Maipo, Rapel, Maule, and Bío-Bío. Labels, thus, must carry the *regional* designation if the grapes from which the wine is made come from various areas in the region; but if the source of the grapes is more specific, the *subregional* designation may be shown.

In the Maipo region, the officially designated subregions are Isla de Maipo, Santiago, Pirque, Buin, Santa Ana, and Llano del Maipo (Fig. 4.4). Some of the best wines from this region are made at Pirque and Santa Ana in the valley of the Maipo River, and also in the urban shadow of Santiago itself. Urban growth has consumed many of Chile's historic vineyards, but some survive in suburban Macul, east of the capital (M on Figure 4.4). Not all of the Santiago region's prominent winegrowing centers were given subregion status; for example, the town of Linderos, south of Buin, is known for its quality wines (L on Figure 4.4). But Linderos is not among Santiago's subregional designations.

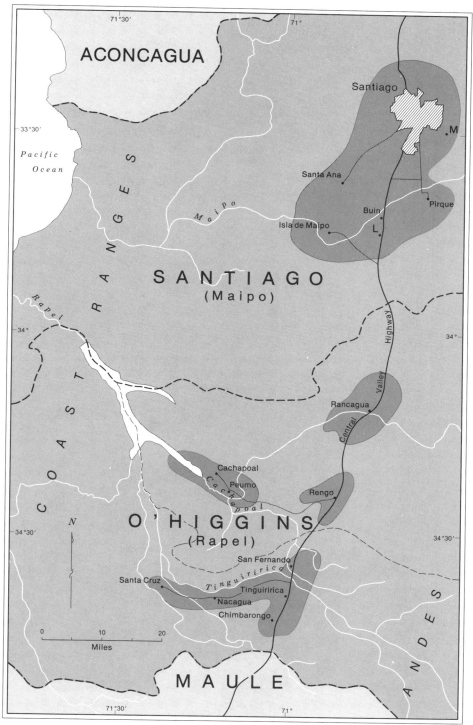

Figure 4.4. Maipo and Rapel wine districts and the city of Santiago, Chile.

VIÑA LINDEROS

Cabernet-Sauvignon
—*nombre varietal*—

para guarda

Las características de este vino corresponden completamente a las de su variedad y no han sido empañadas por el gusto a roble americano; además, ya cumplió con su período de maduración en vasija y desarrollará un gran potencial de envejecimiento si es guardado en botella ("para guarda"). Se recomienda mantener las botellas en posición horizontal, en un lugar donde no hayan grandes variaciones de temperatura.

Producido y embotellado en origen por Viña Linderos
Viñedos Ortiz S.A. - teléfonos 61665 y 87256

Contenido 0,7 L   LINDEROS-MAIPO-CHILE   Grado alcohólico 12° GL

Imp. Meza

Linderos is a respected viticultural name in Chile. This label identifies a Cabernet Sauvignon from that locale, made by Viñedos Ortiz.

The Rapel region (VI), consisting of the old provinces of O'Higgins and Colchagua, is essentially the basin of the Rapel River and is thus appropriately named, although the Rio Rapel becomes the Tinguiririca River upstream (see Fig. 4.4). As the Tinguiririca, the Rapel River flows through the middle of the former Colchagua Province, is joined by the Cachapoal, and then for a short distance forms the boundary between the two former provinces. The designated wine regions lie in the zone where this extensive river system crosses the Central Valley.

There are ten designated subregions in the Rapel region, of which four lie in what was O'Higgins Province. Rancagua, the regional capital, lies amid vineyards on the Cachapoal River. Downstream lie Peumo and Cachapoal. In Colchagua, the subregions flank the upper Rapel (Tinguiririca) River, including San Fernando, Tinguiririca, and Chimbarongo along the highway and Nancagua and Santa Cruz to the west, downstream. It is noteworthy that none of these designations (except

The best Chilean red wines are aged for years in wood and bottle. The once-reliable system of label identification (reserva, gran reserva) no longer applies, and a new system is being devised. Here, Cabernet Sauvignon rests in barrels in the cellars of Undurraga. (Photograph by Edwin W. Snider.)

Santa Cruz, the westernmost) affects the vineyards of the coastal ranges. In these latitudes, the coastal cordillera's vineyards consist almost entirely of lesser varieties such as the País and Torontel, and the wines do not merit subregion status.

The Maule region (VII) includes its four old provinces plus Nuble, and no fewer than thirteen designations. The key artery in this region is the Maule River, which has its source in the Andes of Talca Province, forms part of the boundary between Talca and Linares, and reaches the sea in the former Maule Province. The Río Maule is often regarded to be the southern boundary of the "true" Regadío or Central winegrowing zone, but the officially designated Maule viticulture region extends not only beyond the Maule River, but even beyond the borders of Region VII to incorporate Nuble as well.

This is why the Maule region carries so many viticultural designations. At the heart of it lies the regional capital, Talca, the best-known of the subregions, with nearby San Clemente upstream along the Río Maule, San Javier to the south, and Molina to the north. Most of the important winegrowing districts lie along or near the main route that extends north-south through the Central Valley; the hub of the vineyards lies in the zone where the Maule River and its tributaries cross the valley from east to west. Such familiar places as Curicó (the old provincial capital) and nearby Lontué, Linares (another former provincial capital), Parral, and Chillán (Nuble's focus) are all designated viticulture centers as well. Less well known are the designations of Sagrada Familia, Quillón, and Villa Alegre. Of particular interest is the subregion designation awarded to Cauquenes in Maule; this subregion represents the wines of the unirrigated vineyards of the coastal range, which here achieve superior character and quality.

The Bío-Bío viticultural region (VIII without Nuble) was awarded just two designations: Yumbel and Coelemu. Both are located in what was Concepcion Province: Yumbel on the slopes of the coastal range on a tributary of the Bío-Bío River, and Coelemu in the northern tip of the province, near the coast on the Ilata River. Viticulturally, these subregions belong with Cauquenes just to the north; these are not Central Valley vineyards but, rather, districts of the moist coastal cordillera.

Vines and Wines

In the mid-1980s Chile had approximately 270,000 acres under the vine, a remarkable 70 percent representing red varieties. Chilean viticulturists differentiate between noble varieties (*Finas*) and ordinary grapes (*Corrientes*). Among the noble reds are the Cabernet Sauvignon, the Cot (the regional name for the Malbec of France), the Merlot, the Petit Verdot, and the Pinot Noir. Ordinary red varieties include the País, Carignan, and Muscat Romano. Recognized as noble white cultivars are the Riesling, the Sauvignon Blanc, the Sémillon, and the Pinot Blanc. Ordinary whites are the Muscats, the Torontel, the "Italia" (Ugni Blanc) and several others of uncertain parentage. Using this rather rough distinction between noble and common grapes, it is estimated that slightly more than one quarter of Chile's vineyard acreage is devoted to the best varieties.[2]

Very little of this acreage lies in the Pisquera zone of the Atacama and Coquimbo regions. Here, on about 12,000 acres, most of them along streams or in oasislike settings, stand the hardy Muscats, Torontel, Folle Blanche, País, and other varieties whose grapes will yield fortified wines. Some vineyards have been planted on higher slopes, as much as 5,000 feet above sea level, in the eastern parts of the region, and a few acres are devoted to the Chenin Blanc. In addition to its fortified wines, the region today also produces some sparkling wines. But the emphasis remains on the Pisco (brandy), destined for the domestic market.

The terrain in these northern regions is rough, rainfall is minimal, and sunshine is plentiful. There is little cloud cover. Yet the Pisquera zone is not as hot as might be imagined. Viticulturists measure the amount of warmth received during the growing season by totalling the number of degrees above 50°F. reached by the average temperature of each successive day, and they call the result the heat summation of a locality. In California's Central Valley, this total usually exceeds 3,500 degrees and even 4,000 at some stations. By comparison, the Atacama-Coquimbo vineyards remain surprisingly cool, their heat summations ranging from 2,880 to 3,060 degrees Fahrenheit.[3] The proximity of the cool waters of the Peru (Humboldt) Current, onshore winds, cold desert nights, and the moderating effect of elevation combine to produce this effect.

The soils of the northern valleys and slopes are suitable, if not exceptionally desirable, for viticulture: there are fertile volcanic soils derived from Andean rocks, sandy soils of river valleys, and some loams. The main difficulty in the north is not temperature, nor is it the soil; rather it is moisture. As would be inferred from

Figure 1.5, the Pisquera zone receives, in an average year, no more than 8 inches of rainfall—less in the far north. That average is not really relevant, however, because variability is high. Some years are comparatively moist, far exceeding the mean. Then follows a series of years in which rainfall is less than half the average. Irrigation can ensure a steady supply of water to the vines, but artificial watering cannot protect the vineyards against another threat posed by the region's environment: violent storms. When the rains do come, they often fall in severe cloudbursts accompanied by destructive winds and damaging sheet floods.

Thus the Atacama and Coquimbo regions truly are part of Chile's viticultural frontier. Some success has been achieved with a specialized product, and certain opportunities remain (the expansion of table grapes is among these), but the natural environment poses a serious challenge to winegrowing.

Chile's zone of premium winegrowing, the Regadío, includes the Aconcagua, Maipo, Rapel, and Maule wine regions. These are the vineyards of the Central Valley, the irrigated lands near the major rivers and unirrigated vines in the coastal cordillera. Actually, the Central Valley begins south of Aconcagua, but the lowland of the Rio Aconcagua shares many environmental characteristics with the stream valleys farther to the south. Hence the Central zone of viticulture begins, in the north, in Aconcagua.

So defined, the Regadío includes more than 110,000 acres of vineyards, of which 94,000 are irrigated and 16,000 are unirrigated. The designated subregions, as noted earlier, are concentrated in the zone where the rivers—the Aconcagua, Maipo, Cachapoal, Tinguiririca-Rapel, Lontué, Maule—traverse the Central Valley. Yields per acre are high (too high for sustained quality in some areas), and the Regadío generates as much as 55 percent of Chile's annual wine production. Thus there *is* variation in Chilean premium wines, the region's relatively dependable climate notwithstanding. Rainfall increases from north to south; it is nearly three times as much in Maule as it is in Aconcagua. The soils of some river valleys are better textured than others. The length and character of the summer-dry season under the Mediterranean regime changes from north to south. Above all, vinicultural practices vary, and certain producers have achieved worldwide reputations for the character and quality of their wines. Therefore the creation of Chilean "denominations of origin" had ample justification.

The Regadío is primarily a red wine–producing zone, and the Cabernet Sauvignon is the most widely cultivated noble variety in the irrigated vineyards. (Overall, the País is the most commonly grown variety; about 90 percent of all unirrigated vineyards stand under País.) But in Chile as elsewhere, the popularity of white wines is growing, and the acreages of Chardonnay, Riesling, Sauvignon Blanc, and Sémillon are expanding. It remains to be seen, however, whether Chile's winegrowers can match their success with red wines where the whites are concerned. Chilean Chardonnays, Rieslings, and sparkling wines have not achieved a reputation comparable to that of the excellent Cabernet Sauvignons.

Thus the Regadío remains of interest primarily as a red wine region. After the Cabernet Sauvignon, the Cot (Malbec) is the most widely grown cultivar, followed by the Merlot. Smaller acreages are devoted to the Carignan, Pinot Noir, and Verdot. These are the varieties introduced by the French advisers of the nineteenth century, and they have been cultivated in accordance with French methodology, principally the Espalier and Guyot systems of vineyard management. The two-armed Espalier and single-armed Guyot systems provide control for limited yield and high quality (the Guyot system has long prevailed in the Médoc). They are integral parts of the Regadío's viticultural landscape.

After the political interlude of the early 1970s, a significant change came to Chilean winegrowing. Lands that hitherto had been reserved for food production were now opened to viticulture, and white cultivars were planted on fertile lowlands. Here an old Spanish training system, the Parrales, was used. The vine grows up tall posts and along horizontal wires. Growth is much more abundant, yields are higher—and the wines are rather less distinguished as a rule.

THE ACONCAGUA REGION

When the Chilean Ministry of Agriculture published its 1980 decree establishing the subregional designations of the Regadío, it did not create any such appellations for the Aconcagua region. This underscores the separateness of the Aconcagua, the way this region stands apart from the Central Valley. Still, the vineyards here produce quality grapes, especially the Cabernet Sauvignon, Cabernet Franc, Merlot, and Malbec; much of the annual harvest becomes part of the wine of Santiago's famous firms and cooperatives. Some Pinot Noir also does well in the cool Aconcagua, where heat summations range from 2,520 to 2,610 degrees Fahrenheit, but most of this small yield is blended with other varietals. The capital city of Aconcagua, the port of Valparaiso, is not one of Chile's leading wine centers, although some noted producers have long been based there. These include Viñedos y Huertos Jose and Vinicola Fernandez, Broquaire and Company; another company, Viña Errazuriz Panquehue, owns vineyards in Aconcagua as well.

The discreteness of the Aconcagua region is emphasized by the allocation of vineyard acreages to particular cultivars (Table 4.1). The País covers more than 56 percent of the vineyard land devoted to red grapes (compared to only 9 percent in the adjacent Maipo region of the Central Valley). Among the white cultivars, ordinary varieties also dominate: the Torontel and Cristal represent 20 percent each; the Muscats, Folle Blanche, and various lesser varieties, another 20 percent. In this company the Sémillon looks positively exalted, covering 35 percent of the white grape acreage.

Were it not for the considerable area of Cabernet Sauvignon, the Aconcagua would not rank as one of Chile's premier winegrowing regions at all. But more than 20 percent of the red grape acreage lies under Cabernet, and another 12 percent is planted to the Cot (Malbec). The Cabernet Sauvignon does well here, and the region's production is in demand by the better winemakers.

Fine as the Cabernets of Aconcagua can be, and prestigious as its vineyards are, the region in recent years has witnessed a significant change in its grapegrowing industry. Table-grape cultivation has expanded markedly, mainly for export to markets in North America, Europe, and even Arab World countries. By 1984, Aconcagua had more than 12,000 acres of land under vines for table-grape production, and growth was continuing—not only in Aconcagua but in the Santiago region and O'Higgins as well. This reflects not just the commercial possibilities of the table

Table 4.1 Areas Devoted to Red Cultivars, by Region (in percentages)

	Coquimbo (IV)	Aconcagua (V)	Maipo (Metro)	Rapel (VI)	Maule (VII)	Bio-Bio (VIII)	Total
Cabernet Sauvignon	1.2	20.4	44.1	47.4	21.9	1.7	16.5
Carignan		2.2	0.5	3.7	2.8	1.1	2.0
Cot		11.8	30.3	12.4	9.2	0.4	6.7
Merlot		2.3	4.7	7.6	2.4		2.0
Pais	88.2	56.5	8.8	21.8	61.5	96.7	70.4
Petit Verdot			2.8	2.6	0.1		0.4
Pinot Noir		1.7	2.6	1.7	0.5	0.1	0.6
Romano (Muscat)		3.4	4.4	2.1	0.8		0.8
Other cultivars	10.6	1.7	1.8	0.7	0.8		0.6

Source: Asociacion de Exportadores y Embotelladores de Vinos de Chile, *El Vino de Chile: Su Industria, Su Mercado* (Santiago, 1983), p. 7.

grape, but also the vagaries of the wine industry, whose economic and political uncertainties have led many a grower to seek a safer alternative.

THE MAIPO REGION

When asked to identify Chile's highest-quality wines, Chileans almost invariably point to the wines of the Maipo Valley, the wines of the Santiago region. Here, at the northern end of the Central Valley, in the hinterland of the capital and in the area where Chile's very first vineyards were planted, the vine still does best, and the wines prove it.

The Maipo River is the prototype for those streams that cross the Central Valley to the south: its basin is extensive, the soils of its valley are deep and range from loamy to gravelly in texture (a calcareous layer, derived from limestone, gives the Maipo's soils added worth), and the terrain is under gentle slopes that promote drainage and permit large-scale viticulture. The growing season brings a heat summation of 2,430 to 2,520 degrees Fahrenheit. The winter is sufficiently cold to rest the vines, but not so cold as to endanger their roots. Summer sunshine is nearly constant, water supply is ample. Small wonder that various authorities have written that Chile may have the world's best winegrowing potential outside France.

Certainly the Maipo region (as the wine region is properly designated) produces wines of distinction and excellence, especially reds from the Cabernet Sauvignon, which have been described as the most Bordeaux-like outside the Médoc. Every official subregion recognized by the government (and some undesignated names as well) produces notable wines.

Chile's first vineyards were planted where Santiago now sprawls, and the earliest experiments by the French advisers who came in the mid-eighteenth century took place here. Many of the old names still are prominent in local winemaking, as several major wine firms have established their headquarters in the capital. Viña Concha y Toro, founded in 1883, is the industry's largest. Viña Undurraga has been

Santa Rita is one of Chile's oldest wine names. The company's wines rank among Chile's finest.

in the same family for over a century. Viña Cousiño Macul is among the most highly regarded. The historic name of Ochagavia also continues to grace a Santiago wine firm, founded in 1851. Other prominent Santiago houses include Viña Santa Rita, founded in 1880 with vineyards south of the city, Viña Canepa, with vines in the Maipo and Maule regions, Viña Manquehue with vineyards in Maipo and Rapel, Viña Tarapaca, Viña Carmen, and Viñedos Ortiz-Viña Linderos. Some respected wine producers do not own vineyards, but market distinguished wines from grapes grown by contract growers, including Santa Carolina and Champagne Supercaseaux, the latter another historic name in Chilean wine lore. Still other firms of strong reputation are headquartered in the Santiago region's smaller towns, such as Viña Santa Ema in Isla de Maipo and Vitivinicola Millahue in Buin.

Santiago, the city, is therfore the central place of Chilean viticulture, even as its suburbs swallow up the vinelands of old. Grapes come to the wineries from far beyond the Maipo because, a comparatively few large firms notwithstanding, thousands of growers own just a few acres of grapes. When the industry enjoys prosperous times, more than 30,000 growers produce wine grapes, and about 15 percent of these go to ten major cooperatives set up for the small growers with government help. The major wine-producing and exporting firms have their own vineyards and,

Lord Cochrane

Cousiño Macul, a Maipo winery headquartered near Santiago, is credited by many specialists as being Chile's qualitative leader. Its premium red wines, especially, may indeed be Chile's best.

in some cases, buy contract growers' grapes as well. Concha y Toro, for example, owns some 3,700 acres of vines. These vineyards lie in the Maipo, Cachapoal, and Tinguiririca valleys and even include a small acreage in the Lontué area of Maule. From these vineyards come many of Concha y Toro's finest wines, but the company produces more wine than its own vines can yield. Hence it also is a significant buyer of quality grapes.

The firm of Cousiño Macul, on the other hand, produces all its fine wines from its own vineyards, which extend over more than 700 acres of Maipo's best land. This is one of the old Chilean firms that trace their beginnings to the roots of the modern industry, when French vines were introduced and French advisers set winegrowing on course. Now, more than 100 years later, French traditions persist—in vineyard management, harvest methods, and winemaking. Luis Cousiño, who founded the company in 1868, foresaw the emergence of an estate that would own the vines, nurture the grapes, and produce, blend, and bottle its wines—in short, an estate in the Bordeaux tradition. The prestige of the present firm evinces the accuracy of his foresight. Cousiño Macul's red wines often are complex, well balanced, and long-lived.

Viña Undurraga is another famous Santiago estate. Five generations of the

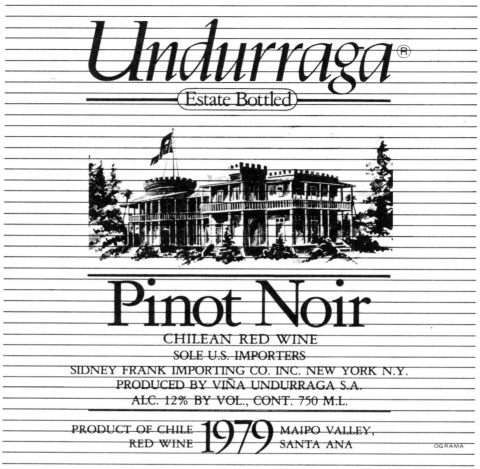

Undurraga is one of Chile's oldest wine firms, and the company maintains a large export trade. Labels such as this are designed especially for the North American market.

Undurraga family have made highly respected wines, both red and white, often marked by a strong aroma and taste of wood. The establishment at Santa Ana is one of the Santiago area's main tourist attractions, and for good reason. Situated in a spacious, parklike garden, the winery is an impressive structure. The bottling plant resembles the most modern of California, but the huge oak vats and barrels are in the old French style. Wines from the Undurraga firm have been exported for many decades (the first consignment to the United States reached the market in 1903), and in recent years about one-fifth of total production has been sold on foreign markets.

Chile's most interesting wines often are blends, such as the Cabernet/Merlot of Cousiño Macul in the Bordeaux tradition, and the Sauvignon Blanc/Sémillon/Riesling as blended by Undurraga. Chilean labels will indicate the varietals used,

Concha y Toro's famed Casillero del Diablo label honors a fine, long-lived Cabernet Sauvignon.

but generic and proprietary names are used as well. Chile is one of the countries that still uses regional (French) appellations: Concha y Toro, for example, markets a "Chilean Burgundy," and Valdivieso uses the Champagne appellation. Among proprietary names, one of the best known is Casillero del Diablo, also of Concha y Toro and used for a prestigious Cabernet Sauvignon. When the original winery was built, it included a large, deep cellar, part of it hidden by a secret entrance. There, the owners stored their best wines, and to deter intruders they spread the story that in those deep recesses lived the devil: this was the "devil's cave." The legend took hold, and today the devil's image, black cape flanked by flaming red, marks the label of Casillero del Diablo. Consumers associate it with a rich, deep, complex Cabernet Sauvignon of dependable flavor and long life.

The Chilean government exercises strict control over vinicultural practices, especially those affecting the export industry. As in France, there are limits on the production per acre, which has the effect of discouraging excessive yields and sustaining quality. Cultivators are compelled to acknowledge overproduction and must dispose of the excess. Wines destined for the export market must achieve prescribed minimum alcohol levels (12.0 percent for reds, 11.5 percent for whites), and the length of aging determines the class of the wine. At the time of writing, the government, in collaboration with leading producers, was preparing new regulations to control the use of terms such as *reserva* and *gran reserva*. For decades, these designations had guaranteed barrel- and bottle-aging. But during the 1970s, their use became corrupted and their dependability declined.

THE RAPEL REGION

The Rapel viticulture region corresponds to administrative region VI, O'Higgins, consisting of the former provinces of O'Higgins and Colchagua. In fact it is the basin of the Rapel-Tinguiririca River and its tributary, the Cachapoal. There are ten subregional designations, emphasizing the importance of this region, which is rather eclipsed by the Maipo-Santiago viticulture region to the north.

The Rapel region is the heart of the Central Valley, its heat summation quite similar to the Maipo's, the soil mainly derived from volcanic rocks, loamy to gravelly in texture. This is a region of true Mediterranean climate, most of the 20 to 25 inches of rain coming in the winter months. Chile's main longitudinal highway traverses the valley from north to south, and along many miles it is flanked by vineyards.

Most of the vines represent red varieties, but there are substantial acreages of whites as well. Among the whites, the Sémillon is by far the most commonly planted (about 77 percent of the total devoted to white cultivars), with the Sauvignon Blanc in second place (less than 11 percent).[4] Among the reds, the Cabernet Sauvignon dominates, although less strongly than in Maipo (more than 47 percent), and the País stands far more extensively than in Maipo, with nearly 22 percent (see Tables 4.1 and 4.2).

There are thousands of small growers in the Rapel region, but large vineyards have been laid out by major wine firms. One of the largest holdings belongs to Agricola Viña Los Vascos, a firm founded in 1892. Some 85 percent of its 425 acres are planted to Cabernet Sauvignon. Los Vascos is a local firm, based in the Rapel region. Another local company is the Sociedad Agricola Santa Elisa, with nearly 700 acres of vineyards, all in the Rapel region. A modern firm (founded in 1978), the Sociedad also concentrates on red wines, with 430 of its 700 acres under Cabernet Sauvignon, 175 acres devoted to Cot and Malbec, and a few experimental acres of Pinot Noir. Several national firms also have vineyards in O'Higgins, including Concha y Toro and Manquehue. Concha y Toro's acreages lie in the Cachapoal-Peumo area, south of Rancagua, and in the Chimbarongo area (see Fig. 4.4).

In the regional perspective of the Central Valley, the Rapel region more strongly resembles the Maipo region to the north than the Maule region to the south: it is a true premium-grape region in which the noble varieties dominate. This is especially clear from Table 4.1, which reveals that the País, the ordinary, blending-wine variety, occupies less than 22 percent of Rapel's vineyard acreage, but nearly 62 percent of Maule's. The Rapel region truly is part of Chile's viticultural core area.

THE MAULE REGION

The Maule viticultural region (administrative region VII) adjoins Rapel to the south. It is a region of numerous official designations and of great vinicultural interest, but its transitional character is evident. Certainly the Maule's superior viticultural land ranks among the best in Chile, but some areas show the effects of an uncertain

Table 4.2 Areas Devoted to White Cultivars, by Region (in percentages)

	Coquimbo (IV)	Aconcagua (V)	Maipo (Metro)	Rapel (VI)	Maule (VII)	Bio-Bio (VIII)	Total
Cristal	0.1	19.9	0.2	0.4	1.2	0.7	1.0
"Italia" (Ugni Blanc)		3.7			1.6	81.6	15.2
Muscat	78.7	5.5	0.7		0.3		10.5
Pinot Blanc		0.7	0.8	0.2	0.4		0.3
Sauvignon Blanc	0.1	6.7	21.6	10.7	14.4	1.4	10.7
Sémillon	0.2	35.0	57.9	77.0	79.1	14.1	53.0
Torontel	4.7	19.9	18.1	8.7	2.3	0.7	6.0
Other cultivars	16.2	8.6	0.7	3.0	0.7	1.5	3.3

Source: Asociacion de Exportadores y Embotelladores de Vinos de Chile, El Vino de Chile: Su Industria, Su Mercado (Santiago, 1983), p. 7.

summer-dry season, excess moisture, and cool ripening seasons. The Maule River, the region's principal artery, often is taken as the southern limit of the "true" Regadío zone, so that the region extends into the Transition zone mapped on Figure 4.3. Thus, some of Maule's official subregion designations lie in the Regadío, and some do not.

Among the noble grapes (thus discounting the País), the Cabernet Sauvignon continues to be the most widely cultivated red variety, but with only 22 percent of the total acreage; the Cot (Malbec) is the only other significant red grape, with less than 10 percent of the area planted to reds. Among the whites, the Sémillon dominates with nearly 80 percent, and the Sauvignon Blanc musters no more than 14 percent. The safe, dependable País is grown on thousands of small plots, and cooperatives play an important role in Maule winemaking.

Two large cooperatives are the Cooperativa Agricola Vitivinicola de Curicó and the C.A.V. de Talca. The C.A.V. de Curicó was established in 1939, and has its headquarters in the old provincial capital. It buys large quantities of grapes and owns 3,500 acres of vineyards, all in the Maule region. Most of these vineyards are devoted to white cultivars: the Sauvignon Blanc occupies well over 1,500 acres and the Sémillon some 1,050 acres. Not much more than 10 percent of the cooperative's vines are Cabernet Sauvignon. The C.A.V. de Talca also is a large vineyard owner, with nearly 3,000 acres, about 1,000 of them under Sémillon and another 500 devoted to the Sauvignon Blanc. The preponderance of white varieties in the cooperatives' vineyards suggests the style of the wines on which they concentrate and the domestic market to which they are directed. "Riesling"-style wines, "rhine" wines, "chablis," and "champagne" sparkling wines all come from the Maule region's cooperatives. The firm named Champagne Valdivieso has, since 1879, produced its sparkling wines from company vineyards in the Maule region; white grapes occupy 165 of its 210 acres.

In the Maule region, too, national wine firms own and manage vineyards. Again Concha y Toro has its share, mainly in the Lontué area in the north. Canepa and Errazuriz Panquehue also have their own vineyards, although they are not Maule-based.

The Cooperativa Agricola Vitivinicola de Talca is one of the district's two largest wineries. Note the Maule designation on this, one of the winery's principal labels.

Two firms that represent the new and the old in Maule are the Sociedad Vinicola Miguel Torres and Viña San Pedro. The Sociedad Vinicola Miguel Torres was founded in 1979 (although its 165 acres of vineyards have stood under vines since 1904). Headquartered in Curicó, the Sociedad began producing wines from its modern, wood and stainless steel winery in 1980, exporting 60 percent of its output. The firm makes a variety of styles, as reflected by the diverse cultivars in its vineyards. About half the acreage is under Sauvignon Blanc and more than a quarter is devoted to Cabernet Sauvignon. Also represented are the Cabernet Franc, Chardonnay, Gewürztraminer, Pinot Noir, and Riesling.

Viña San Pedro represents winegrowing history in Maule, having been founded in 1865 in the Lontué area, on what is perhaps the best land in the region. The firm's more than 800 acres of vineyards are divided almost evenly between Cabernet Sauvignon and Sauvignon Blanc, and from these come its premium wines; grapes are also brought from growers and made into a range of wines sold under proprietary labels such as Gato Blanco (a Sauvignon Blanc/Sémillon blend) and Las Encinas (a Sémillon-based aperitif wine). San Pedro sells its wines principally on the domestic market, exporting only about 2 percent of its output. Its premium wines have been

GATO BLANCO
VIÑA SAN PEDRO
FUNDADA EN 1865

VINO CHILENO DE EXPORTACION-GRAN VINO-ELABORADO Y EMBOTELLADO EN CHILE POR WAGNER STEIN Y CIA. S.A.C.
SANTIAGO CHILE   GRADO ALCOHOLICO 12° G. L.   CONTENIDO NETO 0,70 l.

Viña San Pedro is the oldest winery in the Maule district. Its Gato Blanco label marks a fresh, crisp white wine exported to overseas markets.

awarded numerous prizes and medals at international exhibitions and competitions, proving the capacity of Maule to match the Central Valley's best.

THE BÍO-BÍO REGION

Administrative region VIII, the southernmost viticulture region, is Chile's southern winegrowing frontier. Here lie the unirrigated vineyards of the Secano, and here all the advantages of the Central Valley dissipate. There are only two subregion designations, Yumbel and Coelemu, both situated near the coast against the slopes of the western cordillera. But most winegrowers here, if they have the land to permit it, plant other crops along with grapes, hedging their bets in case the ripening season fails. Viticulture in this region is, indeed, a gamble.

The Bío-Bío River and its basin are the focus of the vineyard zone. The river traverses the region diagonally, from southeast to northwest, and vineyards lie on both its north and south banks. Winegrowing here may be difficult, but there are, nevertheless, as many as 100,000 acres of vineyards in the Secano zone (the total varies as some growers give up on grapes while others plant new vines in supposedly better locales). But the character of the region is revealed more by the kinds of grapes grown here than by the distribution of the vineyards. Among the red cultivars, the País represents no less than 97 percent of the planted acreage, and the Cabernet Sauvignon, the great grape of the Central Valley, less than 2 percent. The white cultivars also are mainly *corriente:* the Italia (a clone of the Ugni Blanc) stands on 82 percent of the acreage, the Sémillon ranking next with a mere 14 percent.

Yields per acre in the Bío-Bío region tend to be small, and the grapes, because of prevailing climatic conditions, often cannot reach the sugar levels required to produce adequate alcohol in the wines. This combination of adversities compels the growers to sell their wines, when they do not attain alcohol levels prescribed by the government, in bulk, to be blended with higher-alcohol wine from northern areas. This is not a profitable proposition, and many growers in the southern region lead a troubled existence, viticulturally and financially.

Viticulture in Chile's southern frontier does not end at the southern border of Bío-Bío. There actually are vineyards in Araucania (Region IX), in the former Malleco and Cautín Provinces. Here the deteriorating climatic conditions of Bío-Bío become so restrictive that only the most persistent growers continue the effort to maintain vineyards. Historically, a succession of comparatively favorable years would lead growers to plant vines, and sometimes such a sequence would last long enough to permit the maturing of the vines and the harvesting of several summers' yields. Then, inevitably, the climatic regime would return to normal, with one cold, wet summer following another. The harvests failed, and the vines stood abandoned— until another series of sunny summers started the cycle over again.

So it was, and still is, on Chile's viticultural frontier, where nature takes back what it has given so generously in the Central Valley.

Ochagavia's Legacy

Chile's vinicultural history is a sequence of ironies and contradictions. When Ochagavia and his colleagues brought French experts and European vines to Chile, France itself was about to be ravaged by the dread disease *phylloxera.* As the Chilean industry developed, guided by the Europeans, *phylloxera* began its global spread, having destroyed the vineyards from Bordeaux to Burgundy and from the Loire to the Midi. *Phylloxera* entered North Africa, Eastern Europe, South Africa, New Zealand. It crossed the Atlantic and attacked California. It reached Argentina, where the growers resisted it by inundating the vineyards, hoping thus to drown the aphid that carried it. But somehow, by a provenance not easily explained, *phylloxera* never did penetrate Chile's vineyards. It is surely an irony that when France's vineyards lay devastated and only North American rootstocks would save the industry, Chile could send European vines to Europe—on their own roots. To this day, Chile's wines represent the only easily accessible wines from *vinifera* grapes that come from ungrafted Cabernets and Chardonnays.

"Chile . . . is a new Oenotria," exclaims Hyams, after chronicling the physical and social advantages for viticulture in a country about to enter its golden age of wine.[5] And yet Chile never has fulfilled its promise or totally realized its potential. In part this must be due to the love-hate relationship between government and industry involving the issue of alcoholism. Another part of it lies in the very nature of Chilean society and its division of wealth: before the political upheavals of the past two decades, Chile had about 30,000 grapegrowers, of whom 17,000 owned vineyards less than 2.5 acres in size, and another 9,000 owned vineyards of 2.5 to 12.5 acres. Such fragmentation may have been made to work in Burgundy, but Chilean geography is something else. Successive governments not only restricted the planting of vines on land deemed essential for food crops, but also began the breakup of the comparatively few (fewer than 100) vineyard estates that had acreages exceeding 500. On the other hand, government support for wine cooperatives allowed thousands of smallholders to stay in the winegrowing business. The contradictions abound.

Another of the ironies lies in Chile's domestic consumption of wine. Few countries in the world can boast of an industry so productive, diverse, and quality-oriented. Chilean wines have achieved recognition around the world, and there are those who argue that the world has not really seen Chile's best. Yet wine consumption in Chile itself has been declining ever since it reached a peak (of 18 gallons per person) in 1962. The decline has been interrupted by temporary reversals, but the overall trend has been downward. And even at its peak, Chile's per-capita consumption ranked far below Argentina (where it has been twice as high in some years) or Spain. Over the past decade, annual wine consumption in Chile has remained below 14 gallons, and in the early 1980s it threatened to go below 12 gallons, a reduction of one-third since 1962. All this happened while wine prices in Chile were (especially considering the quality of the available wine) among the world's lowest.

Other countries, including even France itself, have witnessed a decline in wine consumption in recent years, and undoubtedly Chile's experience has been part of a global tendency. But Chile's case has a unique dimension. Wine production has increased substantially: little more than 30 years ago (in 1952) it was slightly more than 84 million gallons, while 1982 recorded 160 million gallons. Thus, production nearly doubled while domestic consumption was falling rapidly. It is a not unfamiliar combination of circumstances, but no Southern Hemisphere country experienced it more severely than did Chile. The country's population base is not large, so that the industry is strongly affected by a downturn in wine purchases. To cushion the impact, the industry must sell wines on foreign markets—which lie at great distances, where per-capita consumption has also declined, and where competition is intense.

Here, nevertheless, lies Chile's great opportunity. Over may decades, Chilean wines (especially the reds) have become recognized for their quality and, even on those distant foreign markets, for their advantageous values. Chile's *reserva* Cabernet Sauvignons, yielded by vines that never knew *phylloxera* and aged for years in wood and bottle, compare favorably with Cabernets from other world regions priced several times as high. The great names of the Central Valley have achieved a status that would surely bring a smile to the lips of Silvestre Ochagavia Echazareta, gentleman and oenophile, late of Santiago.

5

ARGENTINA:

IN THE SHADOW

OF THE ANDES

Argentina is a land of opportunity and challenge. Opportunity, because its land area is large (more than 1 million square miles), its environments varied, and its resources plentiful. Challenge, because these advantages have been diminished by political troubles and economic policy problems. Practically every enterprise in Argentina has been buffeted by these adversities. The wine industry is no exception.

Yet Argentina has established itself as one of the world's—not just the hemisphere's—leading wine producers by volume. Argentina produces, in an average year, more wine than all other Southern Hemisphere countries combined; its production ranks fifth in the world, if Soviet statistics can be depended upon, fourth if they cannot. Officially, only Italy, France, Spain, and the U.S.S.R. produce more wine than distant Argentina.

Argentina's status among leading wine producers has been achieved during the twentieth century. The industry is old, but its success is recent. Its greatest stimulus was the flood of European immigrants, nearly half of whom originated in Italy, that began after the middle of the nineteenth century and reached a maximum between 1910 and 1939. This immigration brought thousands of farmers with experience in winegrowing to Argentina, and at the same time it created an unprecedented demand for wine on the growing domestic market. The foresight of Tiburcio Benegas, one of Argentina's viticultural pioneers who anticipated his country's rise among world wine producers more than a century ago, has been proven accurate. Today, Argentina is known not only for the quantity of its production and the dependability of its exports to world markets; some of the country's premium wines (*vinos finos* as they are called in Argentina and *reservas* as they are labeled for foreign markets) have attracted attention for their remarkable quality as well.

Argentina's physical geography would not, at first glance, suggest that here lies one of the world's great vineyards. The mountainous walls of the Andes interfere with moisture-bearing winds from the Pacific, to such an extent that a zone of dry steppe adjoins the mountains on Argentina's side (see Fig. 1.5). In some areas east of the Andes the climate is actually desertlike, so that the country's moistest areas lie in the northeast and in the far south. The northeast lies adjacent to Brazil's southernmost states and shares their environment, classified as humid temperate with a warm summer (see Fig. 1.1). This, as has been noted previously, is a difficult environment for winegrowing, and in northeast Argentina the topography does not (as in Brazil) provide microclimatic opportunities for viticulture. The far south of Argentina is too cold for grapegrowing; Patagonia's disadvantages are similar to those of southern Chile.

Hence Argentina's grapegrowers and winemakers must make the best of the country's arid regions in the shadow of the Andes, where the summer sun guarantees a good ripening season and where water must be provided by irrigation. The arid zone along the eastern foot of the Andes is very warm in Argentina's northwest, which lies in the same latitudes as Chile's Atacama Desert and astride the Tropic of Capricorn. Southward, the heat softens somewhat, so that it becomes rather temperate in the provinces of Mendoza and San Juan. Still farther to the south, beyond the valley of the Colorado River (the northern border of Patagonia), the cold winds of higher latitudes begin to make themselves felt.

Thus the province of Mendoza lies in a kind of transition zone between the north's heat and the south's cold, as might be expected from its latitudinal position. Here, in the lee of the towering Andes, the city of Mendoza has become the wine capital of Argentina.

As the map (Figure 5.1) shows, Mendoza's latitude is within a degree of Santiago's (Mendoza, 32° 54'; Santiago 33° 27' S). But the situation of the city of Mendoza so near Santiago on the opposite side of the Andes is not primarily the result of viticulture or wine production. For many years—in fact for centuries after the first Spanish settlement—the small towns of what is now Mendoza Province looked westward, to Santiago and Chile, rather than eastward to the Spanish headquarters on the Plata River and Tucumán. Santiago's influence could extend across the Andes because of the existence of a natural route through the Andes, the Uspallata Pass. This was no facile course, requiring a climb as high as 12,600 feet, but more northerly passes were far higher, and more southerly ones too distant and dangerous. Thus the town of Mendoza was the last stop before entering the Uspallata, and the first settlement reached by those emerging after the arduous crossing.

The original settlement of Mendoza was, in fact, founded by pioneers who came through this Andean pass, and for more than two centuries it and its hinterland

Figure 5.1. *Political divisions and viticulture regions of Argentina.*

remained under Chilean-Spanish administration. Not until 1776 did it become part of the domain of the viceroyalty of Río de la Plata, the nucleus of evolving Argentina. The Uspallata Pass again played an historic role in 1817, when José de San Martín's liberating forces made Mendoza their headquarters and invaded Chile from this base.

Those who crossed the mountains in those early days, in peace or war, could not fail to see the differences between agricultural economies east and west of the Andes. Even in the middle of the nineteenth century, when viticulture on the Chilean side expanded and prospered, Mendoza (the town as well as the province), now separated from Santiago, lay remote and isolated. But change was in the offing. Winegrowers in Mendoza learned of the developments taking place in Chile, and ideas and innovations that had reached Chile from France spread to Mendoza as well—where there were some who paid close attention. Among these was the formidable Benegas, who realized that Mendoza needed not just one, but two stimuli: improved viticultural practices, and better surface connections with Argentina's burgeoning east.

What Mendoza did *not* need was what happened in 1861, when a savage earthquake devastated the town with great loss of life. The city lies in the valley of the Mendoza River at the foot of a spur of the Andes, the Sierra de los Paramillos (Fig. 5.2). This is a geologically active zone, and the 1861 earthquake destroyed virtually every building in the town and surrounding countryside. Out of this disaster came one positive result, however. Rather than haphazardly rebuilding the town, the surviving Mendozans, with help from their government, planned and laid out a modern, spacious, attractive new city with wide, tree-lined avenues, open squares, shady parks, and other amenities designed to make city life pleasant. Today Mendoza is one of South America's most appealing cities, a true wine center that has been likened to France's Aix-en-Provence.[1]

As the city was reborn, its region's chief industry matured. Spurred by local initiative and the knowhow of thousands of immigrants, viticulture (as well as the cultivation of other crops) changed the face of Mendoza's rural countryside, and the vines spread into neighboring San Juan Province as well. The completion of the cross-country railroad (1885) was all the industry needed; it brought an even larger influx of European immigrants and permitted the dispatch of greater volumes of wine to Argentinian and overseas markets. The pattern of the future had been set.

Regions of Argentina

Internationally, Argentina probably is best known for its famous Pampas, the great grassy plains of the east-central part of the country where the Argentinians grazed livestock and planted grain crops. These form one of the Americas' true geographic regions, anchored by the great city of Buenos Aires to the east and bounded by environmental change to the west, north, and south. The Pampas and their cities, towns, communication systems, and farmlands constitute Argentina's core area, just as the valley of Chile is that country's *Nucleo Central*.

Argentina has several other perceptual regions (see inset, Fig. 5.1). Immediately

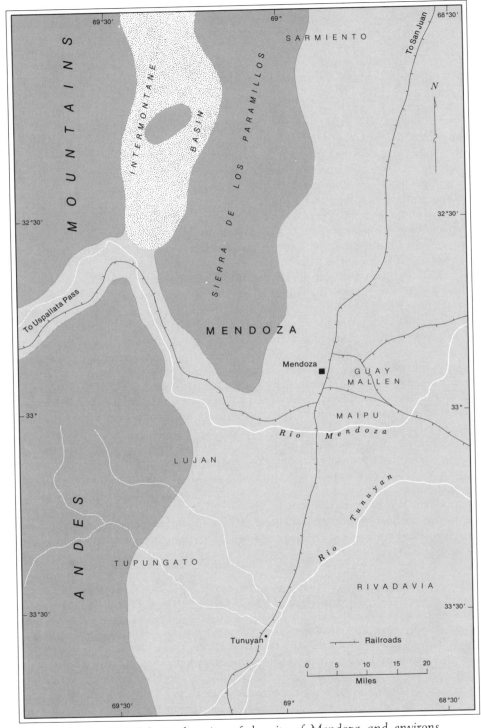

Figure 5.2. Relative location of the city of Mendoza and environs.

to the west of the Pampas lies a three-province region that has for centuries been called the Cuyo, consisting of Mendoza, San Luis, and San Juan provinces. Here the comparatively moist climates of the Pampas yield to the dryness of the Andean piedmont, and irrigation becomes the mainstay of agriculture. Both Pampas and Cuyo are bounded to the south by the Colorado River, which traverses the country from Andes to Atlantic and marks a strong geographic transition. Beyond lie the vast expanses of stormy, cold Patagonia.

Argentina's north contrasts sharply with Patagonia's windswept plateaus and basins. The south is chilled by Antarctic waters; the north is warmed by a tropical sun. Patagonia's cold is dusty and dry; the north's heat ranges from humid to arid. Northern Argentina divides quite clearly into three geographic regions: the so-called Northwest, the Chaco, and "Mesopotamia."

The Northwest witnessed the first penetration of Spanish invaders, and Tucumán for a time was the most important center east of the southern Andes. But apart from its streams and oases, the Northwest is dominated by searing drought and intense heat. The drought yields to somewhat moister conditions eastward, where bush and then trees clothe the countryside. This marks the Chaco, and it extends all the way to the Parana River. Between the Parana and Uruguay rivers lies Argentina's "Mesopotamia," a humid, forested area also called *Entre Rios*, between (the) rivers.

This regional geography quickly explains why Argentina's winegrowing regions have emerged where they did. There are some vineyards on the Pampas' margins in the Province of Córdoba (where Argentinian viticulture may have originated) and, as in Chile, there are vines in the oases of the desert Northwest. Viticulture has even succeeded in Entre Rios and south of the Río Colorado. But the greatest concentration of vineyards lies in the provinces of the Cuyo, where moderate conditions prevail, and where inadequate precipitation can be supplemented by irrigation.

VINEYARD ENVIRONMENTS

The irrigated vineyards at the foot of Argentina's Andes are largest and most numerous in the province of Mendoza, but they actually extend from the far north (Jujuy) to Neuquén and Río Negro in the south, representing a latitudinal range of nearly sixteen degrees (24° south in Jujuy to just north of 40° south in Río Negro). This means that vines are cultivated in every province that adjoins the Andes except southern Patagonia's Chubut and Santa Cruz. The prevailing aridity notwithstanding, this elongated zone exhibits considerable environmental variety.

Even the dryness varies in severity. Although most of the viticulture zone receives a mere 8 inches of (mainly summer) rainfall annually, an average that is not attained in some years, there are places where more precipitation falls. In western Catamarca some areas record an annual mean of 12 inches—still low, but in this arid zone every additional inch of rain is important. In neighboring Salta Province the vineyards receive 8 inches, and to the south in San Juan the average is only 6 inches. In Mendoza Province the average is about 8 inches, but here, too, there are areas, again in the west, where it is as much as 12. Precipitation does not increase significantly in the southernmost viticulture areas of Neuquén and Río Negro.

Drought-dominated climatic regimes are marked not only by low annual average precipitation, but also by high variability. This means that the averages just described are often unattained, while other years are much moister than normal. In turn, this implies that there *are* different vintages in these arid winegrowing zones.

Not only the rainfall, but also the temperature varies. Argentina's vineyards lie in the basins of rivers that emerge from the Andes, and from these same Andean valleys come winds that frequently heat the land even more than the desert sun. Some vineyards are more affected by this phenomenon than others, and certain grape varieties can withstand it better. But elevation has a cooling effect, and there are locales where a combination of slightly higher precipitation and slightly cooler slopes make for better wines. In the south, where the vineyards of Neuquén and Río Negro lie astride the 39th parallel, latitude creates cooler conditions than those of Mendoza and San Juan, again with notable effect on the vines and wines.

The vineyards of the arid zone experience a very warm growing and ripening season each year, but it should not be assumed that the desert-steppe is without a winter. In fact, all four seasons are quite clearly defined here. The summer is hot and mainly cloudless (although most of the limited precipitation does fall in summer), daytime temperatures often exceeding 100°F. At night the mercury may drop as low as 50°F., giving rise to deceptively low heat summations in this parched region. The winter is cold, with an occasional frost, so that the vines benefit from a period of dormancy and renewal. Spring is rarely marked by a damaging late frost, and untimely rain at harvest time is virtually unknown. If there is one serious natural hazard in the region, it is hail, which sometimes accompanies the severe storms that bring the rains. The Parral training system with its overhead trellises provides protection as well as shade for the grapes.

The first vineyards were planted along Mendoza's Andes-fed streams, but today there are 650,000 acres of vines in this province alone—more, obviously, than could be sustained by stream water. The towering, snow-capped Andean mountains that overlook Argentina's wine regions are the source not only of the streams that traverse the desert, but also of a huge natural network of underground drainage that creates a permanent supply of irrigation water. It is not difficult to visualize the physical geography involved: porous rock strata absorb water from melting snow and rain in the high Andes, and gravity carries the water downward—and eastward—in this *aquifer* or water-bearing layer. All that is needed in the adjacent lowland is a borehole; often it is not even necessary to pump the water out, since continuous pressure pushes it up in artesian fashion (Fig. 5.3). There is sufficient water under the surface of Mendoza and its neighboring provinces to vastly expand the grape acreage; Argentinian engineers have dreams of creating a huge lake in one of the region's basins. The snow-capped Andes are the source and sustenance of life in the desert.

Thus the vineyards are watered from several sources: open streams, limited rainfall, artesian wells, and boreholes. In the foothills of the Andean catchment areas, a complex of dams controls much of the surface flow, and in the vineyard zone, more than 30,000 boreholes have been drilled. An elaborate and highly intricate system of irrigation canals and ditches carries the water to virtually all of

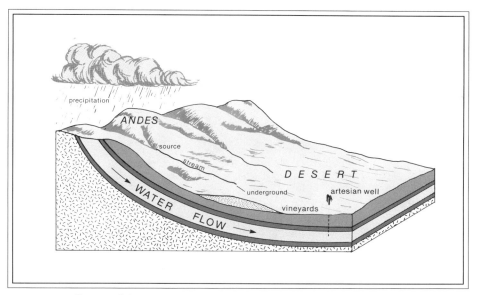

Figure 5.3. Artesian structure of the Andes' eastern flank.

the country's 900,000 acres of vines, a system that has been refined almost continuously since it was begun in the mid-1800s. Today the canal network is augmented by drip-irrigation and sprinkling systems, and an old technique, flooding the entire vineyard, still is used.

The Argentinian winegrowers' ability to flood their flat-lying vineyards proved to be a vital asset when *phylloxera* struck Argentina in the 1890s. By flooding the ground for an extended period, it was possible to drown the aphids that propagate the disease, thus saving the roots that were under attack. The method was so successful that it was even tried in France, but comparatively few French vineyards could be inundated in the same manner (obviously vineyards standing on slopes cannot be flooded at all). Argentina's special physiography thus proved advantageous at a critical time, and *phylloxera*, while it has not been eradicated, was kept at bay.

The soils of Argentina's wine regions vary across the whole textural spectrum, from clayey to silty to sandy, but with a high proportion of loam (a combination of particles of various sizes). Unlike Chile on the Andes' opposite side, the soils are predominantly of alluvial and aeolian (wind-borne) origins; except against the sierras' slopes there are no volcanic or other residual soils. It is important that the soils are deep as well, so that the vines' roots can penetrate without obstruction. In terms of nutrients, there is not the variety found, for example, on the bedrock-based soils of Germany's river slopes, but it is doubtful whether such diversity actually affects wine quality anyway. Many viticulturists hold the view that soil texture is far more important than soil composition, and in this respect Argentina is well endowed. The soils are not only deep, but also loosely compacted and capable of holding adequate moisture in the desert's heat.

The viticultural landscape of Argentina is a vast oasis of green, surrounded by the gray-brown of the desert, set against a background of towering, snow-capped

Verdant vines, the rows stretching to the horizon, roads flanked by irrigation canals and marked by lines of trees that provide some shade relief from the searing summer heat: the viticultural landscape of Mendoza.

mountains reaching for a blue, cloudless sky. The vineyards are flanked by rows of trees nurtured by the same irrigation ditches that sustain the vines, their shade providing some cool relief against the searing sun. It is a landscape that to some extent resembles France's Midi and Australia's Murray region, where stands of the vine are also measured by the mile rather than the acre—except for the incomparable Andean mountain wall that dominates every scene. In all the world, there is nothing to rival it.

VINES AND WINES

In Argentina as in Chile, the Criolla and Muscat were the first grape varieties planted, and both still stand among the vines today. But when the great European immigration gathered momentum, the French, Italian, Spanish, and German cultivars introduced by the settler-farmers soon changed the complexion of Mendoza winegrowing. Argentinians always have had a taste for red wines, and the acreages of Cabernet Sauvignon, Malbec, Merlot, Cabernet Franc, and Syrah (among French grapes), Nebbiolo, Barbera, Sangiovese, and Bonardo (among Italians), and Tempranillo (Spanish) expanded greatly. Among white varieties, the sources also are international: Chardonnay, Sémillon, Sylvaner, Riesling, Ugni Blanc, Muscat of Alexandria, and Torontel.

In the process, this multivarietal diffusion also created confusion. Argentina is not the only winegrowing country in the world where there is uncertainty over the origins and character of certain popular grape cultivars, but the perplexities are a bit more involved here. Argentina's Riesling probably is not even a clone of the White Riesling of Germany; what appears to be the Chenin Blanc is labeled a "Pinot Blanc." In addition,

> there appear to be two very different clones of Cabernet Sauvignon in [Argentina's] vineyards—responsible for wines so blatantly unalike that one wonders why they are allowed to go by the same name. One clone makes a deep, rich, slow-to-mature red quite comparable in taste and texture to a Medoc, the other a short, often astringent product that reminds one, at best, of something from the Midi.[2]

These are growing pains, and in time ampelographic research will solve the mysteries created by the influx of so many varieties. Domestic wines marketed in Argentina tend still to have proprietary names, and local consumers never have been very selective; carrying a varietal name on the label has not been a sales advantage. Thus, the winemakers have been little pressured to be specific about cultivars or blend proportions. The success of Argentinian varietal wines on foreign markets, on the other hand, has demonstrated the potential of *vinos finos* everywhere. Certain cultivars can produce remarkable wines under local conditions.

The most interesting among these may well be the Malbec (spelled Malbeck on Argentinian labels). This is the variety the Chileans call the Cot; here in Argentina, too, it has changed over time, adapted to its regional environment, and established itself as a premium cultivar. In the shadow of the Andes the Malbec is capable of yielding a complex wine, balanced and long-lived, with deep color and strong character. In earlier years, premium Malbecs (and other reds as well) were aged in wood for three to six years, which gave them a dominant woody, even smoky aroma and flavor. This practice is now far less common, and bottle-aging is proving just what long-lived Malbecs are capable of.

The best of the Cabernet Sauvignons, too, are noteworthy wines. Some of Argentina's Cabernets may not rival the Médoc's great growths, but are distinguished wines nevertheless—big, round, full, and durable. Some of these Cabernets are sold on overseas markets, and in competitive tasting competitions they have done remarkably well. Less often seen on Northern Hemisphere markets are Cabernet-based blends, many of which make interesting wines. Cabernet-Malbec blends have achieved a deserved reputation, and the Cabernet also is combined with the Merlot and the Cabernet Franc. In fact, Argentinian winemakers will try almost any combination of potential merit; the Cabernet Sauvignon has even been blended successfully with the Pinot Gris. In Argentina, such combinations are marketed behind proprietary labels and have a loyal following. Chateau Montchenot, a red wine made by the firm Lopez (based in Maipú near Mendoza), consists of a Cabernet-

Obra realizada especialmente por Carlos Torrallardona para Colección Privada.

Colección Privada

1981. Unicamente 144.000 botellas numeradas, atesoran
el vigoroso cuerpo de este vino excepcional
(Cosecha 1975).
Su finísimo corte —Cabernet Sauvignon, Cabernet Franc y
Merlot— asegura, junto con un tranquilo reposo, color,
aroma y sabor incomparables.
Esta botella lleva el Nº

25181

Navarro Correas

Vino Fino Tinto

INDUSTRIA ARGENTINA - ELABORADO Y EMBOTELLADO POR BODEGA
J. EDMUNDO NAVARRO CORREAS S.A. - JUAN B. JUSTO S/Nº - MAIPU -
MENDOZA - I.N.V. Nº B 71-137 - ENVASADO EN ORIGEN - CONT. NETO **750** cm3

Navarro Correas' Vino Fino Tinto, one of Argentina's most interesting blended wines, consists of Cabernet Sauvignon, Cabernet Franc, and Merlot. The wine has spent six years in the barrel and one year in the bottle before release.

Malbec blend. The proprietary label of Valroy, made by the house of Arizu of Mendoza, identifies a blend of the Cabernet Sauvignon, Merlot, and Pinot Noir.

These adventurous blends may, in fact, represent the best of Argentinian viniculture. They are less frequently seen on foreign markets than they deserve; the varietal wines exported by Argentina, good as they often are, hold rather less interest. An Argentine wine labeled a Cabernet Sauvignon proves what that great cultivar, and its vintners, can produce in Argentina. But Cabernet Sauvignons are made in many wine regions of the world. What makes the Argentinian wine especially interesting is local inventiveness in blending toward a particular style.

It may be said that Argentina's white wines have yet to develop a reputation comparable to its reds. In part this is due to a contrast in preferences; local consumers have long liked their wines to show some maderized character, and this has delayed the development of drier, fresher, crisper whites. That these can be made has already been proven, and exported varietal whites, notably the Chardonnay and the Sauvignon Blanc, have found ready acceptance on overseas markets. The Argentinian Riesling, being a Sylvaner misnamed, does not do as well. Neither are the blended whites as interesting as the red wines. Often the combination seems unpromising even before the tasting: Chardonnay with Sylvaner and/or Gewürztraminer; Chardonnay with Chenin Blanc and Pedro Ximenez (the Sherry grape of Spain); Chenin Blanc with Ugni Blanc. None of these blends would do well on Northern Hemisphere markets, but in Argentina they are popular. Even in red wine–drinking Argentina there has been a shift toward white wines, which in the 1980s accounted for nearly 45 percent of all wines sold. "Ordinary" reds still account for about 30 percent, with *vinos finos* (of export quality) about 8 per cent. Rosé wines (mainly made from the Criolla) still have a substantial following, perhaps representing 15 percent of the market, and the remainder of the demand is for sparkling-type wines.

Especially noteworthy is the development of regional styles and identities in Argentina's winegrowing zone. Under the arid climatic regime and the apparent uniformity imposed on viticulture by irrigation, it is remarkable that wines with distinct and consistent regional qualities have developed. Regional character has long been appreciated by Argentinian consumers, and is carefully maintained by the winegrowers. It is further proof that winegrowing in the shadow of the Andes is not merely a matter of monotonous mass-production.

Wine Regions

From the province of Jujuy in the north to Río Negro in the south, Argentina's vineyards extend over nearly 900,000 acres. Expansion has been nearly continuous: in the mid-1930s there were 370,000 acres under vine, and at the end of World War II this had increased slightly to 390,000. Then began a period of rapid growth. In the mid-1950s the acreage surpassed 500,000, in 1970 it approached 750,000, and in the 1980s, as the industry was buffeted by a serious economic downturn, it nevertheless reached 900,000.[3]

Through all this expansion, the province of Mendoza remained the core area of the industry, consistently accounting for about 70 percent of the total acreage. But some of the most significant growth occurred far from Mendoza's heartland, in the frontier provinces of the northwest and northern Patagonia. There, vines were planted in environments not previously tested, and the results were noteworthy. Against the lower slopes of Andean sierras, vines enjoyed the coolness of elevation and southward orientation. Viticulture not only expanded; it also diversified, maximizing the country's limited environmental options.

Thus an Argentinian wine is not simply an Argentinian wine, but a Mendoza or a San Juan or other provincial appellation; furthermore, knowledgable consumers will look on the label for an indication of district or locale for a more specific source. Sometimes that information is provided on a secondary descriptive label on the back of the bottle; Argentina has yet to develop a formal "appellation" system comparable to those devised for Chile or South Africa. It is true that much Argentinian wine is exported as blending, bulk wine, never to be identifiable even as an Argentinian product (and bottled as Japanese or some other "national" wine). But the country's *vinos finos*, and even lesser wines bottled for domestic consumption, have distinct style and character, much of which is attributable to their regional origins.

MENDOZA

The name Mendoza is synonymous with Argentinian wine, and the reasons are many. Here lie the source of the modern industry, the largest vineyard, the *bodegas* of the majority of the winemakers, and the central place of the country's viticulture, the province's capital. Mendoza (the city) is the headquarters of the *Instituto Nacional de Vitivinicultura*, the governing body of the country's wine industry, site of the annual festival of the *vendimia* (harvest), and locus of wineries, coopers, wine trade offices, and countless other wine-related establishments. Much of the urban landscape accommodates a veritable maze of cellars and wine storage facilities.

Even a century ago, when there were just 10,000 acres of vines in Mendoza, the province was Argentina's chief winegrowing region. Since then, acreage has expanded almost without interruption, and Mendoza's lead has grown. The vineyard area exceeded 100,000 acres before 1910 and reached a half-million acres in the late 1960s. It constitutes one of the largest vineyard concentrations in the world, and its enormous harvest requires massive organization. "Massive" is the appropriate word: the bodegas of Mendoza are equipped with huge fermentation and storage vats to handle a production of well over 400 million gallons of wine in an average year (when national production would approach 600 million gallons). In an especially abundant year, such as 1976 or 1979, the yield is even greater, and the bodegas are able to meet the challenge.

It is one of the characteristics of Mendoza's vineyards, and of Argentina generally, that yields per acre are very high, even when the grapes are destined for *vinos finos.* Yields as high as six tons per acre are not unusual, even for the noble varieties; for the Criolla they are still higher. This is more than double the norm in California's premium winegrowing regions and nearly triple those of the communes of the Médoc. Winemakers do not normally equate high yields with high-quality wine, and yet Argentina's prolific vines produce grapes that make some very good wines. It is an interesting aspect of this country's viniculture.

The viticultural geography of Mendoza Province is more complex than its vineyard oases might suggest. The province's nearly 60,000 square miles (slightly larger than Illinois) extend from the Chilean border in the Andes to the Río Salado in the east, and from the San Juan border in the north to the Río Colorado in the south (Fig. 5.4). The drainage pattern reflects the character of climate and soil: many streams that emerge from the Andes disappear as they traverse the desert, victims of porosity and evaporation. Several large rivers that do survive the desert

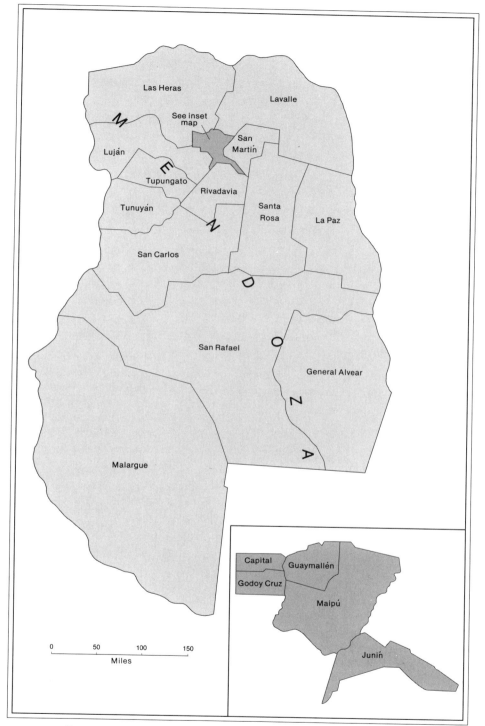

Figure 5.4. The Province of Mendoza and its departments.

crossing are vital to viticulture. The Mendoza River emanates from the Andes just south of the capital, turns north, and enters the San Juan–Desaguadero system which, in turn, becomes the Rio Salado. The Tunuyán River also crosses the province from its Andean source to its merger with the Desaguadero-Salado. To the south, in the middle part of Mendoza, the Diamante and Atuel rivers likewise are perennial (rather than ephemeral) streams. The names of the river valleys often are attached to the vineyards located in their basins, as a matter of regional identification.

Mendoza, like other provinces of Argentina, is divided into departments, and the location of these departments also is a key to the diversity of Mendoza's wines. In Argentina the names of the provincial departments are used as general regional designations; thus a wine may be described as coming from the Mendoza Valley in the Maipú zone, Maipú being a Mendoza department. Including the department called Capital (thus the city and suburbs with very little rural land), Mendoza has seventeen departmental subdivisions, the names of some of which are synonymous with the country's best wines. These include San Martín, Maipú, Luján, Junín, and Tunuyán. The departments usually are named after their own central places; thus the capital of San Martín Department is the town of San Martín, and San Rafael's capital is San Rafael. These towns serve as secondary wine centers and many of them have bodegas, whose fermentation vats tower, gleaming in the sun, over the verdant countryside.

Table 5.1 indicates the quantitative (if not qualitative) contributions of individual Mendoza departments to the province's annual wine-grape harvest. The table reveals the large production of several departments nearest the capital: San Martín ranks first, Maipú second, and less heralded Rivadavia third. The next ranking department is San Rafael of Mendoza's central zone, whose vineyards lie in a zone 130 miles south-southwest of the capital. The table further reflects the wide dispersal of viticulture across the entire province; every department except that of the capital itself contributes to the harvest.

An additional means of locational reference is provided by the "zones" that subdivide the departments. When the railroad to Buenos Aires reached Mendoza, stations along the route were established not only for the towns, but also at rather regular intervals to serve large rural hinterlands. These waystations came to be known by the names of prominent landowners or historical figures. Thus the railroad loop that serves Junín Department passes through that department's Philipps, Andrade, and Medrano "zones," all of them (among others) names of vinicultural consequence. A Mendoza wine, thus, may be known as a Maipú wine from the El Paraíso zone. In the absence of a geographically based appellation-type system, these indicators of origin are useful to the consumer.

Mendoza Province extends over a large area, and with its mountainous west and desert east it has much physiographic variety. Its latitudinal range is great enough to be expressed climatically: the north, which touches 32° south, is significantly warmer than the south, which approaches 38°. The transition is reflected by viticultural routine: in the San Rafael Department, harvesting begins 10 to 15 days after the start of picking in the Mendoza area. It also is revealed by the province's wines. In the heat of the desert, low acid levels are a constant problem and concern, but more so in the north than toward the somewhat cooler south.

Table 5.1   Wine Grapes Contributed to the Annual Mendoza Harvest, by Department, 1975–1983

	Tons	Percent
Capital	0	0.0
General Alvear	139,370	5.50
Godoy Cruz	33,610	1.33
Guay Mallen	165,670	6.54
Junín	171,900	6.79
Las Heras	18,830	0.74
La Paz	7,770	0.31
Lavalle	98,733	3.90
Luján	152,360	6.02
Maipú	413,730	16.34
Rivadavia	352,710	13.93
San Carlos	79,915	3.16
San Martín	491,300	19.40
San Rafael	251,370	9.93
Santa Rosa	71,726	2.84
Tunuyán	24,358	0.97
Tupungato	33,800	1.34
Not determined	24,347	0.96

Source: Instituto Nacional de Vitivinicultura, *Produccion y Elaboracion Vitivinicola* (Mendoza, 1976–1984).

Mendoza exhibits sufficient east-west environmental transition to be reflected in viticulture and wines as well. By general consensus, the province's best wines come from the basins of the Tunuyán and Mendoza rivers, in the southwestern area of northern Mendoza, where the Malbec and Cabernet Sauvignon ripen well. But, as noted earlier, there is some change in precipitation from the flatlands around the capital, where annual totals average about 8 inches, to the hills at the foot of the Andes, where the average is up to 12 inches. To this small but significant moistening should be added the effect of cooling with higher elevation. Southwest of Mendoza City, in the Tupungato Department, lie vineyards nearly 1000 feet above those around the capital (where the elevation is 2700 feet). There, the harvest begins as much as three weeks later, as cooler conditions slow the ripening of the grapes.

It is therefore of more than passing interest to know more than that a wine comes from Mendoza rather than one of Argentina's other wine provinces; the crucial question really is *where* in Mendoza stand the vines from which the wine is made. Mendoza is red wine country; 46 percent of all wine-producing varieties are reds, and fewer than 20 percent are whites, although white acreage is expanding and the red contracting. Argentinian statistics list the Criolla and the Cereza among "rosé" grapes, and these make up the majority of the remaining acreage. White grapes include principally the (probably misnamed) Pedro Ximenez, Chenin Blanc, Sémillon, Palomino, Moscatel, the so-called Riesling, and, increasingly, the Chardonnay.

In addition to the successful Malbec and still-expanding Cabernet Sauvignon, Mendoza's vineyards carry the Lambrusco (the Italian cultivar), Barbera, Tempranillo

(Spanish), Cabernet Franc, Merlot, Pinot Noir, Bonarda, and some Nebbiolo among red varieties. There is a certain spatial variation in this assemblage: the Malbec and Cabernet Sauvignon are concentrated in the northern vineyards centered on the capital and those of the Tupungato-Tunuyán Districts to the southwest. The central winegrowing zone, with the town of San Rafael as its focus, lies in the area where the Diamante and Atuel rivers approach each other quite closely, thus creating a large and productive oasis. The San Rafael District, too, produces *vinos finos*, but there is more Tempranillo here, and sizable stands of the Sémillon along with the omnipresent Criolla. South of San Rafael there is nothing comparable as viticulture becomes infrequent and patchy, until it expands again in the basin of the Río Colorado. Argentina's winemakers produce much more than the bottled *vino fino* varietals seen on foreign markets; they make large quantities of country-style wines for the domestic market and even larger amounts of blending wine and must (grape juice that will be converted into wine in the importing countries) for bulk export. Thus, the noble varieties stand among vast expanses of grapes whose harvest are intended for mass production, thousands of gallons at a time. It is the mainstay of the industry, and this industry ranks third in importance among all of the country's enterprises.

Here some of the world's largest winery facilities tower over the countryside, a constant reminder of the factorylike output of Mendoza. But the province has virtually everything to offer: among its more than 1,300 wineries are small bodegas and huge, ultramodern, computerized wine factories. In the province of Mendoza alone there are storage facilities with a total capacity of well over a *billion* gallons. The enormous vineyard area is divided into more than 32,000 properties, ranging from the vast holdings of major companies to the small parcels of independent growers.

The names of several of Argentina's major firms have become familiar to Northern Hemisphere consumers, because their *vinos finos* have improved greatly over the past two decades and, as values, they are unmatched. If Argentina's Malbecs and Cabernet Sauvignons cannot be compared to the greatest *crus* of Bordeaux or California's best, they nevertheless are very good and interesting wines; and in repeated blind tastings they have at times outranked representative wines from those areas. In a recent, well-publicized tasting, an Argentinian Cabernet Sauvignon stood ahead of a 1974 Cabernet from a leading Napa Valley winery, and very slightly behind another; the price of the Argentinian wine was one-tenth of the California wines. "Measured simply as value for money, the Argentinian wines are in a class by themselves."[4]

The largest winery in the entire Southern Hemisphere may well be Mendoza-based Bodegas y Viñedos (ByV) Peñaflor. The firm also has a large bodega in San Juan and a bottling plant in Buenos Aires. It was founded by an Italian immigrant, Antonio Pulenta, in the early years of the century and has become one of the most modern operations of its kind in the world. Three of its labels seen on overseas markets, Andean, Trapiche, and Fond de Cave, represent dependable varietal wines. Another giant of the industry is ByV Giol, founded in 1894, and now owned and operated by the provincial government of Mendoza. Its best wines are not familiar to overseas consumers but have been awarded prizes in Argentina. Proprietary labels include the Toro Viejo (white and red), Canciller ("Bourgogne" and Cabernet), and

Bodegas y Vinedos Lopez ranks among the leading premium-wine producers in Argentina. This label represents a blend in which Cabernet Sauvignon dominates.

La Colina (Pinot Rouge, a Pinot Noir–dominated blend). Noted for its quality wines is ByV Lopez, a family firm since its founding in 1898. Lopez is not as large as Peñaflor or Giol but, as in the case of Chile's Cousiño Macul, the firm's fine wines are held in high esteem. The Lopez vineyards lie in several departments where conditions suit particular cultivars, including San Martín and Rivadavia. One of its labels is Chateau Montchenot (red and white), another is Chateau Vieux, a Malbec-based blend of considerable merit. Other Lopez wines not normally seen outside the country are Vasco Viejo (red and white) and Rincon Famoso (red and rosé). In general the Lopez firm is respected for its considerable success with the Malbec, but its white *vinos finos* also have a large following in Argentina. A good example of a smaller, quality Mendoza firm is Orfila, another family winery. Orfila owns several vineyards with vines more than a half-century old, and others with younger vines. The firm also purchases grapes from growers who have sold their harvests to Orfila for decades, ensuring quality control. Orfila makes excellent Cabernets and Cabernet-Malbec blends.

Chateau Orfila

1978
CABERNET SAUVIGNON
OF ARGENTINA

BOTTLED AT THE CHATEAU VINYARDS
IN MENDOZA

A TOTAL OF 78,230 BOTTLES WERE
PRODUCED FROM THIS VINTAGE
THIS BOTTLE NUMBER IS *10994*

PRODUCED AND BOTTLED BY **JOSE ORFILA LTD.** MENDOZA ARGENTINA
ALCOHOL 12³⁰% BY VOL. NET. CONTENT. 750 ml PRODUCE OF ARGENTINA
IMPORTED BY JOSEPH VICTORI WINES INC. BROOKLYN - N.Y. 11231

Orfila is an important name in international diplomatic circles and in Mendoza wine. This Cabernet Sauvignon by Orfila was made from grapes grown in the department of Junín. It is a good example of a traditional Argentinian Cabernet, popular at home and a good value abroad.

Another noted Mendoza wine firm is Pascual Toso Vineyards, whose Toso Cabernet won a gold medal at the first National Wine Competition of 1978. This wine comes from the Barrancas zone in the Maipú Department, where the vines were originally planted in the 1890s. Toso's Malbec also is a very good wine, and in Argentina such wines as Toso's Bar-le-Duc and Toso Viejo are highly regarded. *Bodegas y Viñedos* Flichman produces successful Syrahs and Merlots, both of which have won gold medals. The Furlotti firm, with vineyards in Maipú and Agrelo, is noted for its Cabernet Sauvignon and its proprietary Ponte Vecchio and Val de Loire labels. Also prominent are *ByV* La Rural, with part of its vineyard in the hills of Tupungato and excellent varietal reds and whites; *ByV* Arizu, with bodegas at Godoy Cruz in Mendoza, San Rafael, and Río Negro and the noted Valroy label for its Cabernet and Chardonnay, and gold-medal–winning Cava Privada Rouge, a blend; and *ByV* Santa Ana, known for its Pinots and its sparkling wine from Chardonnay.

A number of other Mendoza wineries merit attention. The name of Benegas still remains associated with winegrowing through the Federico Benegas label, known for its good Merlots. Fine sparkling wines, Argentinian "Champagnes," are made by Crillon and more recently by a Moët & Chandon subsidiary, M. Chandon. Good Sherry-style wines are made by La Esmeralda's San Juan bodega (the firm is headquartered in Córdoba and has extensive vineyards in Mendoza). Espiño is a major name in Luján, and Arnaldo Etchart produces premium wines from several vineyards: Cabernet Sauvignon in Luján, Merlot in Tupungato, and Malbec in Maipú. The Norton label also signifies premium winegrowing, and the Norton vineyards at Perdriel are among Mendoza's most favored. Pacifico Tittarelli markets a noted Cabernet.

Mendoza's San Rafael zone, 130 miles to the southeast, boasts some major names as well. The leader is the Suter Winery, which releases prize-winning *vinos finos* from the Malbec, Syrah, Sémillon, "Riesling," and Pinot Blanc. Suter's Valle Hermoso, a long-lived white, is a remarkable wine. Bianchi, a firm dating from 1910, has recently modernized its facilities and now produces a noted red (Bianchi Particular) from Cabernet Sauvignon, and a fresh Chablis-style wine. Gargiulo, Goyenechea (with its "Aberdeen Angus" line), Lavaque, Mahia Hermanos, Rodas, and Sainte Sylvie (with its Santa Silvia "Excelente 98" Gran Tinto) lend further distinction to Mendoza's "other" viticulture zone.[5]

Numerous additional bodegas produce noteworthy wines not seen on foreign markets. Argentina delayed far too long the development of an appellation system, so that label interpretation is difficult. Those interesting blends that do not reach overseas consumers are not normally described on the label, so that neither geographic origin nor varietal combination is revealed. But some bodegas specialize in particular cultivars and bottle these *vinos finos* as varietals: *ByV* Bragagnolo's Barbera, Biondolillo's Cabernet Sauvignon, the Cooperative Viñateros Unidos' Sémillon, La Chimba's Malvasia, Corinto's Chardonnay, Borbore's Barbera, Valenti's Pinot Blanc, and Gargiulo's Pinot Noir are among these. In the vineyard and in the winery, Argentina's industry is progressive and up to date. The label on the bottle reveals how long its classificatory modernization is overdue.

SAN JUAN

The province of San Juan adjoins Mendoza to the north, where summer temperatures are even warmer and rainfall is even lower, averaging barely 6 inches over most of the area. Hot, desiccating winds are a greater danger to the vine than violent hailstorms. Winter is comparatively mild. The capital, historic San Juan, is located on the San Juan River, one of the province's two major streams (the other, the

Goyenechea's vineyards and bodega lie in the San Rafael zone of Mendoza. This rather unusual label represents one of Goyenechea's three major lines (the other two are Goyenechea and Marques del Nevado). It is recognized in Argentina as a premium Cabernet, and is now seen on foreign markets.

Río Blanco, flows across San Juan only to terminate in a basin of interior drainage in the extreme southeast corner). The Río San Juan is the vital water source for the province's viticulture, supplemented of course by wells. The viticulture area lies concentrated in the south and consists of about 160,000 acres, nearly one-fifth of the country's total.

San Juan ranks second only to Mendoza as a wine region of Argentina, but its viticultural landscape is quite different. A much larger part of the overall grape harvest is marketed fresh or as raisins; the wine grapes cultivated here are not the

Huge bunches, high yields: mark of Argentina's viticulture. Rigorous training and pruning by several quality-oriented growers have contributed to the production of premium wines that have made their mark on world markets as excellent values.

reds of Mendoza, but the high-sugar whites whose juice is suitable for concentration and distillation. A few *vinos finos* are produced by bodegas specializing in premium wines, but the main objective is volume. Naturally the Criolla and the Cereza are ubiquitous, and the dominant white grape varieties also include the Pedro Ximenez, Muscats, and Torrontés (the Torontel of the Chilean side of the Andes). The small acreage of reds, less than 10 percent of the total, contains Barbera, Nebbiolo, Malbec, and several small parcels of lesser varieties. If this combination of cultivars is reminiscent of the Chilean Pisquera zone, the comparison is apt: San Juan lies exactly opposite Chile's Coquimbo.

The cultural landscape evinces the vineyards' composition. Mendoza's vines are trained, over more than two-thirds of the area, on the high-low Espalier system, whereas the Parral system is almost universal in San Juan. There is very little pruning, so that the vines here grow luxuriantly, budding without inhibition and producing enormous harvests per acre, even by Argentinian standards.

San Juan Province is Argentina's largest exporter of concentrated musts, grape juice that will be converted into wine in the importing countries (Venezuela, Japan, and the United Kingdom have been major buyers). Well over 80 percent of all of Argentina's concentrated must exports come from San Juan, and only about 15 percent from Mendoza. This alone reflects the vinicultural contrasts between the two neighboring wine regions, but San Juan's table wines and *vinos finos* should not be forgotten. Brandies and Sherry-type wines from San Juan are popular on the domestic market, and some wineries have built open-air, solera-style aging systems. And among San Juan's more than 370 wineries some produce *vinos finos* from the comparatively small red grape vineyards of the province. These are often good wines, rarely seen outside Argentina but certainly the equal of many of Mendoza's export wines. In a few limited areas of San Juan there are microclimates that provide the opportunity to raise better grapes; it is then up to the winemakers to make the most of the harvest. Some succeed admirably.

San Juan's vineyards are divided into nearly 14,000 properties, so that the grapegrowing region is even more fragmented than Mendoza's. Large companies own substantial tracts, but many small parcels are owned by independent growers. This, too, encourages the highest possible yields; when growers are paid by weight of the harvest, they tend to be unreceptive to pruning prescriptions.

A majority of the province's vineyards lie in the basin of the San Juan River. As in Mendoza, however, harvest statistics are revealing for what they record about the diffusion of viticulture in the province. All but one of San Juan's eighteen departments annually report a wine-grape harvest to the INV. The Capital Department, which includes a large rural area, is the most productive of all, followed by San Martín, Caucete, Santa Lucia, Pocito, and Albardon. The Zonda and Ullun zones, important producing areas, lie in Rivadavia and Ullun departments respectively, but the Tulum zone, most of it in Albardon, also produces the province's largest table-grape harvest. Again the data reflect quantity and dispersal, not quality. A labeling system based on geographic origin will benefit especially those quality-oriented bodegas that make the best of San Juan's challenging (and far from uniform) environment.

Among prominent names in San Juan is Santiago Graffigna, a firm dating from the 1860s, and known for its ordinary but dependable Colón line and its more expensive, limited-production Graffigna line. Its Graffigna Tinta, a Malbec, is a good example of that style. Other San Juan wineries include Duc de Saint-Remy and El Parque.

LA RIOJA

The province of La Rioja lies to the north and east of San Juan, and reaches farther into the lowlands east of the Andes than does its southern neighbor (Fig. 5.5). Temperatures in the lowlands are hotter still than those in San Juan, and rainfall averages a mere 8 inches, but these are not the real limitations on viticulture. The

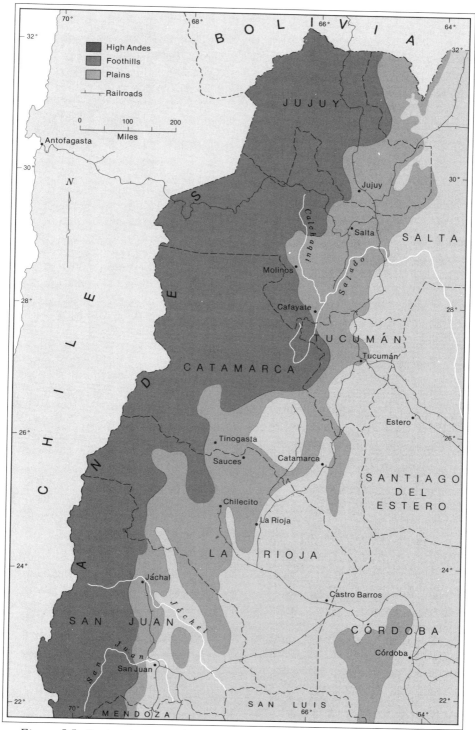

Figure 5.5. *Regional topography in the northern viticulture areas of Argentina.*

necessary investments in water control, well drilling, and irrigation-system development have not yet been made. La Rioja's natural environments are quite similar to those of San Juan, and where the vine has been planted, it has done well.

The natural valley-oases of La Rioja are among Argentina's historic viticultural sites, and grapegrowing here predates Mendoza by centuries. But progress has been slow. Today there are some 20,000 acres of land under the vine in La Rioja, divided into the smallholdings of nearly 5,500 owners and the larger vineyards of several major bodegas. There are about fifty wineries in the province. By Argentinian standards, these figures are low, but they should be viewed in another context. La Rioja's vineyard acreage still is larger than the entire area under vines in New Zealand, where fewer than 15,000 acres sustain an entire national industry.

La Rioja, nevertheless, remains a viticultural frontier. In the irrigated vineyards stand the Torrontés, Criolla, Cereza, the Muscat of Alexandria, and the Pedro Ximenez, all able to survive and produce in the heat and mainly trained on Parral trellises. Small acreages of Malbec, Barbera, and Bonarda are cultivated on high Espalier, but the great majority of La Rioja's wines are high-alcohol, low-acid, sweet-tasting, white table wines that may have no prospect on international markets but have won approval on the domestic scene.

The great majority of La Rioja's wines come from the most productive department, Chilecito, extending west of the capital city (also called La Rioja). Chilecito contributes nearly three-quarters of the province's entire annual harvest from valleys that benefit from slight elevation above the eastern flatlands. Of some additional interest are the departments of Castro Barros and Saragasta in the western foothills, and San Blas de los Sauces in the far north, where production is small but the focus is on specialized training and pruning for quality wines; here the potential of La Rioja is in evidence.

THE NORTHWEST

The provinces of Catamarca, Salta, and Jujuy are grouped together as a single wine region, a practice of the INV based, primarily, on the relatively small dimensions of the industry here. The total wine-grape acreage in the three provinces is about 14,000 acres, more than 9,000 of these in Catamarca and a mere 1,000 in Jujuy. Catamarca, southernmost of the three northwestern provinces, also has the majority of the region's forty wineries. In this remotest viticultural frontier, Catamarca is the leading area.

Distance and isolation have undoubtedly had an impact on the wine industry of the Northwest, because the region contains some promising environments yet to be developed. Here, on the western flank of the Chaco and against the east-facing slopes of the Andes, conditions are more like those of Mendoza than in La Rioja or even San Juan; there is somewhat more rainfall, there are cooler valley microclimates, and there is more environmental diversity.

This diversity is well illustrated by the two separate winegrowing zones of Catamarca. The capital city lies in the southeastern corner of the province, and in this vicinity grapes are grown for the table and for fortified beverages. In the western foothills, temperatures are cooler, rainfall reaches as much as 15 inches (the average is 12), and here lie 90 percent of the province's vineyards for wine production. The Tinogasta Department is the entire Northwest's most productive zone. In addition to the Criollas and the Cerezas, Muscats and Torrontés, there also are stands of Malbec and Barbera, and even the Cabernet Sauvignon makes a reappearance.

The vineyards of the province of Salta lie in the same environmental zone as Tinogasta, again in the western foothills. Here the valleys of the Calchaqui River and its tributaries accommodate the vines of Molinos, San Carlos, and Cafayate departments (Cafayate is the most important), and the region's suitability for viticulture is evident. Watered by streams and springs, cooled by elevation, and ripened by a summer sun that is not excessively hot, grapes ranging from the ordinary to the noble ripen to yield a range of wines, among which some are quite remarkable. Salta has been proven capable of producing *vinos finos* that can stand with the best of Mendoza. Cafayate has four noteworthy bodegas: La Rosa, which makes pleasant whites from Torrontés and a good Cabernet Sauvignon; La Banda, marketing the Vasija Secreto label's reds and whites; El Recreo, whose Buen Retiro red is a good wine; and Arnaldo Etchart, producing good Malbecs.

Jujuy Province is not a wine-producing area as yet, but the potential exists here as well. Jujuy's grape-growing area is almost entirely devoted to table grapes, although there is some small amount of local winemaking. The vineyards lie between the capital, San Salvador de Jujuy, and the southern border of the province (see Fig. 5.5).

Although the three provinces of the Northwest are traditionally combined as a single viticultural region, they are likely, eventually, to achieve recognition as individual Argentinian appellations. Each has well-defined and distinct winegrowing regions, varietal combinations, and vinicultural products. Geography, in the form of distance, remoteness, and comparative inaccessibility, has been the Northwest's adversary. Time and environment will prove its crucial allies.

RÍO NEGRO

South of Mendoza lies what may be Argentina's most promising viticultural frontier of all. The Río Colorado is traditionally taken as the northern boundary of Patagonia, and that very name suggests another kind of isolation. But Patagonia's northernmost provinces—Neuquén and Río Negro—present environmental alternatives not found to the north. Here, astride the 39th parallel, the summer heat ameliorates, the winter intensifies, and the grapes are not pushed by a relentless sun toward a high-sugar and low-acid combination. There is no problem with the sugar—ripening is complete. What is really different is the acid level. Cooler temperatures, slower ripening, and general environmental moderation produce very good balance with adequate acid in the grapes.

As in the case of the Northwest, this southern region consists of more than one province, but again as in the north, only one of them is really important. The main vineyards lie in Río Negro, and the viticulture zone extends slightly into adjoining Neuquén (Fig. 5.6). Río Negro has more than 45,000 acres of vines; Neuquén fewer than 2,000. Río Negro has more than 3,500 individual vineyards; Neuquén only about 250. Thus Río Negro ranks third, behind San Juan, among

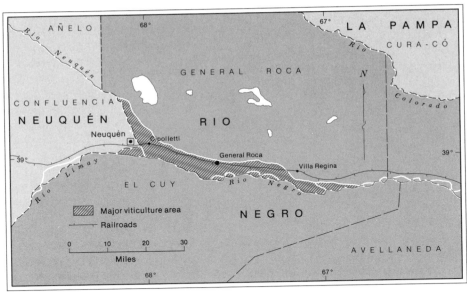

Figure 5.6. The winegrowing districts of Río Negro and Neuquén, Argentina.

wine regions in Argentina, accounting for about 5 percent of the total vineyard area.

Although conditions are cooler here, rainfall remains slight (the familiar average of 8 inches prevails) and irrigation is essential. The vital stream is the Río Negro, product of two Andean tributaries (the Neuquén and Limay rivers). The two tributaries join near the capital city of Neuquén in the appropriately named department of Confluencia, where the Río Negro enters a wide flood plain on its way to its merger with the Río Colorado. The soils in the Río Negro's basin vary somewhat: north of the river they contain more gravel and have a sandy texture, whereas those on the south bank are finer grained. This difference gives rise to some interesting viticultural contrasts, since the northern soils (*costa*) are better textured and the southern soils (*barda*) are more nutrient-rich. Here, under the controlled irrigation that has been elevated to an art as well as a science by Argentinian winegrowers, may lie the best answer to the debate over the role of soil composition in wine quality.

If Río Negro presents winegrowers with an environmental hazard, it is related to the intensified winters at these latitudes. Late spring frosts and early fall freezes have in some seasons damaged buds and grapes, but the spring damage may have a somewhat positive impact by reducing yields and intensifying the wines. In Río Negro, therefore, vintage years do matter.

The viticultural landscape presents quite a contrast to the Parral-dominated north. In Rio Negro–Neuquén, there is little Criolla: the grapes are mainly Malbec, Barbera, Syrah, Pinot Noir, Merlot and, increasingly, Cabernet Sauvignon among the red cultivars, and Chenin Blanc, Sémillon, Malvasia, Pedro Ximenez, and Torrontés among the whites. These are trained on the Espalier system (low for two-thirds of the vines, high for one-fifth), and Guyot-pruned. Other systems, including some Parral, are in use in the high-yield vineyards of Torrontés and Pedro Ximenez.

In the 1980s Río Negro's production of grapes exceeded 120,000 tons annually, while Neuquén's output (all of it from Confluencia) was below 4,000—a good measure of the dominance of Río Negro Province in this region. And about 90 percent of Río Negro's yield normally comes from a single department, General Roca, which extends from the Negro River northward, immediately east of Neuquén. Each of Río Negro's five other departments also contributes to the province's output, Pichi Mahuida and Avellaneda (both fronting the river downstream from General Roca) ranking next. Two leading wineries are Canale, whose Cabernet Intimo and Gran Vino (Pinot Noir, Pinot Gris and Merlot) prove what the region can produce; and the Cooperativa Colonia Choel Choel.[6]

The Río Negro-Neuquén region produces noteworthy *vinos finos*, in some ways the most interesting of Argentina's wines—but few of these find their way to overseas consumers. It is evidence of the growing sophistication of the domestic market that the region's table wines have become accepted and even popular: these are not the nondescript white country wines of more northerly origins. In many ways Río Negro exemplifies the best of Argentinian viniculture.

BEYOND ANDEAN SHADOWS

In one way or another all the western vineyards of Argentina, from Jujuy to Río Negro, are affected by the Andes Mountains. But there are some grapegrowing areas—very few—elsewhere in the country, away from the Andes' lee. The most productive of these is in Córdoba Province, where several vineyards lie scattered north of the capital and near the boundary with San Luis in the west, around Villa Dolores. Between Córdoba and Mendoza, in the province of San Luis, small vineyards lie near the capital of the same name. North of Córdoba is the historic province of Santiago del Estero, where Argentina's first vines may have stood; today production is very small, and nearly half the tiny output of grapes is destined for the table. Some vineyards even overlook the Parana River in the department of San Nicolas of northern Buenos Aires Province, in the region traditionally called *Litoral*, which extends into Santa Fe Province. In Santa Fe, too, and even in Entre Ríos across the river, an attempt at viticulture is being made. None of this can compare with the enormous industry of Mendoza and its neighbors, but it is further evidence of Argentina's productive capacity.

Problems and Potentials

Argentina's wine industry has experienced a century of growth and success based on a unique combination of Italian viticulture and Spanish viniculture. Italian traditions and cultivars fashioned the cultural landscape, but in the bodegas Spanish practices prevailed. It is no accident that Argentina's wineries are called bodegas and not *fattoria* or *castelli*. This is why an old Spanish winemaking custom—the lengthy aging of wine (white as well as red) in wood—has long been a feature of Argentinian viniculture. The aroma and flavor this imparts to local wines are preferred by the great majority of Argentinian consumers, and the domestic market is vital to the industry, bulk exports notwithstanding. In the absence of pressure from the home market, winemakers will be reluctant to tamper with tradition.

But the growing importance of exports of premium wines (and to some extent their acceptance by a fraction of the home market) has caused a reconsideration of established practice. The most successful red wines on foreign markets are those that have some wood aging, but not as much as five years or more; the most salable whites are fresh and dry, not old and maderized. It is a reality on virtually every major international market, and it has led to changes in aging methods in the export-oriented bodegas of Spain's Rioja region, the original source of Argentina's wine technology. Spanish Rioja's success on world markets always has been a guide for Argentina's premium winegrowers, and the improved quality and international recognition of Argentina's *vinos finos* have also generated new directions in Argentinian winemaking.

Other new directions will be geographic and ampelographic. The southernmost, coolest region for viticulture (Río Negro) has possibilities that will be more fully exploited to produce the kinds of fresh, crisp white wines to match Argentina's best reds. This will be linked with an overall rationalization of Argentina's viticultural geography, so that regional specialization will develop more strongly. Certain cultivars that do not (yet) stand among Argentina's most successful may emerge in the process, such as the Ruby Cabernet (a cross between Cabernet Sauvignon and Carginnan) and the Emerald Riesling (a cross between the White Riesling and the Muscadel). Research and experimentation will uncover Argentina's unexploited potential, of which the Neuquén-Río Negro region may hold the key.

A growing awareness of the need for change in other areas of the wine industry also is evident. As was for many decades the case in the United States, Argentinian wines mainly destined for local consumption have long been marketed as "Chablis," "Rhine," "Beaujolais," "Rioja" (an imitation not seen in California), "Margaux," and other foreign, mainly French, appellations. Sparkling wine is labeled Champagne; there has even been an Argentinian "Asti Espumante." Even varietal labels may not reveal reality: a "Riesling" may not contain anything other than Sémillon and/or Sauvignon Blanc. It is a situation that has for many years required modification, especially since these imitative designations are used in place of geographic identifications. Thus an Argentinian consumer might satisfy a preference for a particular regional wine simply by knowing that the bodega on the label is located in a certain province or town; normally there is no mention at all of more specific geographic locales such as departments. Yet the advantages of such labeling have been proved repeatedly: the practice builds consumer confidence and loyalty.

This is an anomalous situation, because the Argentinian wine industry is otherwise quite strictly, even severely, controlled by the various arms of the *Instituto Nacional Vitivinicultura*. With its headquarters in the city of Mendoza, the INV has agencies in more than forty locations in the wine regions, and it operates ten laboratories throughout the area. It is staffed by a veritable army of bureaucrats, inspectors, and technicians, who control virtually every aspect of winegrowing. Replacement of cultivars or the planting of new vineyards may not take place

Argentina's vineyards, cellars, and outlets are kept under constant INV surveillance. Vineyard practices are checked, cellar techniques are monitored (sugaring is strictly prohibited), and retail stocks are subject to inspection. The viticultural landscape seems to reflect this atmosphere of order and control.

without INV approval. Vineyard care, pruning, harvesting, and even the transportation of the grapes to the bodegas is supervised. Harvest decisions are not simply made by the viticulturist; they must be approved by the INV. The *Instituto* stipulates the alcoholic content the marketed wines must have, and decides when wine may be released for sale. It enforces the ban on Chaptalization. All of this is constantly checked by INV representatives who appear unannounced in wineries and wine shops and subject the content of vats and bottles to analyses. No wine may be dispatched from one locale to another without INV authorization, and all wine, stored, aging, bottled, or otherwise, must be registered. A winegrower who violates the regulations of the INV is subject to severe punishment, and not merely a fine in serious cases.

Financial transactions involving bodegas, labor relations, and winery administration also are under the scrutiny of the INV. The upper echelon of the *Instituto* has always had direct links with the Buenos Aires government (especially military governments whose retirees often were appointed as INV officials), so that the organization has functioned as a government-within-a-government. The power of the INV is evidence of the importance of the wine industry in Argentina's total economy.

That power is used not only to regulate and control, but also to support and assist. The INV has effectively coordinated the work of public and private organizations in the wine industry, funding cooperative ventures in such areas as promotion and advertising, market allocation, and communication. The INV has been very effective in areas of research and development, assisting winegrowers by providing facilities for the testing of field conditions and by conducting much-needed ampelographic studies. In addition, the *Instituto* makes available grants and scholarships to organizations and individuals working in oenological areas.

The INV has recognized the growing importance of Argentina's export wines, and a special office has been created to regulate and assist this sector of the industry. Controls over the production of *vinos finos* are even more stringent than those governing viniculture overall, and one result has been the dependability of Argentina's premium wines on international markets. Another result has been the price control that makes these wines such attractive alternatives among wines costing several times as much. Again the INV assists the exporters as well as controlling them: much of the visibility of Argentinian *vinos finos* in North America and Europe results from promotional efforts under INV auspices.

Even the INV, however, could not protect the wine industry against the vagaries of politics and economics that have plagued Argentina in recent decades. Argentina has been described as the most mismanaged country in the world, and whether or not that assessment is accurate or fair, there can be no doubt that national political and economic problems have had an impact on the wine industry. Inflation rates in the late 1970s hovered around 150 percent, and there were wealthy investors who seized on this opportunity to speculate. One of these was Hector Greco, who built a financial, industrial, and agricultural empire of which wine was a cornerstone. He broke the hold of major companies over Mendoza's wine industry, buying out seven wine firms and amassing an inventory of 290 million gallons of wine. Using his Banco de los Andes and its assets, he outbid competitors for grapes, undercut their sales by lowering his own wine prices, and then acquired them as they foundered. At the January 1979 harvest, growers had received an average of U.S. $0.90 per gallon of their (ordinary) wine; the effect of Greco's bidding was to raise that figure to $2.65 in January 1980, an unprecedented tripling in just one year. But Argentinian consumers resisted the rising market prices, and this caused the first ripple of concern. Then Greco's financial empire collapsed as depositors, fearful of bank failures, withdrew their savings. Wine prices fell to $0.80, lower even than they had been before Greco's intervention. Mendoza's heady boom was over.

Recovery was slow, and much damage had been done to the industry generally. Small growers were in debt, and when the next harvest was taken, the situation worsened. Consumer demand remained weak, and the large bodegas did not buy their usual quotas of bulk wine from the smaller vintners. They, in turn, did not buy from the individual growers. In early 1982 wine was selling at less than $1.00 per gallon in Mendoza stores, and cost only slightly more in Buenos Aires. What Argentina's wine industry needed most was a larger export trade of premium wines, but only about 5 percent of the vineyard acreage was devoted to noble grapes. The industry also needed relief from its long-term dependence on quantity (at the expense of quality) on the domestic market. The task for the *Instituto* is obvious: the expansion of premium-quality grapes at the expense of lesser varieties, and the rigorous standardization of domestic "appellations." The future of one of the world's great wine industries depends on this campaign.

6

BRAZIL:

VITICULTURE EMERGENT

B razil is South America's largest and most populous country, a nation three times as large as Argentina and Chile combined. The great majority of Brazil's 127 million people trace their ancestries to European countries where wine is an integral part of culture: Portugal, Italy, Germany. And yet Brazil's wine industry developed but slowly, as did Brazilian tastes for good wine. Perhaps the early problems of winegrowers in southern Brazil (see Chapter 2) constituted the crucial setback. Possibly the later dominance of American cultivars and hybrids produced wines for which the locals had no taste. Many Brazilians probably had the urge, in the melting pot of their fermenting culture, to turn to something new and different rather than the old and familiar.

Undoubtedly the geographic environment had much to do with it as well. Brazil, for all its European (and African) legacies, is a tropical country, straddling the equator in the north and escaping the tropics only in the far south. Wine is not a warm-weather libation (a chilled dry white may be perfect for these conditions, but such luxury was out of the reach of most Brazilians until quite recently), and drinking habits turned elsewhere. When Brazil entered its modern era of rapid growth and urban-industrial expansion, its long-forgotten wine industry experienced a revival to match. Today Brazil produces more than half as much wine as Chile, and more than twice as much as it did just twenty years ago. Not only has the domestic market recognized the quality of Brazil's wines, but Brazilian wines have succeeded on foreign markets as well, especially in Canada but also in the United States of America.

Almadén

ADEGA REGIONAL DE VINHOS FINOS

VINHEDOS PRÓPRIOS - PALOMAS - SANTANA DO LIVRAMENTO, RS

1983

Sauvignon Blanc

Palomas

VINHO FINO DE ORIGEM CONTROLADA

VINHO BRANCO FINO DE MESA
PRODUZIDO E ENGARRAFADO NA ORIGEM POR:
ALMADÉN
DIVISÃO DA NATIONAL DISTILLERS DO BRASIL IND. E COM. LTDA.

GRADUAÇÃO ALCOÓLICA 12° G.L. - CONTEÚDO: 720 ml
Indústria Brasileira

This Almadén (Brasil) label symbolizes the new era in Brazilian winegrowing. In southern Rio Grande do Sul, a major experiment by National Distillers' Brazilian subsidiary is under way with the planting of large acreages of premium grapes.

Brazil's relative location on the South American landmass suggests some of the environmental obstacles facing the country's grapegrowers. There is no Mediterranean zone in the country (see Fig. 1.1), nor is there a dry climatic regime comparable to Argentina's Andean rainshadow. North of the equator, Brazil reaches just slightly beyond 5° north latitude, and the entire countryside is clothed in rainforest. South of the Tropic of Capricorn, the country's southernmost town of Santa Vitoria do Palmar lies as far south as 33° 31', but on the lagoon-studded coast adjacent to Uruguay. Brazil's highest latitudes thus lie opposite the lowest-latitude grapegrowing zones of Argentina (La Rioja–Catamarca) and Chile (Coquimbo). This is not the most encouraging of comparisons, and the climatic map indicates the consequences: southern Brazil's climate resembles that of much of the southeastern United States, eastern Australia, and eastern China. The symbols on the map tell the story: summers are moist and warm, winters are cool, and there is no pronounced dry season to favor the ripening grapes. Such a regime, propitious for the cultivation of many other crops, is not the best for viticulture. First the missionary settlers, then the Portuguese immigrants, and later the Italian winegrowers discovered this in turn.

But winegrowers are not easily discouraged. The Spanish missionaries who came to what is today southernmost Brazil via Chile and Argentina realized that they had reached the least suitable of viticultural environments, but they nurtured their Criolla vines nevertheless, and some of their plantings were still bearing when the Portuguese arrived. The Portuguese, who imported cultivars of *vinifera* more familiar to them than the Criolla, saw the mildew envelop their grape bunches and the rot destroy their harvests. They persevered, but in the 1830s they were forced to turn to American hybrids as their fledgling industry was about to be wiped out. The American variety that rescued the industry was the Isabella, which came to southern Brazil via Portugal, where it had been introduced with some success. The Isabella is a Labrusca-based hybrid whose disease-resistance and abundant yield made it suitable for southern Brazil's problematic environment, and soon it replaced virtually every *vinifera* vine in the region's vineyards. But the wine vinted from the Isabella grapes had the "foxy" taste characteristic of Labruscas, and it never gained wide acceptance in Brazil. When the next immigrant-winegrowers, the Italians, arrived in the region they were determined to find locales where their European varieties would survive and yield.

The Italian immigration, which gained full force in the 1870s, had the same effect it had in Argentina, except that its dimensions were smaller. Many of the Italian settlers in Brazil's southernmost province were winegrowers, but Rio Grande do Sul was no Mendoza waiting to be opened up. The Italians concluded that the winegrowers preceding them had not identified the best locales for viticulture in the province, and as they searched for the microclimates that would overcome the most unfavorable aspects of the overall environment, they clustered in the highlands north of the Jacui River. There they developed what was to become the heartland of Brazilian winegrowing.

Regional Geography

Brazil is a federal republic with 22 states, four federal territories, and one federal district (containing the capital, Brasilia). Geographers recognize six traditional regions: the overpopulated, stressed Northeast, the country's historic heartland; the North, consisting mainly of the forested Amazon Basin; the Interior, the extensive plainlands of the Mato Grosso; the Southeast, centered on the former capital city of Rio de Janeiro and including the industrial region of Minas Gerais; São Paulo, focus of Brazil's modern core area; and the South (Fig. 6.1). The South consists of three states: Rio Grande do Sul, the country's most productive wine region; Santa Catarina, also a wine-producing state; and Paraná, less important as a wine-producing state.

As a region, the South contains Brazil's viticultural heartland, but wine is made elsewhere also. In São Paulo there are two major wine-producing areas, centered on the towns of São Roque (about 25 miles west of São Paulo's urban area) and

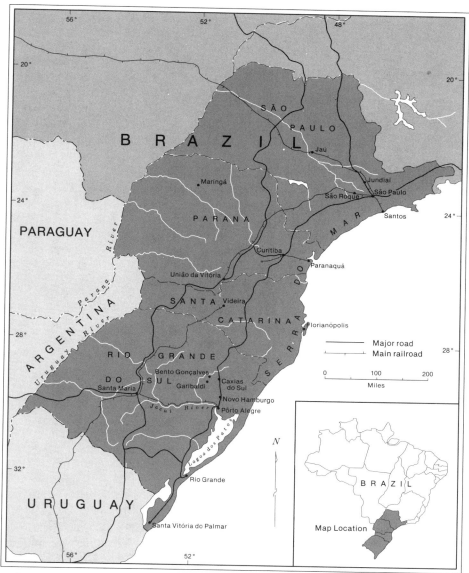

Figure 6.1. The great majority of Brazil's vineyards lie in the southern states of Brazil, primarily Rio Grande do Sul.

Jundiai (about the same distance to the north-northwest). Some wine is produced in the state of Minas Gerais in the town of Andredas as well. Some wine grapes (but mostly table grapes) are grown in the valley of the São Francisco River in the state of Pernambuco. And for several years a viticultural experiment has been in progress in the near-equatorial state of Bahia. There, an attempt is being made to ripen and harvest grapes during each of the two dry seasons of the savanna climatic regime which, as Figure 3.1 shows, prevails over Brazil's Northeast. If this double-

Bento Gonçalves, center of the wine industry of Rio Grande do Sul.

cropping experiment, unique in the field of viticulture, were to succeed over the long term, the implications would be incalculable.[1] The map of world wine production would be reshaped.

Thus Brazil's viticulture zone extends over a wide latitudinal range, beginning well within the tropics and ending where many wine reigons elsewhere begin: around 30° south. The environmental challenge is difficult, but the winegrowers' skills are meeting it.

RIO GRANDE DO SUL

The state of Rio Grande do Sul remains the heartland of Brazilian viticulture. The capital of the state, the city of Porto Alegre (2.5 million), marks an important physiographic transition that explains the location of the main winegrowing areas. Brazil's eastern margin is marked by a conspicuous escarpment separating a narrow coastal lowland from extensive interior highlands. That escarpment's southern end lies in the approximate latitude of Porto Alegre. North of the city it forms the east-facing edge of the Serra do Mar, an appropriately named upland whose influence on regional drainage can be clearly discerned from Figure 6.1. Many streams flow westward into the Uruguay River rather than eastward to the Atlantic Ocean; much of the land of southern Brazil slopes gently westward, not seaward. That pattern ends with the eastward-flowing Jacui River, which drains central Rio Grande do Sul and flows into the Guaiba estuary and thence into the Lagoa dos Patos at Porto Alegre.

North of the capital lies a dendritic system of Jacui tributaries, among them the Rio das Antas, and in the highlands separating these rivers the Italian winegrowers found the viticultural environments they were looking for. In this area, at the Southern end of the great *Planalto*, lie the towns whose names are synonymous with wine in Brazil: Bento Gonçalves, Caxias do Sul, Garibaldi, and others. This is Brazil's "wine triangle," where more than 40 percent of all grapes (including table grapes) are cultivated. Clustered here are nearly 350 of the country's 600 wine producers, including the most prestigious names in the industry. Many of these producers are small, local operations that make and sell some wine in addition to other agricultural products, but others specialize in wine, exporting blending wine to other Brazilian states and bottled wine overseas.

It is appropriate to reflect on the climatic environments under which Brazil's grapes are grown. Brazil's "frost boundary" (that is, the line north of which no frost normally occurs) lies across northern Parana and southern São Paulo states, thus accentuating the regional boundary of the Brazilian South. But while the South thus records occasional below-freezing temperatures, the climate classified as Cfa (see Figure 1.5); winters are considerably warmer even than in Argentina's Mendoza. At Porto Alegre, the coolest month of the year averages about 56°F., and the warmest month records a 76°F. average. Summer humidity is high, even under the somewhat cooler conditions of the uplands between the Jacui tributaries, and summer rain is not uncommon. The natural vegetation is a semideciduous forest. These are the circumstances that led Brazil's Italian immigrant-winegrowers to look for the most suitable microclimates of Rio Grande do Sul, a search that led to the development of the wine triangle.[2]

The regional viticultural geography of Rio Grande do Sul displays a concentration in the Caixas do Sul area, comprising the municipalities of Bento Gonçalves, Garibaldi, Flores da Cunha, Farroupilha, and Caixas itself. This is the old core area of winegrowing, and a second, pioneer zone has emerged more recently along the southern border of the state. There, the districts of Guarai, Santana do Livramento, Dom Pedrito, Bage, and Pinheiro Machado (and to a lesser extent Herval and Piratini) now contain significant vineyards, including a major venture by Almaden, the Brazilian subsidiary of National Distillers (Fig. 6.2).

Today Rio Grande do Sul is a patchwork of major firms and companies, cooperatives, small individual winemakers, contract growers, and grape farmers. There are about 40 major wine firms in Brazil, many of which are headquartered in one of the towns of the wine triangle or in Porto Alegre. Foreign investment and involvement also have changed the regional map. National Distillers (United States), Cinzano (Italy), and Moët & Chandon (France) are among foreign corporations that have had a positive impact on viticultural, vinicultural, and marketing practices.

In 1911 an important development occurred with the establishment of the Cooperativa Agricola de Caixas, earliest of the cooperatives that enabled winegrowers to share facilities and market their harvests dependably. Among major firms headquartered in Rio Grande do Sul are the Cooperativas Vinicola Garibaldi and Aurora. Based in Bento Gonçalves, Aurora was founded in 1931 as a cooperative by a small groups of winegrowers in the area, and fifty years later the firm had more than 1000 member-winegrowing families. Like other major Brazilian wine firms, Aurora has company-owned vineyards as well (about 12,000 acres in 1984) and continues

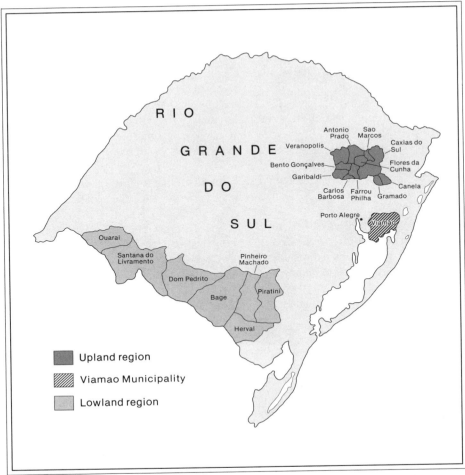

Figure 6.2. Winegrowing districts in Rio Grande do Sul, Brazil.

to expand. In 1983 Aurora purchased the large, Heublein-owned Dreher firm, thereby doubling the grape acreage under its control and extending its influence over regional viticulture. Dreher is known, in part, for its introduction of large-scale cultivation of Cabernet Sauvignon and Merlot cultivars in the late 1960s, and the marketing of its claret-style Castel Marjolet when the vines began to yield. Since the mid-1970s, Castel Marjolet (70 percent Cabernet, 30 percent Merlot) has been exported to overseas markets, especially Canada and the United States.

Other well-known Brazilian wine firms centered in Rio Grande do Sul include, in addition to the Garibaldi Cooperative, the Companhia (Cia) Vinícola Rio Grandense, Cia Vinícola San Gabriel, Cia Monaco Vinhedos, Fontanive & Cia, Vinhos Finos Santa Rosa, and Champagne Georges Aubert. Among these, the Rio Grandense firm pioneered the development of premium cultivars. As long ago as the early 1930s, Rio Grandense had planted more than 125 acres to vinifera such as Cabernet Sauvignon, Merlot, and Trebbiano. Its Granja União line of fine wines stood as a standard for the industry.

Viticultural landscape in Brazil's wine triangle. Contrasts in shades of green reveal American and vinifera varieties.

Brazil's wine industry displays all the earmarks of its rapid and sometimes chaotic transformation and modernization. The percentage of Labrusca vines among cultivars is declining, although the Isabella and its cousins still may represent about half of the total acreage. Research and experimentation have begun to reveal the possibilities for *vinifera* in Rio Grande do Sul, and while bulk wines remain Labrusca-based, the *vinhos finos* are derived from nobler grapes. Aurora's vineyards of Barbera are expanding, and this cultivar may be the red grape of the future for southern Brazil, although the Nebbiolo, too, has proven its adaptability. The Cabernet Franc and the Merlot also have succeeded here, and Aurora's Cabernet Rouge is a blend of 80 percent Cabernet Franc and 20 percent Merlot. Among the whites (overall, Brazil's winegrowers have been much less successful with white wines), the Muscat still dominates, but the Trebbiano has been able to adjust to local conditions, and there also is some Sémillon. Aurora's Rafaella Valli Chablis Blanc is 75 percent Trebbiano and 25 percent Sémillon. Dreher's Castel Marjolet was something of a breakthrough, made possible through the investments by Heublein during the 1970s. In the 1980s the large-scale venture of National Distillers, in the especially favorable microclimate in Santana do Livramento, promised to produce more than 2.5 million gallons of quality wine for the domestic Brazilian market, representing fully one-fifth of current local consumption. At the other end of the spectrum is the remarkable venture by Oscar Guglielmone, who wanted to produce "chateau" wines in the state and built, thirteen miles outside Porto Alegre, a full-scale replica of a medieval castle. There he produced, sparing no expense, some hundreds of bottles of (Italian) Piedmont-style Nebbiolo and (French) Bordeaux-style Cabernet Sauvignon.

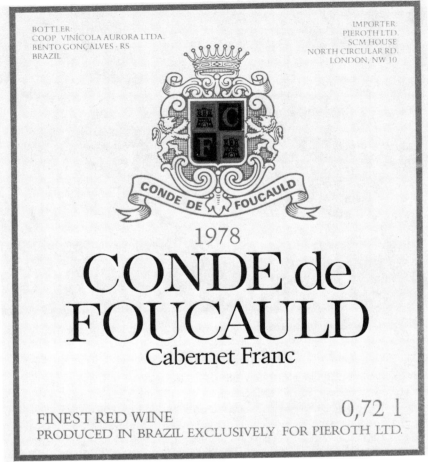

BOTTLER:
COOP. VINÍCOLA AURORA LTDA.
BENTO GONÇALVES - RS
BRAZIL

IMPORTER:
PIEROTH LTD.
SCM HOUSE
NORTH CIRCULAR RD.
LONDON, NW 10

CONDE DE FOUCAULD

1978

CONDE de FOUCAULD
Cabernet Franc

FINEST RED WINE   0,72 1
PRODUCED IN BRAZIL EXCLUSIVELY FOR PIEROTH LTD.

Aurora's Conde de Foucauld line includes several of Brazil's best Vinhos Finos, including this vintage Cabernet Franc.

Such are the growing pains (or perhaps pleasures) of Rio Grande do Sul, still the heartland of Brazilian winegrowing and the basis for optimism regarding its future (Table 6.1).

SANTA CATARINA

Rio Grande do Sul's northern neighbor, the state of Santa Catarina, was settled by fewer Italians and more Germans, and the viticulture map reflects this. The German farmers concentrated on the cultivation of grains (mainly rye and corn) and the raising of pigs. But some Italians did migrate to Santa Catarina, and there were German farmers who tried their hand at viticulture as well.

Santa Catarina is the smallest in area of the three states of the South, but it has considerable relief. The central part of the state is a divide between rivers and

Table 6.1   Viticulture in Brazil, by State

State	Planted area (acres)	Production (tons)	Percent of production
Rio Grande do Sul	100,000	430,000	63
São Paulo	27,000	150,000	22
Santa Catarina	15,000	77,000	11
Paraná	5,000	17,000	2.5
Minas Gerais	1,300	3,500	0.5
Pernambuco	1,000	4,600	0.7
Other states	200	800[a]	0.1

[a] Table and raisin grapes only. All states listed produce wine as well as table grapes.

Source: Extrapolated from 1980 statistics published by the Instituto Brasileiro de Geografia e Estatistica. Figures rounded to the nearest thousand.

streams to the north and south; in the east the escarpment of the Serra do Mar is quite pronounced. Just west of the town of Cacador the elevation reaches over 4400 feet, and on the divide to the south, altitudes about 3500 feet are common. Here, on the railroad line south of Cacador, lies the wine center of Videira—hardly comparable to Bento Gonçalves or Caixa do Sul, but unmistakably the focus of a viticulture region. Nearly all the vineyards of Santa Catarina lie in the valley of the Peixe River.

In Santa Catarina as in Rio Grande do Sul, elevation provides the crucial cooling that so greatly helps the grapegrower. Throughout Brazil's South the harvest begins in January and is over by the end of February. Only a small part of the harvest is vinified in the state (by small, family wineries); the bulk of it is sent to the large wineries of São Paulo for fermentation. In the past, those grapes did not arrive at their destinations in good condition; fermentation would begin prematurely and loss would be considerable, both quantitatively and qualitatively. But modern means of transportation, part of the industry's overall modernization, have remedied this, and the winegrowers of Santa Catarina are now in much better position to share in the rewards of this progress.

The great majority of cultivators in the state are members of one of several growers' associations, chiefly the Cooperativa Agropecuaria Videirense, which negotiate with purchasers of wine grapes on behalf of their producers. Wines made in the state are not normally seen on overseas markets.

PARANÁ

The northernmost state of Brazil's southern region lies astride the Tropic of Capricorn—and the state's main wine center lies at exactly 23½° south, on a river divide in the northwest. Paraná's viticulture is insignificant compared to its southern neighbors (and compared to São Paulo as well), but the Diamante firm has a production facility in the town of Maringa. Paraná's environment does not generally favor viticulture. Temperatures are high (though ameliorated somewhat by elevation toward the interior); rainfall is heavier than desirable (although a winter dry spell develops in the northwest). Thus Paraná's economy has developed in other directions, principally the cultivation of much of Brazil's enormous coffee harvest. Some viticulture does occur, however, and the state must be counted among Brazil's wine producers. The cultivars are non-vinifera, as American varieties only can withstand Paraná's unfavorable climate.

SÃO PAULO

It is axiomatic that wine production occurs near major, urban population clusters, whether the natural environment is favorable or not. From Tokyo to the Transvaal, large cities have stimulated winemaking in areas that would, but for their presence, have been used for other purposes.

So it is in the state of São Paulo in Brazil. A glance at the list of addresses of the country's nearly 600 wine producers indicates that well over 100 of these firms are located in São Paulo state, suggesting the existence here of a second, competing viticulture area to Rio Grande do Sul. But further investigation soon dispels that impression. Certainly wine grapes can be—and are—grown in São Paulo. But much of the state's wine production is achieved with grapes or juice imported from the south.

A number of São Paulo's wine producers are located in the great metropolis that anchors the state in the east, but others cluster some distance away. To the west, about 25 miles from the city center, lies the town of São Roque, a rural center of wine production in the urban shadow. To the north-northwest, on the railroad line that eventually connects Brazil to Bolivia, lies Jundiai, a second focus of wine production. Much further away, not far from the geometrical center of the state, lies Jau in the highlands. Other municipalities where winegrowing occurs are Louveira, Itatiba, Jarinu, Cabreúva, Vinhedo, Valinhos, and Atibaia. The Niagara is the main cultivar, and rosé wines dominate production.

São Paulo has many wine producers, but they tend to be makers of bulk wines, subsidiaries of international firms, and producers of alcoholic beverages among which wine is just one line of products. Some do specialize in winemaking, however, including Vitivinicola Cereser (Jundiai); others are diversified industries such as Passarin and Antonio Borin (Jundiai) and Bebidas Primor (Jau). These are not the premier names in Brazilian winegrowing, but they are associated with large-volume production and distribution. São Paulo's wine industry is the product of its huge market, not any favorable environments.

The Evolving Wine Industry

Brazil's total vineyard acreage devoted to grapes now exceeds 180,000 acres, which is two-thirds the size of the viticulture area in Chile. Winemaking and marketing employ more than 650,000 workers, directly and indirectly, so that the industry is by no means inconsequential in the overall economy. Annual production of wine

The vineyards of the Bento Gonçalves area lie near the southern margin of the Planalto, inland from the Serra do Mar and in the valleys of the Jacui River's tributaries. Here, the slopes lie draped under the vine, symbolizing the maturity and stability of the industry.

has fluctuated, but displays a long-term increase from less than 50 million gallons in the 1960s to more than 80 million gallons in the 1980s. This is more than half the volume produced by Chile, three-quarters of that of Australia, and seven times that of New Zealand. In 1974, when Brazil had an especially bountiful harvest and Australia a small one, Brazil actually outproduced Australia. All this underscores the fact that Brazil has taken its place among major wine producers of the Southern Hemisphere. Indeed, by volume its wine industry is larger than the industries of several European countries.

But when it comes to home consumption, Brazil ranks much lower. It was noted previously that Chile's wine industry has suffered because domestic consumption had declined to 12 gallons per capita annually, and that Argentina's traditionally prodigious consumption also had slackened, to about 20 gallons. In the early 1980s Brazil's domestic consumption of wine was just 0.7 gallon per person. This astoundingly low figure should be seen in context of the country's large population, of course: Brazil has nearly 130 million inhabitants, so that total wine consumption is about 90 million gallons per year, not an insignificant volume. But the productive capacity of the wine industry is much greater, so that Brazil is among those countries seeking to increase their exports to foreign markets.

Brazil's tiny per-capita consumption does suggest the enormous untapped potential of the domestic market. Even the slightest increase in domestic acceptance of wines will translate into a large growth of overall consumption, because population numbers are so high. In Chile, a one-gallon per-capita increase in consumption

PRODUCT OF BRAZIL

PRODUCED AND BOTTLED BY HEUBLEIN DO BRASIL
BENTO GONÇALVES, RIO GRANDE DO SUL, BRAZIL.
ALCOHOL 12% BY VOLUME, CONTENTS: 750 ml (24,5 FL. OZS.)
IMPORTED BY INTERNATIONAL VINTAGE WINE COMPANY, HARTFORD, CONN.

Castel Marjolet, a Heublein wine (before Heublein's purchase by Aurora), was among the first successful Brazilian exports.

amounts to a total increase of 12 million gallons per year. In Brazil, such an increase would involve a demand for an additional 130 million gallons. Brazil may be in search of export markets, but its greatest opportunity lies at home.

In order to realize this potential, the development of the industry, its modernization and promotion already under way, must continue. Already, much progress has been made, and for this the foreign companies present in Brazil are substantially responsible. While most grapes in Brazil still are picked by hand, new plantings are row-spaced to permit mechanical harvesting in the future. Long-distance transportation of grapes from growers to wineries (for example from Santa Catarina to São Paulo) now takes place under conditions that prevent loss of juice and premature fermentation. Viniculture methods also are much improved, and wineries have been modernized. Stainless-steel tanks replace the old wooden barrels, reducing oxidation risks and enhancing control over the winemaking process. (The "burned" quality of Brazilian wines was commonplace, especially of the whites). From storage to bottling to packaging, Brazil's wineries have adopted contemporary techniques and methods, and the wines have begun to prove what the country is capable of.

As is so often the case, however, these viti-vinicultural developments are not yet matched by improved classification and labeling practices. The major wine legislation was promulgated in 1973, and it has been modified repeatedly since then without addressing several key areas. As a result, Brazilian wines are marketed behind a profusion (and confusion) of labels. In general terms, these may be grouped into four categories: the generics, bearing the names of European wines or wine regions; the varietals, identifying the grape used in the making of the wine; the descriptives, identifying a wine simply as "dry red" or "sweet white"; and the imitatives, using terms such as "castel," "clos," or "chateau" to create a European impression. Proprietary names and terms are used in all four categories, but the name of the winery does not always appear on the label, so that familiarity with the proprietary "line" is important.

According to the 1973 legislation, Brazilian wines are classified into three major categories: Vinho de Consumo Corrente, Vinho Especial, and Vinho Fino. The Vinho de Consumo Corrente is Brazil's coarsest wine, made exclusively from American and hybrid grapes. Vinhos Especiais are of somewhat better quality, have some regional characteristics, and are still (but decreasingly) made with American and hybrid varieties. Vinhos Finos are wines of the highest quality, made exclusively from vinifera grapes. In the early 1980s, as much as 20 percent of total production was annually classified as Vinho Fino—a percentage far too large in view of the very limited production of genuinely fine wines. In the case of varietal Vinhos Finos, at least 60 percent of the wine must be made from the grape specified on the label.

Brazilian table wines are more practically classified as *vinhos finos*; *vinhos de mesa* or table wines, representing a wide range in quality; and *vinhos comum*, the lowest-quality bulk wine that "sometimes resembles natural grape juice rather than the fermented version."[3] Much table wine and all common wine is still made from Labrusca varieties, but the one-fifth of annual production that classifies as *vinhos finos* (or *premiados*), and made entirely from *vinifera* cultivars, includes a small percentage of interesting varietal wines. The Cabernet Franc has been especially successful, and perhaps this will be Brazil's equivalent of Argentina's Malbec—the beginnings of a regional association. In the early 1980s, 40 percent of these fine wines were reds, 35 percent were whites, and 25 percent were rosés. Over the past decade, the proportion of reds has been slowly increasing, mainly at the expense of the whites (rosé production also has increased somewhat). This undoubtedly reflects the tarnished reputation of Brazilian white wines because of their maderized character, and the success of red cultivars in the newly developed vineyards.[4]

Brazil's winegrowers have proven, however, that very good, clean white wines can be made. Several blended whites of the 1979 vintage were favorably received in overseas competitions and tastings, and showed good acidity, pale color, and no trace of the oxidation that so often marked Brazilian whites of earlier years.[5] The finer whites are made from the Trebbiano, Sémillon, Riesling (probably misnamed), Peverella, and the Malvasia, with the Muscat (Moscato) for the more traditional, darker, frequently maderized table wines.

The Italian heritage of Brazilian viticulture is reflected by the red cultivars used in *vinho fino* production as well. The Barbera and Bonardo are extensively planted, and some of Brazil's Barberas have been favorably compared with their Italian counterparts. The expansion of Cabernet Sauvignon, Merlot, and Cabernet

In three generations the Aurora Cooperative has grown enormously, reflecting the prosperity of Rio Grande do Sul and the well-being of its wine industry. A comparison between this photograph of Aurora's cellars in Bento Gonçalves in the early 1980s and that in Chapter 2 suggests the pace of progress. (Photograph courtesy of M. and K. Rudolph and Cooperativa Aurora.)

Certain Brazilian labels so resemble German counterparts that consumers are occasionally confused. Imitation French and Italian labels also abound in Brazil.

Pipa n.º 114

CLOS des NOBLES

Reservado:

Tipo: *Vinho Fino Tinto de Mesa Seco*

Classificação: *Vinífera de qualidade superior*

Vindima: *1980*

Uva: **Cabernet Franc**

Local de Origem: *Bento Gonçalves, R.G.Sul*

Observações: *Engarrafado no inverno de 1982*

Análise:

Grad. Alc.	pH	Ac. T	Ext. Sec.
11,50	3,20	78	20,58

Anotações do Degustador: *Agradável, com equilíbrio e generosidade, apto a desenvolver excepcionais qualidades.*

Mestre de Chai   Enólogo

Produzido e engarrafado por
Cooperativa Vinicola AURORA Ltda.   Rua Olavo Bilac, 449/500
Registro do Produto no M.A. n.º 00029882 - C.G.C.M.F. n.º 87 547 188/0001-70

Industria Brasileira — CONTEÚDO 720 ml

Clos des Nobles, a Vinho Fino Cabernet Franc, is a true Brazilian premium wine. The label represents an innovation in Brazilian labeling practices. The Cabernet Franc has been Brazil's most successful varietal red.

Franc marks the modern era of Brazilian winegrowing, and the increasing orientation to the export market.

But the largest acreage of wine grapes still is planted to North American and American-French hybrid varieties, and from these the large volume of common wines is made. The Labrusca's relatives require less care in the warm and often humid climate of Brazil, and thus the Dutchess, Niagara, Delaware, Concord, and various Seibels fill the vineyards with vines whose grapes are destined for the bulk market, along with other lesser cultivars such as the Herbemont (an Aestivalis-based hybrid) and a Couderc (a Rupestris-based cross). The American connection that rescued the industry in the 1880s has not been broken, the industry's modernization notwithstanding.

Because of the transitional character of Brazilian labeling practices (the government plays an important role in quality control and will undoubtedly move to institute an "appellation"-type classification system), familiarity with the leading producers and their labels is the consumer's strongest ally. Many oenophiles would recognize the Companhia Vinicola Rio Grandense, Cooperativa Vinicola Aurora (now merged with Dreher), Cia Mônaco Vinhedos, Vinhos Finos Santa Rosa, and the Cooperative Vinicola Garibaldi as among the leaders; also recognized are the names of Luiz Antunes, Luiz Michielon, and Ernesto Mosele. Qualitatively less ambitious but also producing good wines are the Sociedade Brasileiro de Vinhos, the Sociedade Vinhos Unico, and VINOSUL (Central Vinicola do Sul).

To know proprietary labels is to know the products of these growers and vintners. Rio Grandense markets its red and white *vinhos finos* under the Granja União label, but without complete information concerning varietal(s). The red is Cabernet-based. Aurora's Conde de Foucauld label is used for a good Cabernet and for its "Champanha." Aurora also markets a "Riesling"-based Johannesberg (*sic*) in the characteristic, slender, German-style bottle. Another Aurora proprietary label is Mont Chatel, used for red, rosé, and white table wines. Its limited-production *Clos de Nobles* represents the informative labeling not yet common in Brazil. The Garibaldi firm has marketed a German-style imitation called *Nachtliebwein*, and Santa Rosa's *Chateau Lacave* is actually a sparkling rosé of uncertain origin and unreported vintage. An unusual use of a regional name not likely to be found outside Brazil is *Algarve*, a "vinho verde branco" from Monaco made to resemble the Portuguese version.

Missing from these labels (and present on very few Brazilian bottles) is vintage information. Brazilian winegrowers argue that climatic conditions do not vary sufficiently from year to year to make vintage dating relevant (a view not confirmed by weather data); further, most Brazilian wines are blends of various vintages. Still, vintage information is useful to the consumer because it indicates the age of the wine in cask and/or bottle. The practice of vintage dating will undoubtedly become more common, especially since some wineries now hold their *vinhos finos* for as long as five years in barrel and bottle before release on the market. And vintage dating is virtually indispensable for success on international markets, so that exported wines normally carry this information.

The changing, emerging Brazilian wine industry still shows some signs of immaturity, but its progress over the past two decades has been nothing less than spectacular. What is needed now is a campaign of public education in Brazil itself, to realize the enormous potential of one of the great latent markets in the Western world.[6]

7

SOUTH AFRICA:
WINES OF THE CAPE

At the southern end of the African continent lies South Africa's Cape Province, outgrowth of the historic Cape of Good Hope. Near the tip of the Cape is the San Francisco of Africa, the city of Cape Town. Here, in the shadows of towering Table Mountain, landed Jan van Riebeeck and his settler party in 1652. Here, on the shores of one of the world's most beautiful bays, the Europeans and Africans made earliest contact and accommodation. Here were planted the first vines, and before the end of that memorable decade the Cape's first wines were vinted.

Today, nearly three and a half centuries later, the vineyards of the Cape clothe the slopes and valleys of an incomparable, dramatic landscape. Magnificent mountains, snow-dusted in winter, rise above a rolling, vine-draped countryside. Standing amid the vines are the modest, whitewashed estates built in the unique Cape-Dutch style, a legacy of centuries. In the autumn, when the leaves turn golden and the cloud-puffed skies signal the onset of a Mediterranean winter, memories of the Côte d'Or fade against such unsurpassed beauty.

The countryside of the Cape has been described as the ultimate cultural landscape of viticulture, the supreme achievement of a noble industry. Such accolades lead to high expectations of the wines created from these favorable environments. The wines of the Cape, notably the reds, meet that challenge. At their best, they rank with the hemisphere's greatest. The ordinary wines of the region are, in general, far better than their equivalents elsewhere. The reputation lost after the eighteenth century is reviving in the twentieth.

Indeed, it is probable that South Africa may be able to produce wines superior even to the best of its current vintages. Recent research results suggest that areas of the Cape that may present the most propitious environments for viticulture are not fully exploited. This relates to a complicated combination of circumstances involving history and tradition, economics and industry governance, to be explored later in this chapter. Quantitatively, South Africa produces, in an average year, slightly more wine than Chile and substantially more than Australia. But South Africa's wine-consuming population is comparatively small. Wine has not yet become a popular libation among the country's African peoples, whose preference is for beer; official estimates indicate that less than 10 percent of domestic consumption of wine is attributable to the African market. Even among South Africans of European ancestry, wine has not yet become an essential ingredient of lifestyle. Among the country's major population sectors, the Coloureds of the Cape—the people of mixed European-African and Southeast Asian ancestry—have adopted wine more than any other. Without their participation, South Africa's per-capita consumption (2.2 gallons annually) would be even lower.

Such limitations, and memories of crises past, have imposed caution and restraint on the South African wine industry. Undoubtedly, the Cape could produce more quality wine than it does, and recent developments on the banks of the Orange River, far from the viticultural heartland, have illustrated the country's remaining potential, at least quantitatively. But the risk of overproduction and the uncertainty of export options have controlled the expansion nature would sustain.

Nature is certainly kind to the Cape's winegrowers. The winegrowing region may not be large, but it is favored by a combination of climate, slope, and soil that permits the cultivation of a considerable range of red and white varieties, especially in the coastal zone. At the heart of the region lies a zone of true Mediterranean climate, but unlike its Chilean equivalent there is enough summer moisture over much of this area to allow grape cultivation without irrigation. (Artificial watering occurs even where it is not strictly necessary.) The Mediterranean regime extends from approximately 31° south latitude to the tip of the continent, and from about 22° east longitude to the west coast (see Fig. 1.6). This, as the map indicates, includes not only the grape-growing areas of the Cape, but also a patchwork of intervening mountains, and these highlands contribute importantly to the precipitation pattern and cloud cover. Microclimates at the Cape vary strongly and over short distances. So do the soils, which (to generalize) suffer from excess acidity and require lime treatment for optimum production.

The viticulture region coincides approximately with the zone of winter-maximum rainfall, but in this zone the annual precipitation varies from as little as 4 inches in the interior plains to as much as 80 inches in the mountains. Vines are grown from near sea level to 1700 feet in the foothills. The mountains of the southwestern Cape form several belts, of which the outermost is most significant as a viticultural marker. This L-shaped chain extends north-south to the vicinity of Stellenbosch (20 miles east of Cape Town), where it forms an irregular jumble of ranges that eventually combines in an eastward axis called the Riviersonderendberge (Fig. 7.1). Between this first set of ranges and the ocean lies what may be called the coastal zone of South African winegrowing, and it contains the most important districts. Here, in the environs and hinterland of Cape Town, annual rainfall ranges from

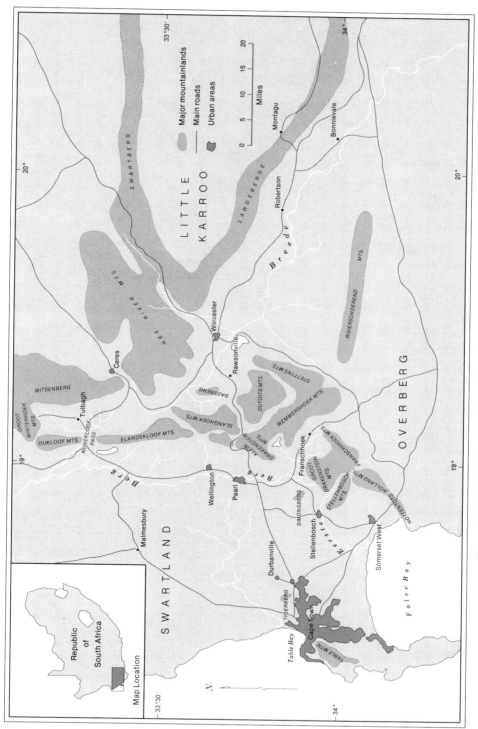

Figure 7.1. *Physical geography of the Cape wine region, South Africa.*

Groot Constantia, oldest of South Africa's wine estates. The Manor House now is a museum, but the winery produces premium wines from Constantia's vineyards immediately adjacent.

20 to 25 inches, but as much as one-fifth to one-quarter of this precipitation can fall during the summer ripening season. This is enough to permit nonirrigated viticulture, and more than 50 percent of the total vineyard area of South Africa lies in this zone. The famous names of South African wine, such as Stellenbosch, Constantia, Durbanville, and Somerset West, lie in this, the country's premier red wine-producing area. Nestled in mountain-cupped valleys are Franschhoek and Tulbagh, favored by microclimates.

But annual rainfall declines both northward, in the direction of Olifants River, and eastward, toward Swellendam and the Little (Klein) Karroo. The Cape Mediterranean region is surrounded on all sides by B (steppe) climes, so that there is not, as in France, California, and Chile, the transition to moister, cooler, higher-latitude conditions. There is no equivalent to Oregon or Bío-Bío in South Africa. Rainfall declines not only toward the north and east, but also toward the interior. Behind that first "L" of mountains lie valleys cooled by elevation (commonly 1000 feet and more) but cut off from the rains: annual precipitation in these vinelands is just 8 to 15 inches, and irrigation is essential here. Still, about one-third of the country's total vineyard acreage lies in this interior zone, which historically has produced mainly distilled wines.

For centuries the Cape was South Africa's sole wine-producing region, but this is no longer true. In recent years a new viticulture area has emerged on the banks of the Orange River, some 500 miles north-northeast of Cape Town. This is desert country, with about 8 inches of summer rainfall and high temperatures. In the past, only raisin production took place here, but wine for distillation is now

PRODUCE
OF ZIMBABWE

IMPORTED BY
KENYA WINE AGENCIES
LIMITED NAIROBI

ZANIA
DRY STEEN
WHITE TABLE WINE

720 ml

The Zimbabwe wine industry not only serves the domestic market, but following independence has found foreign outlets as well. Exports are yet small, but they are symbolically important. This Zania white, made from the South African cultivar the Steen, is sold in Kenya.

made in some quantity. And wineries have been established successfully even farther from the Cape. An example is the Loopspruit winery in the Bronkhorstspruit area about 60 miles east of the capital, Pretoria, in the Transvaal. There, on the South African highveld under Cwb climatic conditions (see Fig. 1.6), fortified wines and some table wines are produced from cultivars that are more commonly associated with the Cape.

South Africa is not any longer the only southern African country to produce wines. In recent years Zimbabwe (formerly Rhodesia) has taken its place as a wine producer, albeit on a very small scale. The industry developed during the pre-independence period of economic isolation, although the first commercial production occurred even earlier, in 1963, near the capital of Salisbury (now Harare). The first vines planted were of the Labrusca variety, the Isabella, but *vinifera* soon replaced them. In the early 1980s 800 acres were under the vine in the country, about 200 each planted to the South African varieties, the Pinotage and the Steen, and the remainder to the Cabernet Franc and Cabernet Sauvignon, Clairette Blanche, Colombard, Hanepoot (a South African clone of the Muscat d'Alexandrie), and Riesling. The acreage is owned by a surprisingly large number of growers; in 1980 eighty-nine grapegrowers owned a reported 644,000 vines.[1] Among prominent producers is Monis Wineries, which in 1983 won a medal for its Vat 10 Colombard at the Fourteenth International Wine and Spirit Competition in the United Kingdom. Monis's Mukuyu Cabernet, matured for fourteen months in imported French oak barrels, is Zimbabwe's most noted red wine, proof that good red wine can be made in the country. Today the fledgling industry is protected by heavy duties on South African and other foreign wines.

The Cape, however, remains Africa's premier winegrowing region, its 250,000 acres of vineyards devoted to wine grapes just slightly fewer than Chile's. In the mid-1970s the Cape for the first time outproduced Algeria's declining industry, and since then South Africa has been the continent's leader in every (viti- and vinicultural) respect.

Regional Geography

South Africa's traditional regions have their basis not only in history, but also in physical geography. In Africa it is often said that "it's the altitude that counts, not the latitude," and anyone who has seen the snows of Kilimanjaro, in sight of the equator, can attest to the truth of that statement. South Africa is not an equatorial country, and most of it actually lies outside the tropics (the Tropic of Capricorn lies across the Northern Transvaal). Still, elevation means much here as well. The South Africans differentiate between the plateau country of the interior, the "highveld" consisting of grassy plains a mile above sea level, and the "lowveld" at lesser elevations, where it is warmer and the vegetation reflects the difference. This is the "bushveld," another regional term for the lowveld. Highveld and lowveld are separated by the Great Escarpment, the sometimes spectacular wall that rims the plateau. Where this escarpment descends steplike to lower elevations, South Africans recognize a "middleveld" between highveld and lowveld.

In the interior, the Kalahari's desert dryness dominates the landscape, yielding southward to the Great Karroo of the Cape, another vast, steppelike expanse. The parallel mountain ranges of the southern Cape Province, trending east-west until they collide in Cape Town's hinterland, signal the end of the Great Karroo and the beginning of the Cape's varied topography. Streams occupy the valleys, making irrigated agriculture possible, and ribbons of green lie in marked contrast to the gray-brown slopes. In the far south, the last two major mountain ranges are so far apart that what lies between them is a basin, not merely a valley. Appropriately, this is called the Little Karroo, its landscape (where unirrigated and uncultivated) resembling the interior Cape farther North. The Southwestern Cape (or the Western Province, as it is also named) is the heartland of South African winegrowing, and viticulture is one of the dominant features that make *Die Kaap* what it is.

Viticulture in the Cape region extends as far north as the vicinity of Vredendal in the bend of the Olifants River, more than 150 miles north of Cape Town, and as far east as the area of Oudtshoorn in the Little Karroo, over 250 miles from Table Bay. Thus winegrowing occurs in a zone well over 400 miles in length, L-shaped as it conforms to regional topography, and mostly within 80 miles of the coast. Environmental contrasts in this zone are strong, so that the range of wine styles is large. In the comparatively cool region between the coast and the first mountains, table wines of premium quality are made. In the warmer, drier areas north and east of this core area, and in the mountain-enclosed interior, excellent sherries, dessert Muscats, and brandies are produced. But such a generalization does an injustice to the Cape's versatility. Some fine table wines come from areas that would seem destined to produce only fortifieds.

In the 1920s the K.W.V. salvaged and resurrected a troubled industry, but the modern viticultural map of South Africa did not take shape until the 1970s. Legislation toward a South African *appellation* system actually was created as early as 1957, when the industry experienced considerable growth, but the work leading to the rules now in force began with committee deliberations, under government auspices, in the late 1960s. The South African Wine of Origin System that emerged from these preparations has much merit not only because of its geographical structure, but also because of the unique way a wine's status is conveyed to the consumer. It took effect in 1973.

The geographical structure that forms the basis of the South African system is depicted on Figure 7.2, but the apparently simple map conceals a number of complications. The legislation of 1973 established a five-level regional hierarchy, later reduced to four, of which the districts shown on the map were the cornerstone. Currently it involves four spatial units (the region, district, ward, and estate) and thus bears resemblance to the French *Appellation d'Origine Contrôlée* system. In the early 1980s there were six regions, eleven districts, 19 wards, and about 70 registered estates.

What complicates the map (Fig. 7.2) is that while three regions consist, logically, of combinations of adjoining districts, three others are single-district regions and appear, cartographically at least, as districts, not regions. A further complication involves the nonconformity between multidistrict regions and district boundaries. Part of Tulbagh District, for example, lies in the Boberg Region; part also lies in the Breede River Valley Region. The six regions of South African winegrowing are:

1. Little Karroo
2. Olifants River
3. Boberg (Paarl and Tulbagh districts)
4. Breede River Valley (Tulbagh, Paarl, Worcester, Robertson, and Swellendam districts, all or in part)
5. Coastal (Constantia, Paarl, Stellenbosch, Durbanville, and Swartland districts, all or in part)
6. Lower Orange River

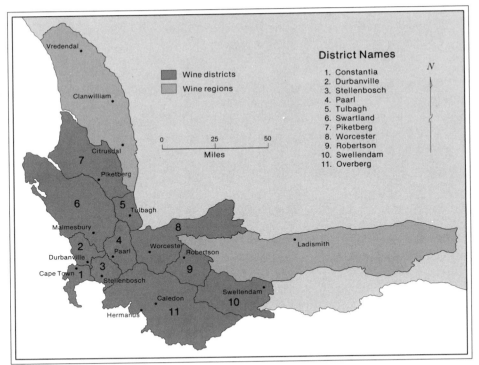

Figure 7.2. Officially designated wine districts and regions of the Cape, South Africa.

The eleven districts of the Cape include the most prestigious names in South African wine. Constantia is the site of historic Groot Constantia; Stellenbosch carries the name of one of the founders of the Cape's wine industry; Paarl contains the headquarters of the K.W.V.; mountain-cradled Tulbagh produces some famed estate wines. Mountain crests and river courses form the physiographic guidelines for the district boundaries, so that the map reflects prevailing topographical orientations. The smallest of the districts lie in the hinterland of Cape Town, where the two axes of the "L" meet; the larger ones lie to the north and east. The eleven districts are:

1. Constantia
2. Durbanville
3. Stellenbosch
4. Paarl
5. Tulbagh
6. Swartland
7. Piketberg (Piquetberg)
8. Worcester
9. Robertson
10. Swellendam
11. Overberg

The next-ranking spatial unit in the regional hierarchy is the ward. With one exception, these wards are subdivisions of districts or regions, based on clustered microclimates, soil distributions, and associated wine styles. These wards, somewhat similar in concept to the commune in French legislation, are still being delimited,

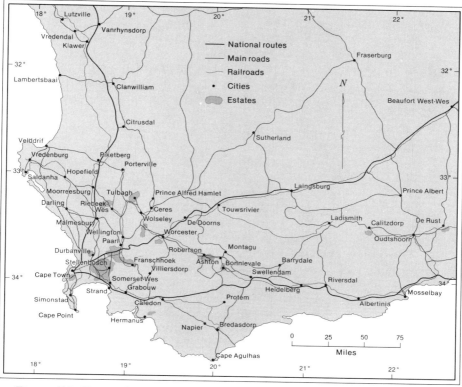

Figure 7.3. Regional geography and the distribution of estates in the Cape, South Africa.

and their names have not yet become as familiar in South African wine geography as the districts and regions. In time, that will undoubtedly change. The most recent enumeration of wards is as follows:

1. Aan-de-Doorns (Worcester)
2. Boesmansrivier (Robertson)
3. Bonnievale (Swellendam)
4. Cederberg (Olifants River)
5. Eilandia (Robertson)
6. Franschhoek (Paarl)
7. Goree (Robertson)
8. Goudini (Worcester)
9. Groenekloof (Swartland)
10. Hoopsrivier (Robertson)
11. McGregor (Robertson)
12. Nuy (Worcester)
13. Riebeekberg (Swartland)
14. Riverside (Robertson)
15. Scherpenheuvel (Worcester)
16. Slanghoek (Worcester)
17. Simonsberg-Stellenbosch (Stellenbosch)
18. Vaalharts (No Region or District)
19. Vinkrivier (Robertson)

The most prestigious designated appellation in South Africa is the estate. This was one of the real innovations of the Wine of Origin legislation, designed to promote quality and acknowledge the excellence achieved by some winegrowers. Under the terms of the legislation, an estate must consist of a single cultivated area, or a contiguous cluster of parcels farmed as a single unit (some noncontiguous parcels also have been approved when they satisfied certain requirements). Viticulturally, there are conditions as well. All the grapes in an estate wine must be harvested from that estate's vineyards; no purchase of grapes, not even from controlled contract growers, is permitted. Qualitatively, the estate wine must meet high specifications, in both analysis and taste. These requirements are tested by the official agency of the government, the Wine and Spirit Board, before approval is given for the wine to be marketed as an estate wine. There is no restriction on the style of wine estates may produce. Cultivar (varietal) wines, blends, fortified wines, sparkling wines, Sherry- and Port-style wines, late-harvest wines, and other kinds of wine all can carry the coveted estate designation.

When the Wine of Origin legislation took effect in 1973, only fourteen wine farms satisfied the requirements for estate designation. Over the past dozen years that number has grown as applications have been examined and approved, and in 1983 it approached seventy.[2] This, however, understates the situation somewhat. Several wine farms cannot meet the exacting requirements of the official legislation, for example regarding the adjacency and proximity of vineyard parcels, but nevertheless produce estate-quality, premium wines. These operate as unregistered estates, and while they cannot carry the official estate designation, they remain competitive because the quality of their wines assures recognition on the market.

The distribution of estates (Fig. 7.3) emphasizes their concentration in the Stellenbosch-Paarl-Robertson districts and also their dispersal as far north as Tulbagh and as far east as the eastern Little Karroo. The district with the largest number of estates, Stellenbosch, has been described as the Napa Valley of South Africa. Here lie such illustrious estates as Kanonkop, Simonsig, Alto, Overgaauw, and Vergenoegd. But Stellenbosch does not have a monopoly over quality. South Africa's best comes from widely scattered sources.

The question of control does affect estates and grapegrowers alike. In South Africa, anyone growing grapes for wine production is (and, indeed, must by law be) a member of the official cooperative winegrowers association, the K.W.V. A wine farm must have a production quota, allotted to it by the K.W.V., and a licence to grow grapes. Even the approximately eighty estates (registered and unregistered) are not exempt from quota restrictions. The other winegrowers (about 7,500) deliver their grapes to a K.W.V. cooperative or directly to a licensed merchant. Quantity (filling the assigned quota) tends to become a dominant concern, and quality may thus suffer.

The first of the Cape's wine cooperatives was established as long ago as 1905, even before the K.W.V. came into being. In the past, all the wine made in the cooperative cellars was sold in bulk to large wine companies, which would in turn sell it under their corporate labels. Today a half-dozen of these wineries, now numbering more than seventy, market a small part of what they produce (about 5 percent) under their own labels. Some of this wine is quite good and holds interest because of its local (albeit district, not vineyard) identity.

Most of what the cooperatives produce does continue to be sold to wine companies called, in South Africa, "producing (or producer-) wholesalers." The name is appropriate, because these companies function as producers for member-growers and act as wholesalers of cooperative-made wine, as well. To some extent

The Zonnebloem label is one of the most prestigious from Stellenbosch Farmers' Winery.

they resemble the "shippers" of Burgundy, but there are important differences. The most famous of these merchants, for many decades, was the Stellenbosch Farmers' Winery. Its history goes back as far as 1867, when a wine farm, Oude Libertas, began to make wine not only from its own grapes, but also from grapes harvested by growers nearby. In the 1920s the firm, still not very successful, was taken over and developed by W. C. Winshaw, a Tulane-educated Kentuckian, into a large and powerful organization. It absorbed other wine firms and thus acquired a Paarl estate of high repute, Nederburg. The headquarters of S.F.W. remained at Oude Libertas, however, and its reputation for quality wines was sustained by its premium line. Its Oude Libertas, Zonnebloem, and Nederburg labels have won numerous medals and awards, and the names of firms acquired over the years (Monis, Sedgwick's) continued to grace S.F.W. labels. One of Nederburg's triumphs is the fabled late-harvest Edelkeur, a honeyed nectar that matches Europe's best.

The other major producer-wholesaler in South Africa, Oude Meester, was established in 1970 from a merger of a number of older wine firms. Its subsidiary, Die Bergkelder, was opened in 1968 for the production of two labels, one of which (Fleur du Cap) has long been sold on the American market. Oude Meester, through its Bergkelder auxiliary, also acquired joint marketing rights to the wines of seventeen Cape estates. Indeed, Die Bergkelder does far more than merely marketing the labels of its seventeen estates; it also "processes" their wines. The grapes are crushed on the estate (thus satisfying the requirement for "estate" status); then the juice is

ALLESVERLOREN ESTATE · S.F. MALAN

Allesverloren

SWARTLAND ROOD

RED WINE · VIN ROUGE

Allesverloren is grown and made on
the Allesverloren Wine Estate and bottled
by The Bergkelder Ltd. Stellenbosch

e
0,75ℓ

A23

PRODUCT OF THE REPUBLIC OF SOUTH AFRICA

WINE OF ORIGIN SWARTLAND

Allesverloren Estate lies in the Swartland district, but its wines
are bottled at Die Bergkelder in Stellenbosch. Die Bergkelder,
in addition to its bottling and marketing of seventeen estate
wines, releases wines under its own proprietary labels, such as
the Stellenryck line.

WINE OF ORIGIN SUPERIOR COASTAL REGION

STELLENRYCK

Blanc Fumé

1981

PRODUCED AND BOTTLED IN THE REPUBLIC OF SOUTH AFRICA

A23

PRODUCED AND BOTTLED
BY THE BERGKELDER LIMITED
STELLENBOSCH

tank-trucked to Die Bergkelder for malolactic fermentation, acid adjustment, aging, and bottling. It might be argued that this rather dilutes the image of estate rank.

In 1980 a major event in South African wine circles occurred when Stellenbosch Farmers' Winery and Oude Meester were themselves absorbed into a huge new company, Cape Wine and Distillers. This enormous firm dwarfs the remaining merchants (Gilbey's, Douglas Green, Union Wine, and others). The K.W.V. holds a 30 percent share in C.W.D., changing significantly the relationship between K.W.V. and its two major competitors. Under the new arrangement, however, both the Stellenbosch Wine Trust and Oude Meester will continue to produce wines under their time-honored labels.

But the most significant aspect of the situation concerns the extraordinary producer monopoly it creates. Since the formation of the C.W.D., the K.W.V. also has a stake in the wholesaling of wines on the local market. Because the K.W.V. can set total production limits, through the quota system introduced in 1957, the growers are in the privileged position of being protected from the rigors of the free-market economy. New growers can enter the circle only by purchasing (or inheriting) a farm with a K.W.V. quota. Thus areas that have no such quota, some of them potentially among South Africa's best, cannot be exploited. (In Australia, the southward march of viticulture into Coonawarra, southern Victoria, and Tasmania has faced no such artificial barriers.) Further, much of the total quota is taken up by the vineyards of the interior, where hot-climate, distilling grapes are grown. There is no qualitative differentiation. Many of the distilling-wine producers manage to remain in business because they produce a certain volume of table wine (usually quite modest), whose price is artificially sustained by the K.W.V.–ordained minimum for the domestic market. For a country so dedicated to the free enterprise system, the wine industry holds some surprises.

The regional and economic geographies of South African viticulture thus continue to change. The list of recognized estates lengthens; new wards continue to be delimited; the district and regional map is modified. Relationships between the K.W.V. and other major wine organizations have yet to stabilize over the long term. The South African wine industry has a lengthy history, but its modern resurgence has been comparatively brief. Its organizational modernization is of even more recent vintage; in fact, it is still incomplete.

Districts and Regions

Although the map of South Africa's areas of origin is still in the making, its essential outlines (see Fig. 7.2) are firmly entrenched. The districts and regions it delimits have strong individuality. Every district has a particular combination of environments and viticultural traditions. That distinctiveness is reflected by the wines each district yields. Stellenbosch's red table wines, Tulbagh's whites and "Sherries," Paarl's white table wines, Swartland's "Ports," and Robertson's dessert wines exemplify the relationships between viticultural district and wine style. This link between viticultural locale and wine styles lies in the geography of each district. In truth, the geographic associations are yet formative, and are represented by a minority of significantly distinct styles. But the pattern is set and maturing.

STELLENBOSCH DISTRICT

Stellenbosch merits pride of place in any discussion of South Africa's wine districts. Viticulture dominates the cultural landscape as in no other district except part of Constantia. A few fields of tobacco and vegetables (and forests planted on higher mountain slopes) form the sole exception to a land use pattern almost completely devoted to the cultivation of the noble grape. The map goes far to explain this: Stellenbosch District has an especially favorable location on the northeast shore of False Bay. Open to maritime influences from the south, the district is cradled to the east by mountain ranges that extend from the very coastline northward (as the Hottentots-Holland Range) and continue toward Paarl (in the Groot Drakenstein and Simonsberg Ranges). From this eastern chain several mountain belts trend roughly westward, into the heart of the district. One of these, the Stellenbosch Mountains, eventually turns northwest. At the end of this range lies the town of Stellenbosch, the historic wine center and focus of the district. The Eerste River, the major stream here, originates in the eastern highlands and rounds the Stellenbosch Mountains at the point where Stellenbosch is located (Fig. 7.4). Toward the west, the relief becomes much lower, and the dunes of the Cape Flats form the western limit of winegrowing.

The topographic diversity of the district is matched by its pedologic variety, the vines standing on granite-derived soils in the hilly east, sandstone-based soils in the lower west, and alluvial soils in the valley of the Eerste River. Many of Stellenbosch's greatest red wines come from vineyards that clothe the eastern slopes, while good whites are produced from sandy soils of the lower west. Soils, however, are less important than climate, and in this respect the district is one of the most favored areas of the Cape. Those west-facing slopes are warmed by the afternoon sunshine, and from False Bay come moisture-laden sea breezes that help the grapes mature through the dry Mediterranean summer. Hence the vineyards extend to very near the shore of False Bay, and there are those who believe that South Africa's very best red wines come from vines that overlook the water, notably those of Vergenoegd, Overgaauw, and Meerlust.

But Stellenbosch's Mediterranean climate differs considerably from that of the heartland of the Cabernet Sauvignon, the Médoc. The regime is more consistently Mediterranean, its precipitation lower (the district average is 20 inches annually, somewhat more against the eastern slopes and rather less in the west), and its summers drier. Even more striking is the heat summation of Stellenbosch locales. The Bordeaux average is just over 2500 (°F) degree-days, placing it in the transition between Region I (coolest) and Region II. Stellenbosch locales record such readings as 3160 (Firgrove) and 3416 (Koelenhof), so that many of the Cape's most prestigious estates lie under the conditions of Region III.[3] These conditions (which prevail especially in the interior sections) are much warmer than those considered optimal for Cabernet Sauvignon grapes, but Stellenbosch's quality reds belie such disadvantages. It is all the more remarkable that, under the microclimates in the eastern foothills, some hectares of vines yield excellent harvests without artificial watering.

The climate of the Stellenbosch District does, however, have its adverse side. The feared "Southeaster," a powerful spring wind that can bring intense, damaging rainshowers, afflicts Stellenbosch's vintages recurrently. Destructive hailstorms also

Figure 7.4. Regional geography of Stellenbosch District and the distribution of leading estates.

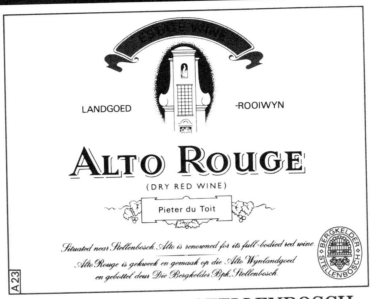

WINE OF ORIGIN STELLENBOSCH

Alto is one of the leading estates in Stellenbosch District. Alto Rouge is a blend of Cabernet Sauvignon, Shiraz, and Tinta Barocca.

occur. And those same moist breezes that moderate the summer heat can increase the risk of mildew. When the normal regime breaks down and the summer is cool and rainy (as happened in 1977), the district's exposure to the sea can be detrimental. Some estates in that exceptionally bad year lost their entire Cabernet harvest to the downy mildew, as only the earlier-ripening varieties survived.

None of this threatens Stellenbosch's position as the leading viticultural district of South Africa. About 40 percent of all the registered estates lie within its boundaries, and also some famed unregistered wine farms whose wine (but not layout) would qualify for estate rank. Among the great names of Stellenbosch are Alto, an elongated vineyard on the lower slopes of the Helderberg Mountains south of the town and very near False Bay; Kanonkop, with its unirrigated vineyard standing on several different soil types (all treated heavily with lime) and at elevations ranging 400 feet; Meerlust, dating to the late 1600s and still a leading name in Cape winemaking, its irrigated vines yielding superb Cabernets and Pinotages; Overgaauw, long known for its crisp white wines but also bottling premium reds; and Simonsig, northwest of Stellenbosch and known for its good white and lighter-bodied red wines. Among the unregistered estates, the most prominent is Delheim, a fragmented wine farm that does not meet the contiguity requirements of the 1973 legislation but does produce superior wines that match the best of the district.

The dominance of winegrowing in the economy of Stellenbosch District is revealed not only in its cultural landscape, but also in the character of its central place, the town of Stellenbosch. The University of Stellenbosch has a School of Viticulture and Oenology, the only program of its kind in the country. The government-operated National Institute for Viticulture and Oenology is located at Nietvoorbij in suburban Stellenbosch. And the country's first *route du vin*, the Stellenbosch Wine Route, was inaugurated in 1971. The Wine Route facilitates and organizes tours of the district by local and foreign visitors; a dozen estates and farms and several cooperative wineries have joined in this effort to provide an overview of the district's wine scene.

Stellenbosch District lies at the juxtaposition of the two axes of the Cape's L-shaped viticulture zone, open to the ocean, protected by mountains, favored by climate and soil. After Constantia it is the oldest South African winegrowing district, and its long traditions are etched into the cultural landscape of town and countryside. The quality wines of Stellenbosch's estate are the pride of the Cape.

PAARL

The Paarl District adjoins Stellenbosch to the north, and in some respects resembles its southern neighbor (Fig. 7.5). As in Stellenbosch, its eastern border is defined by the crests of mountain ranges. Again as in Stellenbosch, a single major stream (the Berg River) and its tributaries dominate the drainage system, although the Berg River, unlike the Eerste River, flows northward from its mountainous, southeastern source. The central place of the district, also named Paarl, adjoins the Berg River. Although more than 40 miles from the ocean, the cooling breezes that bring relief to Stellenbosch also reach Paarl, though much less effectively. Paarl's environs are substantially warmer than those of Stellenbosch. The Mediterranean climatic regime brings more moisture to the southeast (25 to 30 inches annually) than to the significantly drier northwest. Granite-based soils on the eastern mountain slopes give way westward to sandstone-derived soils and some alluvium in the lower valley.

Paarl and Stellenbosch districts also share a lengthy viticultural history. Paarl's southeastern ward is Franschhoek, where Simon van der Stel in 1687 awarded the first farms to French Huguenot settlers. Wines (and fine brandies) have been made here for nearly three centuries, contributing importantly to the Cape's early reputation for these commodities.

But the differences between Paarl and Stellenbosch are perhaps more significant than the similarities. Paarl District is an important winegrowing area, but viticulture does not dominate the cultural landscape as it does in Stellenbosch. Fruits other than the wine grape (apples, pears, prunes) occupy substantial acreages, table grapes are produced in large quantities, grain crops appear in the drier northwest, and forestry is an important industry in the district. Winegrowing predominates among these enterprises, but the economy is mixed.

Even the viticultural pattern itself is not simply a continuation of Stellenbosch's. Whereas Stellenbosch is famed for its great red wines, and large vineyards are

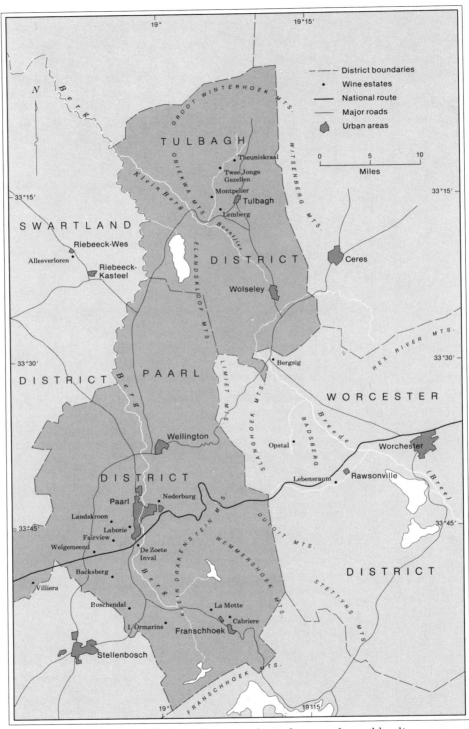

Figure 7.5. *Paarl and Tulbagh Districts: physical geography and leading estates.*

The Backsberg label is one of Paarl's most prestigious. The estate, known for its fine red wines as well as whites, was among the first to produce a varietal Chardonnay.

planted to the Cabernet Sauvignon, Pinotage, Cinsaut, Merlot, some Cabernet Franc, and other red cultivars, Paarl is better known for its white wines. Among these, of course, are the district's "Sherries," evidence of the high, Jerez-like heat summations of its warmer sectors. Thus the Steen, Palomino, Sémillon, Colombard, and Riesling are prominent here although, in recent years, the acreages of Cabernet Sauvignon, Pinotage, and Shiraz have expanded and Paarl's reds are now better known. What these plantings have proven is that Paarl can produce excellent red wines in a class with those of Stellenbosch.

The pattern of viticulture differs in another way. Again compared to Stellenbosch, fewer Paarl winegrowers produce and bottle their own wines; the majority market them through one of the several cooperatives in the district. Thus there are not as many estates (a dozen in 1984), and not as many truly prominent names on the wine map. Backsberg and Boschendal probably are the most prestigious estate names in Paarl. Backsberg produces notable whites from the Chardonnay and Sauvignon Blanc and fine, lighter-style reds from the Cabernet Sauvignon and Pinotage. A stand of Pinot Noir soon will complement this line. Boschendal is the largest wine estate in South Africa, although only about 650 of its 7500 acres are

Boschendal Estate, one of Paarl's leading wineries, on a moody winter day. (Photograph by D. Rallis.)

LA CONCORDE

KWV

STEEN

WHITE TABLE WINE

COASTAL REGION WINE OF ORIGIN

NET CONTENTS 750 ml (25,4 fl oz)

ALCOHOL 11% BY VOLUME

PRODUCED AND BOTTLED IN THE REPUBLIC OF SOUTH AFRICA

A100

IMPORTED BY GLOBAL DISTRIBUTORS INC, BIRMINGHAM, ALABAMA, USA

CAPE F & L W

The K.W.V. bottles wines under its own labels in its massive Paarl cellars. This Steen, under a label graced by the association's La Concorde headquarters building, is seen on U.S. markets.

planted to wine grapes (table grapes and other fruits also are produced). Situated in the Franschhoek area of Paarl, between the Simonsberg Mountains and the Berg River, Boschendal's vines stand under a variety of microclimates that permit the cultivation of a large range of wine grapes. Known for its good white wines, Boschendal also markets a noted Cabernet Sauvignon. But what may be the best-known name of all in Paarl District, Nederburg, is not a registered estate but a property of Stellenbosch Farmers' Winery. It is something of an irony that this, the brightest star in the firmament of S.F.W., is located in Paarl; and its wines, ranging from complex, long-lived Cabernets to steely Sauvignon Blancs, prove what the district is capable of.

The town of Paarl, positioned approximately at the center of the district, is the headquarters of the enormous Cooperative Winegrowers' Association, the K.W.V. Not only the K.W.V.'s administrative center, but also its enormous winery is located at Paarl. The dimensions of this complex, its storage capacity, and its output go far to explain why Paarl is a name synonymous with wine in South Africa. The facilities, including offices, laboratories, winery, and cellar, cover more than 40 acres. Storage capacity exceeds 60 million gallons. About 7500 members, including estates and smaller cooperatives as well as individual growers, belong to this giant organization, the dominant force in the South African wine industry. An attraction of world class, the K.W.V.'s establishment draws tens of thousands of visitors annually to Paarl.

These visitors also may avail themselves of the second of the Cape's official wine routes, the Paarl Wineway. This route begins at the Backsberg Estate and visits a cross-section of other estates and several cooperatives, the towns of Franschhoek and Wellington as well as Paarl, and ends at K.W.V.'s Laborie, a "wine house" complete with winery and cellar, tasting room, restaurant, and, in the eighteenth-century manor house, a national museum.

Thus Paarl represents the size and strength of the South African wine industry, its modernization, efficiency, and stability. This is the center of gravity of Cape viticulture, the crucible of decision-making, a mirror for the domestic market (the preponderance of white cultivars accurately reflects consumer preference in the Republic). The map suggests that Paarl lies at the heart of Cape viticulture; the district's prosperous cultural landscapes confirm it.

CONSTANTIA

Constantia District is the source, the original vineyard of the Cape. It extends over the neck of the Cape Peninsula south of Cape Town, whose suburbs have engulfed many of the acres on which the vines once stood. Today Groot Constantia is the only registered estate of this historic district, and winegrowing is the sole agricultural industry to have survived (however diminished) Cape Town's encroachment. But viticulture's revival in Constantia is no longer confined to this single estate, as the thriving Alphen winery attests.

The vineyards destroyed by the city's expansion lay on some of the Cape's most favored acres. With the Atlantic Ocean to the west and False Bay to the east of the peninsula, no vines stood (or stand today) more than five miles from the water, so that the hot Mediterranean summer is moderated even more than in Stellenbosch by cool, moist breezes. Annual rainfall in Groot Constantia's vineyards averages as much as 35 inches, so that irrigation is not necessary. Most of the vines stand in soils derived from sandstone, but some others grow on granite-based soils. Constantia underscores the secondary significance of soil as opposed to microclimate: the same Cabernet Sauvignon that does so well in the granitic soils of Stellenbosch produces magnificently on sandstone-based soils here. This is due, without doubt, to the special combination of east-facing slopes, a southerly location, maritime exposure, and hence a comparatively lengthy, slow ripening season. Constantia classifies as Region II in the heat summation system, and harvesting begins as much as three weeks later than in Paarl or Stellenbosch. The result is an array of remarkable wines, red (notably the medium-bodied Cabernet Sauvignon and Pinotage) as well as white (White Riesling, Sauvignon Blanc, Steen).

Groot Constantia is something more than just another registered estate, even apart from its distinguished history. In 1975 the government established the Groot Constantia Control Board, whose objective it was (and is) to restore the estate to its former glory, to consolidate its land and protect it against urban sprawl, and to produce premium wines to rank among the Cape's best. The manor house continues to serve as a museum, and Constantia's legacy is carefully preserved. But change and modernization have been necessary as well; new vineyard plantings have been made, some acreages of particular cultivars have been relocated to benefit from available microclimates, and a new, although architecturally ugly, technological state-

The new winery building of Groot Constantia Estate stands in stark contrast to the serene beauty of the manor house.

of-the-art cellar was opened in 1982. The Control Board continues to manage Groot Constantia as if it were a privately owned estate, producing and marketing new as well as established lines of Constantia wine. Among the new wines are the improved whites; in addition to the varietal reds, the estate now produces a Shiraz-based blend not unlike several Australian styles, and a Cabernet-based blend in the style of Médoc. These blends are among the most interesting wines made at the Cape today.

DURBANVILLE

With Constantia, Durbanville is the other wine district in the shadow of Cape Town. In fact, the two districts often are described together, giving the impression that a Constantia-Durbanville District exists. And it is true that Durbanville, Constantia's northern neighbor, lies enmeshed in Cape Town's expansion to the northeast as Constantia does to the south. Constantia's green vineyard oasis south of Cape Town is matched by the pockets of vines of Durbanville to the north.

Ample justification exists, however, to separate the two historic districts. In the first place, Constantia is protected by legislation from further urban invasion. Durbanville's winegrowers face the urban tide without such assistance. Environmentally, Durbanville is drier and warmer than Constantia. The annual rainfall of 20 inches in Durbanville's vineyards is less than two-thirds the average recorded at Constantia. But the two districts' vineyards do share a viticultural quality: no irrigation is used, not even in the dry vinelands of Durbanville, where a moisture-retaining, clay-layered soil makes up for the paucity of precipitation.

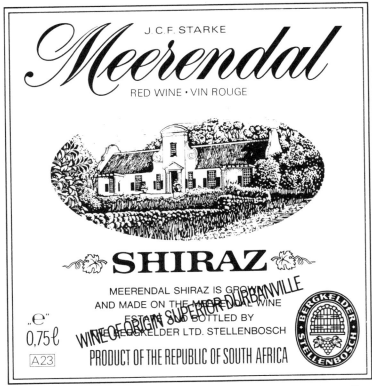

Meerendal is one of only two registered estates in Durbanville. Its wines are bottled and marketed through Die Bergkelder in Stellenbosch.

Durbanville's comparatively small vineyards lie on the slopes of a line of hills that extend northward from the Tigerberg north of Cape Town and east of Table Bay. Cooling sea breezes reach the vines, just 12 miles from the ocean, and heavy dews contribute to the moisture budget. As in Constantia, both red and white cultivars are grown, but the red wines have long been regarded as the better. This may change as promising plantings of Sauvignon Blanc and Chardonnay reach maturity.

Two estates grace the Durbanville wine scene: Diemersdal and Meerendal, situated just a mile apart and within sight of the Durbanville built-up area. The situation is all too reminiscent of similar circumstances near such cities as Santiago, Adelaide, Lisbon, and San Francisco, where premium vinelands were lost to urban sprawl. For the moment, Diemersdal and Meerendal have yet to sustain such an impact. Diemersdal has been a farm for nearly three centuries, and a winery for more than two; to this day it is a mixed farm, the vineyards adjoining grain fields and pastureland. Meerendal was the first estate to be registered in the district, and it has long been known for its Pinotage and Shiraz, and more recently its Cabernet Sauvignon. Meerendal, too, is a mixed farm, with viticulture supplemented by wheat fields and sheep and cattle grazing. This is another point of difference between

The vineyards of Tulbagh are cradled by high mountains that help create especially favorable microclimates. (Photograph by D. Rallis.)

Constantia (where viticulture is the only form of agriculture to survive) and Durbanville, where the rural Cape really begins.

TULBAGH

Tulbagh is one of the Cape's most interesting wine districts. Physiographically, Tulbagh straddles the coastal and intermontane zones of Cape viticulture. Its western boundary is the Berg River, flowing northward from Paarl. Some vines stand in the valley soils, but the major winegrowing zone lies in the east, where the town and environs of Tulbagh lie in a mountain-encircled basin. This basin is entered through the Nuwekloof Pass across the continuation of those mountains that form the eastern borders of Stellenbosch and Paarl—the north-south axis of the familiar "L." Cradling the vineyards are the majestic Witsenberg Mountains to the east and the Winterhoek Mountains to the north; to the south, the district's boundary is less pronounced but coincides approximately with the divide between two river systems. The Tulbagh basin's streams flow westward, through the pass, to join the Berg River. The other river, the Breede (or Breë) River, flows between the ranges in a southeasterly direction and is, as will be noted later, crucial to viticulture in districts to the east.

The floor of the Tulbagh basin lies below 1000 feet in elevation, but the surrounding mountains reach 6000 feet, so the Tulbagh District presents a great variety of microclimates. Snow covers the encircling ranges during the winter, ensuring a supply of meltwater for irrigation during the dry season. This is important,

THEUNISKRAAL

ESTATE WINE

LANDGOED -WITWYN

THEUNISKRAAL
RIESLING

Jordaan Broers

Theuniskraal geleë in die Tulbaghvallei,
is al vir meer as 'n eeu as puik wynplaas bekend en vir baie jare reeds word
Theuniskraal Landgoedwyne na die buiteland uitgevoer

Theuniskraal Riesling is grown and made on the Theuniskraal
Estate and bottled by The Bergkelder Ltd. Stellenbosch

WYN VAN OORSPRONG TULBAGH

Theuniskraal is Tulbagh's northernmost estate. Under its comparatively cool microclimate it produces noted Rieslings.

because here, behind the first range, annual rainfall averages a mere 15 inches (less in some areas). Most of Tulbagh's vines are irrigated, but even here certain favored locales permit viticulture without artificial watering. The vines spread from the basin floor around Tulbagh up the mountain valleys, where elevation moderates the summer's heat, and where orographic precipitation augments the Mediterranean regime's deficient moisture supply. Soils are mainly derived from sandstone, with a shale base on the lower mountain slopes and alluvium in the stream valleys.

Although winegrowing is Tulbagh's leading industry, other fruits also are cultivated. This is South Africa's major prune orchard, and table grapes also are produced in quantity, especially in the area of Wolseley in the southern sector of the district. But Tulbagh has long been known for its excellent Sherry-style wines; South African "Sherries" are reputed to be virtually indistinguishable from those of Spain, and may well be the best made anywhere outside Jerez itself. Premium white table wines also are produced. The chief cultivars of Tulbagh, naturally, are the Steen, Palomino, Hanepoot (Muscat d'Alexandrie), Sémillon, and the Clairette Blanche. Winegrowers who produce and market their own wines have proven, however, that Tulbagh's microclimates can support such cultivars as the White Riesling, Gewürztraminer, Chardonnay, Sauvignon Blanc, and even the Pinot Noir and Cabernet Sauvignon. The fine wines made from these varieties evince Tulbagh's capacities.

Tulbagh's estates exemplify the best in Cape-Dutch architecture, hallmark of South Africa's viticultural landscape. (Photograph by D. Rallis.)

Tulbagh has four registered estates and several other wine farms that market their own wines, but the majority of the harvest is vinted cooperatively. All four of the estates lie north of Tulbagh town, in the Winterhoek cul-de-sac. The most prominent is Twee Jonge Gezellen, one of South Africa's most innovative and progressive wineries, with vineyards extending from alluvial valley soils to stony mountain soils as high as 5000 feet above sea level. The estate's prize-winning white wines are famous and sought after throughout South Africa. Although more than a dozen cultivars are planted (and over 30 have been subject to experimentation), the key varieties are the Gewürztraminer, Riesling, Sauvignon Blanc, Sémillon and, soon, the younger Chardonnay. Varietal as well as blended wines are made by the winery whose technical innovations started something of a revolution in Cape winemaking. The Theuniskraal Estate is the northernmost of the three Tulbagh estates, and its reputation was built on its excellent Rieslings. Theuniskraal lies on the left bank of the Kleinberg River, and its soils are alluvial and fertile; the vineyards are irrigated. In recent years other varietal wines, especially the Gewürztraminer, Steen, and Sémillon (including some noted late-harvest styles) have extended the estate's line. The third of the registered estates is Montpellier, also located very near the Kleinberg River, and also known for its Rieslings and Chenin Blancs (the French variety, not the Steen). The newest of Tulbagh's estates, Lemberg, was registered in 1983.

Like Argentina's Mendoza, Tulbagh lies near a junction of mountain and plain. On 29 September 1969 Tulbagh experienced Mendoza's fate: a devastating earthquake shook the district and destroyed and damaged many of its historic homes and wineries. Although some of the old structures were beyond repair, others could be restored—and some were long overdue for refurbishing, in any case. The government and the K.W.V. sprang into action with loans and assistance, and in some ways the quake was a blessing in disguise. Out of the destruction came the K.W.V.'s first "wine house" for visitors, the restored eighteenth-century Paddagang in Tulbagh town. Today the renovated manor houses of the estates and wine farms symbolize Tulbagh's leadership in the modernization of Cape winemaking.

SWARTLAND

North of Durbanville, Paarl, and Tulbagh, along the Atlantic Ocean's coastline, lie three viticulture areas, two classified as districts (Swartland and Piketberg) and one as a region (Olifants River). Swartland is the official name of the district centered on the town of Malmesbury. The district formerly was known as Malmesbury after its central place, but was renamed as part of the legislation of 1973. Its eastern and northern boundaries are defined by the Berg River, which reaches the sea at Saint Helena Bay.

Swartland is not primarily wine country; its major industries are wheat farming, sheep raising, and dairying for the nearby urban markets. But viticulture has had a foothold here for decades, and considerable growth has marked the industry in recent years. The vineyards lie mainly in the southern part of the district, north and east of Malmesbury and in the area of Darling, nearer the coast. The climate remains Mediterranean, but rainfall is a mere 10 inches per year; yet vines are grown without irrigation in some favored areas. The cool Atlantic breezes, cool nights and mornings, and heavy dew formation contribute to this.

Swartland has proven itself capable of yielding characteristically heavy, alcoholic red grape wines and dry whites, as well as distilling wine. There are two cooperative wineries near Malmesbury, and several growers produce and market their wines themselves. One of these has been awarded estate status: Allesverloren Estate is highly regarded for its Port-style wines and, more recently, for its full-bodied red table wines, notably the Tinta Barocca and Cabernet Sauvignon. The estate lies some 30 miles from the ocean and in the east (lee) side of the Kasteelberg, and yet the vines are not irrigated. On the stony slopes now stand Pinotage and Carignan, Ruby Cabernet and Shiraz, even Sauvignon Blanc and Steen. Allesverloren is proof of the potential of the long-dormant Swartland District.

PIQUETBERG

North of Swartland, across the Berg River, lies the Piquetberg District. One might wonder how an area so comparatively unsuited to winegrowing could be accorded a status equal to Stellenbosch and Tulbagh; here temperatures are higher still than in Swartland, annual rainfall is even lower (7 inches), and irrigation is essential. Most of the limited viticultural development has taken place in the vicinity of the villages of Piketberg and Porterville, and the sole cooperative winery, located at Porterville, vints almost all the grapes harvested here. There grapes are mainly Muscats, the Palomino, the Steen (some dry white wines are made), and the Cinsaut.

Dessert wines and distilling wine constitute the bulk of production. No estate award has been made in Piquetberg.

OLIFANTS RIVER

Adjoining Piquetberg to the north is an area that, appropriately, does not rank as a wine district, but rather as a region: Olifants River. This is essentially the valley and basin of the Olifants River, which flows northward from a U-shaped highland zone around the village of Citrusdal and eventually turns westward to the Atlantic Ocean.

Citrusdal is appropriately named, for this is orange, grapefruit, and tangerine producing country, and viticulture is of lesser importance. The climate suggests the main reason: not only is it hot here, but rainfall varies from a maximum of about 10 inches annually at Citrusdal to 2 inches in the northwestern part of the region.

Nevertheless, Olifants River region produces finished wine in addition to distilling wine and concentrated juice. In the past the irrigated vineyards in the alluvial soils on the river's banks yielded mainly Muscats (and Sultanas for drying), but more recently the Palomino and Steen have been successfully introduced, and some red varieties (the Cinsaut among them) have further diversified the wine scene. No estates have been awarded to any of the few growers who market their own wine, but there are six cooperatives to serve the great majority of grape farmers.

WORCESTER

Tulbagh, with its pivotal location, adjoins all three of the northern areas just enumerated; it also borders Paarl and, to the southeast, the district of Worcester. As the map suggests, Worcester District has an irregular, elongated shape that reflects the jumble of valleys and mountains in which it lies. In fact, the important part of the district, viticulturally, is the west, centered on the town of Worcester. Here lies the valley of the Breede River, the dominant stream in this intermontane area. The eastern extension of the district is the Hex River Valley, where table grape production is virtually the only agricultural activity.

The western part of Worcester District receives much more moisture than the east, accounting for the concentration of winegrowing here. Around Worcester the annual precipitation averages nearly 30 inches, but in the Hex River Valley to the east it declines to less than 10 inches. The Breede River has a deep and wide valley, and much of the viticulture area lies below 1000 feet in elevation; heat summations here are remarkably high. At Rawsonville, west of Worcester town, the degree-day reading is 3658°F., which represents Region IV and places Worcester in the same category as many of California's Central Valley locales. This explains Worcester's long-established reputation for fortified sweet wines and brandies, but recently the pattern has been changing. Dry white wines and quality reds have taken their place among Worcester's premium wines.

On the basis of quantity, Worcester District is the leading wine-producing area in South Africa, contributing nearly 25 percent of the country's average annual vintage. The vineyards total nearly 45,000 acres (nearly double the Napa Valley plantings) and there are twenty cooperatives in the district, including a large K.W.V. establishment at Worcester. These cooperative wineries crush the bulk of the harvest, but there are several independent wine farmers and three registered estates.

The estates of Worcester lie in the western part of the district: Lebensraum just south of Rawsonville, Opstal on the western slope of the Badsberg in a U-shaped valley, and Bergsig in the Breede River Valley, near the border of Tulbagh District. Bergsig's vineyards stand in the alluvial valley of the river as well as in granite-based soils on higher slopes; the estate produces quantity from the fertile alluvium and quality from the higher ground. Irrigation supplements the fairly substantial rainfall, and one aspect of the microclimate is especially significant: between the high mountains, summer breezes almost constantly waft over the vineyards, the air cooled by the funnel effect of the topography. Opstal's acreage extends from the high, west-facing slopes of the Badsberg, across the valley, to east-facing slopes on the opposite bank of the valley stream, elevations ranging from over 2700 to below 1000 feet. The high mountain crests cast hours of shadow over the vineyards, so that the hours of sunlight are limited to the middle of the day. East- and west-facing slopes are carefully exploited for their microclimates; table wines (mainly white) come from the vines facing east, fortified wines from those facing west. In this valley the advantage is not in the warmth of the setting sun; it lies in the coolness of shade and cloud. Lebensraum, just outside the village of Rawsonville, has long been known for its excellent Hanepoot (Muscat) dessert wines, made from the Muscat d'Alexandrie which does especially well in the valley soils, irrigated and cooled by summer southeasterlies that penetrate this part of the district.

Worcester District is among the most scenic of South African wine areas, the vineyards carpeting the valley floors and draping the foothills of towering mountains. This is the more functional, less ornate face of Cape viticulture, a cultural landscape adorned with fewer architectural landmarks but reflective of the real dimensions, efficiency, and modernity of the industry.

ROBERTSON

The Breede River, flowing southeastward through western Worcester District, turns east between two of the Cape's major mountain ranges: the Langeberge to the north, and the Riviersonderend Mountains to the south. Here lies the wine distrtict of Robertson, centered on the town of the same name. The vines stand amid fruit farms (notably peaches and apricots) and pasturelands; canning factories as well as cooperative wineries serve the farmers. At first glance, the Mediterranean climate here does not appear promising: rainfall averages under 15 inches annually, heat summations are high (nearly 3900°F. at the town of Robertson), and the alluvial soils of the Breede River are not the best for quality wine production.

Yet Robertson District produces some noted wines, boasts no fewer than twelve registered estates, and records a steadily growing quality-wine production. This is related in part to the spread of the vines from the valley soils to the somewhat higher ground adjacent, where the so-called Karroo soils, derived mainly from shales among the layered rocks constituting the mountains, support the better

WINE OF ORIGIN ROBERTSON

Zandvliet's Shiraz has for years been one of South Africa's finest wines from this cultivar (that produces such noted wines especially in Australia). Zandvliet Estate is located in Robertson District, where the grapes are grown, but Zandvliet is among those estates whose wines are bottled at Die Bergkelder.

cultivars. Robertson's soils, in these locales, have a higher lime content than virtually any other Cape soils, accounting for much of viticulture's success here. It also is a matter of technology. Improved irrigation methods and modern winemaking techniques have made possible what was previously beyond the growers' reach.

Robertson District has a strong reputation for its "Muscadel" wines, its dessert wines generally, its "Sherries," and its brandies. South Africa's Muscadel is a sweet wine style made from a cultivar called the Muscadel at the Cape, but which is in fact the Muscat de Frontignan of France. Mont Blois, one of the Cape's most picturesque estates, is especially highly regarded for its superior Muscadels, principally its white (both white and red Muscadels are vinted). "Sherries" of high quality are made by some estates (notably Weltevrede) and by several of Robertson's cooperative wineries, and the largest brandy distillery in South Africa is located in the town of Robertson. But the potential for dry table wines brought new vigor to the district's industry, and estates that had been known for superior Muscadels began to diversify their lines.

SOUTH AFRICAN NAMES FOR FRENCH CULTIVARS

France	South Africa
Chenin Blanc	Steen
Cinsaut	Hermitage
Muscat d'Alexandrie	Hanepoot
Muscat de Frontignan	Muscadel
Sémillon	Greengrape

Robertson's dozen estates lie in the eastern part of the district, from the vicinity of the town, mainly along the river, toward the area known as Bonnievale, across the border in Swellendam District. Viticulture began in the fertile alluvial soils where water was available from the stream, but in time the riverbank vines were replaced by other crops, and the vineyards spread to higher ground as irrigation systems expanded and improved. Some of the farms were originally intended for viticulture, but environmental problems forced their owners to plant other crops; many of these farms have returned to winegrowing since. One of the best known (initially for its Muscadels) is Mont Blois, where vineyards stood as long ago as 1884, when the wine was destined for the brandy distillery. A dam was built to create a dependable water supply through the dry summer, and the farm began to produce its now-famed Muscadels. Estate status came in 1973, and the vineyards of Mont Blois today look very different: in addition to the Muscadels there are acres of Steen, Palomino, Hanepoot (Muscat d'Alexandrie), Chardonnay, Sauvignon Blanc, Riesling, Colombard, and Cinsaut. Drip irrigation and cold fermentation have revolutionized winemaking in environments such as Robertson's.

Nor is this transformation confined to white cultivars and wines. The Zandvliet Estate, near Ashton in the eastern margin of Robertson District, receives about 8 inches of rain; for many years this was a mixed farm where horse breeding and peach orchards supplemented the income derived from the dessert wines also grown here. In the 1960s the estate turned to white table-wine production, and in the 1970s it began to produce its first varietal red, a Shiraz. Zandvliet Shiraz has been awarded the highest official rating repeatedly, beginning with the 1975 vintage, and its success has led to the planting of Cabernet Sauvignon and Pinot Noir in what would not long ago have been regarded as an inappropriate location.

Thus Robertson today is a winegrowing district very different from just two decades ago. De Wetshof is a good example of the change. Perhaps the most progressive of Robertson estates, it still produces its remarkable Muscadels and late-harvest wines, but today De Wetshof's cellars also produce dry Rhine Rieslings,

Sauvignon Blancs, and Chardonnays. The estate was the first to market a Chardonnay, and it achieved the "Superior" rating with each of its premium whites. It also has proven capable of creating distinguished reds. The district's future is bright.

SWELLENDAM

Still farther down the Breede River Valley, southeast of Robertson, lies the Swellendam District. Like Robertson, the district is defined by the valley between the Langeberge to the north and the extension of the Riviersonderend Mountains to the south, and here, as in Robertson, the crucial stream is the Breede River with its tributaries. One of the Cape's designated wards, Bonnievale, occupies the northwestern corner of Swellendam's viticulture area. The town of Swellendam lies in the northeast, and another viticulture zone extends between the capital and Suurbraak on the Breede River tributary.

The Bonnievale area is the principal winegrowing zone in a district that shares some features with neighboring Robertson. Summers are warm, rainfall is light (about 15 inches annually), and irrigation is necessary. Unlike Robertson, however, no registered estates exist in Swellendam. White cultivars are planted for the production of fortified and distilling wines and some dry white wines, but there is as yet no achievement with red wine comparable to Robertson's. A few winegrowers bottle their own wines and market them through one of several wholesalers, and five cooperative wineries handle the harvest of other grape farmers. All these are situated in or near Bonnievale, the viticultural heart of a district where fruit orchards, citrus groves, wheat fields, and pasturelands outnumber vineyard acreages.

OVERBERG

The southernmost wine district of South Africa is Overberg, which borders Stellenbosch, Paarl, Worcester, Robertson, and Swellendam to the north and lies open to the ocean in the south. This district formerly was known as Caledon, after the Divisional Council capital, and was renamed after the 1973 legislation was adopted. It is a large area, extending from the coast to the Riviersonderend Mountains, its topography marked by a series of east-west trending mountains and hills, with wide valleys intervening. The centrally positioned among these valleys is known as the Overberg, and hence the wine district's name.

Overberg District is not a winegrowing area to compare to the other ten districts. It has a history of intermittent winegrowing that faded out when the advantages of the fertile soils and watered valleys of the interior became known. There are no registered estates, not even a cooperative winery in the district today. And yet this may be one of the Cape's most promising areas for premium wine production. Overberg is exceptionally cool, its heat summation adding up to Region II status with, in several small areas, patches of Region I. That coolness has its price: the area lies directly in the path of the full force of the Cape's Southeaster, and the high winds can make farming difficult. To the winegrower interested primarily in quantity of production, as was the rule in earlier times, this is not an attractive locale.

Nevertheless, the great wines of the Northern Hemisphere are produced in the cool conditions of Regions I and II, and the Overberg District is of interest to winemakers who put quality above all else. In 1974 a vineyard experiment began just north of the town of Hermanus on Walker Bay. Two parcels were laid out as part of Hamilton Russell Vineyards: one on a south-facing hillslope, the other on slightly west-facing valley land. An interesting result soon was obtained: the Bordeaux cultivars (Cabernet Sauvignon, Merlot, Malbec, Cabernet Franc) did not ripen sufficiently, failed, and had to be replaced. This related to an aspect of the local microclimate. Although in heat summation Region II, the Walker Bay area experiences a dramatic temperature decrease in March, just when the late-ripening Cabernet Sauvignon should be maturing. Pinot Noir did better, and Chardonnay and Sauvignon Blanc proved well suited to the local conditions. Although Hamilton Russell is not a registered estate, this attempt to exploit one of the Cape's most challenging environments has attracted much attention.

LITTLE KARROO

The easternmost contiguous Cape winegrowing area, like the northernmost, is not classified as a district but, rather, as a region. It also is the largest. The Little Karroo (or Klein Karroo in Afrikaans) is small only by South African standards. The region extends as a vast basin across the heart of the southern Cape Province, between the Langeberge to the south and the Swartberg–Groot Swartberge range to the north. These ranges have crestlines as high as 4500 to 5500 feet, and the Little Karroo lies remote from the maritime influences that influence many other Cape winegrowing zones.

Environmental conditions vary considerably across the 200-mile Little Karroo region, both topographically and climatically. The region is large, and viticulture is widely dispersed. It reaches as far east as the Oudtshoorn area, better known for its ostrich farms than its wines. In many areas the terrain is too hilly for irrigation, water supply is undependable, or remoteness inhibits agriculture. Precipitation in the Little Karroo averages about 8 inches annually, most of it coming in March or April; winters are quite cold, but spring warmth comes early. Exposure and slope orientation are important elements of Little Karroo microclimates; all winegrowers in the area know the advantages of southeast-facing slopes and the natural ventilation brought by remnants of the Cape Southeaster reaching here. West-facing slopes are significantly warmer. This is a relatively high-latitude steppe climate, so that nights do tend to be cool, giving more moderate head summations than might otherwise be the case. Oudtshoorn, midway in the easternmost winegrowing area, records 3857°F., still Region IV—which is lower than some California Central Valley locales.

Winegrowing occurs in scattered, stream-valley ribbons from west of Montagu (where elevation brings substantial cooling) at one end of the Little Karroo region to east of De Rust at the other. The K.W.V. has a winery at Montagu, and seven other cooperative wineries are in the area. The beginning of winegrowing here is a saga of frontier trial; nineteenth-century brandy makers carted their barrels on week-long treks to the railhead at Worcester. Just two decades ago this still was almost exclusively a fortified wine, brandy, and distilling wine area, but vinicultural modernization changed the Little Karroo, as it changed Robertson and other interior districts. Today the cooperative wineries still market their Muscadels, but crisp, dry white wines from the Colombard, Steen, and Palomino, pleasant rosés, and even some reds (mainly from the Cinsaut) are also produced.

The Little Karroo may not have district status, but it does have three registered estates. Two of these, Boplaas and Die Krans, are located near the village of Calitzdorp, about 40 miles west of Oudtshoorn, and the third, Doornkraal, just outside De Rust about 25 miles to the east. Boplaas produces a Port made from Pinotage grapes, and a good Sauvignon Blanc; Die Krans, adjacent to Boplaas, also markets Port and Sherry as well as Muscadel wines, but red table wines are becoming a major part of its line. The Tinta Barocca, a red wine cultivar developed for warm regions in South Africa and especially successful in interior districts, is among the varietal reds of note from the Little Karroo, and growers, Die Krans included, are developing it.[4] Doornkraal, in the eastern Little Karroo, continues to be known for its excellent sweet wines, including red and white Muscadels and Ports.

One of the problems associated with the low-rainfall regimes is their variability and susceptibility to sudden, intense storms. On 25 and 26 January, 1981, torrential rains struck the interior districts of the Cape, causing major loss of life, unprecedented flooding, and the destruction of farmlands and crops in stream valleys. Vineyards in the Breede River Valley and in the Little Karroo were devastated, including many newly planted red grapes; thus the diversification program at many wineries was set back. The worst damage, however, was in the Little Karroo's Montagu area, where not only vines, but entire soil horizons were washed away and bedrock cropped out where vineyards once stood. Winegrowers whose vineyards were merely flooded, the crop lost to rot, were fortunate. The usually predictable climate of the Cape does have its hazards.

THE MULTIDISTRICT REGIONS

Little Karroo and Olifants River appear on the map as Cape wine districts but are, in fact, classified as regions. There are four other regions in the South African Wine of Origin system, of which three consist of clusters of districts and one lies far from this core area, along the Orange River.

The Cape's multidistrict regions exist to permit the production of wine from contiguous districts that possess certain physiographic or vinicultural similarities. The *Boberg* Region thus constitutes the upper course and basin of the Berg River (Boberg means Upper Berg) and combines the Paarl and Tulbagh districts. Importantly, this regional appellation is established only for the production of fortified wines. The *Breede River* Region constitutes the catchment basin of the Breede River from southern Tulbagh District through Worcester and Robertson to the Bonnievale Ward of Swelllendam. So defined, this region generates about one-third of the entire national vintage annually. The *Coastal* Region creates a unit for the Cape's historic wine districts, including Stellenbosch and Paarl, Constantia and Durbanville and, by more recent addition, Swartland.

THE LOWER ORANGE RIVER

A discrete region has been established for the vineyards far from the Cape's viticultural heartland. Grapes have been grown in the irrigated alluvial soils of the

Orange River Valley for many years, but for purposes other than winemaking: they were destined for the table or for raisin production. Then the possibilities for winegrowing were recognized, and the comparative proximity of this area to the large Witwaterstrand market provided a geographic incentive as well. Soon the Sultanas and Muscats were supplemented with the Steen and Colombard. The viticulture region centers on the town of Upington, a lengthy ribbon of green sustained by a series of dams that provide the irrigation water. Bulk and distilling wine remains the chief objective in this area, which has region status but is in no way comparable to the multidistrict regions of the Cape proper.

Wines of Origin

The regional framework originally established with the 1973 legislation was only one part of the Wine of Origin system developed by South Africa's oenologists. The other dimension had to do with wine classification and labeling. The regional source of wine is a crucial aspect of any appellation scheme, but it does not provide all the necessary information. Cultivar data, vintage facts, and some qualitative assessment are useful to the consumer.

When the South African Wine of Origin (W.O.) system was introduced, label information was not always reliable. A varietal wine might contain an unspecified percentage of the stated cultivar. The term "estate" had no legal or official basis. There was little (other than reputation and demand) to distinguish excellent wines from ordinary ones.

The South African government in 1973 introduced a wholly new program of wine certification as part of the W.O. system. This involves the attachment of a small, brightly colored seal on the neck of the bottle. If the label on the bottle contains specific information (such as a vintage year, a cultivar, or "estate" bottling), the official seal of the Wine and Spirit Board certifies that such information is accurate and in accordance with legal requirements. The system is not without flaws, but in the Southern Hemisphere nothing comparable has been created, and South Africa is far ahead in the area of classification and labeling precision. On the international market, South African wines are immediately recognized by their seal; the consumer can tell at a glance whether a wine is of (designated) superior quality or not.

The W.O. system is not without flaws. The most serious of these, undoubtedly, is the absence of controls over yields, irrigation practices, and other viticultural procedures. This is one of the cornerstones of the French A.O.C. system, and its exclusion in South Africa weakens the W.O. system.

Certification is a detailed process that demands much of the winegrower, who must keep record of the progress of the harvest even before the grapes are ripe; throughout the winemaking process such documentation also must be kept. Ultimately the wine will be assessed by representatives of the Board, to determine whether it meets the basic specifications of the seal and, more particularly, if it is of sufficiently high quality to be awarded the coveted (and official) "Superior-Superieur" seal. Again, this certification is an assessment *only* of the final product, regardless of vineyard practices and cellar techniques. And the board's tasting panels include not only government officials, but also producers, a combination that is open to criticism.

THE OFFICIAL CONTROL SEALS OF THE WINE & SPIRIT BOARD

These seals appear on the neck capsules of all bottles of wine certified and approved by the Government-appointed Wine & Spirit Board. They are official certification of authenticity of claims relating to origin, variety and vintage made on the label.

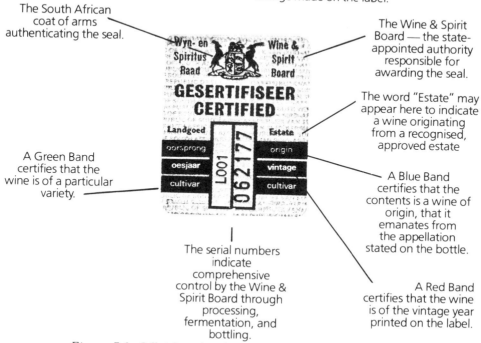

The South African coat of arms authenticating the seal.

The Wine & Spirit Board — the state-appointed authority responsible for awarding the seal.

The word "Estate" may appear here to indicate a wine originating from a recognised, approved estate

A Green Band certifies that the wine is of a particular variety.

A Blue Band certifies that the contents is a wine of origin, that it emanates from the appellation stated on the bottle.

The serial numbers indicate comprehensive control by the Wine & Spirit Board through processing, fermentation, and bottling.

A Red Band certifies that the wine is of the vintage year printed on the label.

Figure 7.6. Official seals of South African wine legislation.

The official control seal of the Wine and Spirit Board (Fig. 7.6) consists of three colored bands and, if appropriate, a fourth, written line to confirm the estate origin of a wine. The three bands (blue for origin, red for vintage, green for cultivar) confirm that what the label asserts has been certified as accurate by the board. The blue band certifies that the wine originates from the region, district, or ward specified on the winegrower's label. The red band verifies the vintage year (thus a nonvintage wine would not carry a red band). The green band will not be present unless the wine is made from at least 75 percent of the cultivar stated on the label. Above the three bands the word "Estate-Landgoed" signals that the source of the wine is one of the Cape's prestigious registered estates.

Until 1982, the term "Superior-Superieur" was placed below the three colored bands if a wine was judged, by official tasting panels representing the board, to be of truly exceptional quality. The practice of awarding "superior" ranking continues, but a special seal has been designed to distinguish more clearly between these exceptional wines and other wines. The seal has the same bands, but its background is gold. Recognition is thus given to the small minority of South African wines to achieve this status.

Winegrowers are not compelled to submit their wines for certification, and many bottles of Cape wine come on the market without the W.O. seal. Such wines may also cost less; the consumer simply is alerted to the absence of the guarantee the W.O. seal provides.

The combination of regional designations and W.O. certification constitutes a most satisfactory solution to problems of classification and labeling. It may be argued that the "Superior" designation has its pitfalls, because some wines do improve in the bottle, and others, after auspicious beginnings, fade more quickly than an exceptional wine should. On the other hand, the W.O.S. designation provides a strong incentive for winemakers to produce quality wines: prices for superior wines are substantially higher than for wines without such rank.

Cultivar and Climate

The Cape environment has been proven capable of yielding world-class wines, and few areas of the world have been subjected to closer scientific scrutiny than the wine districts of South Africa. And yet questions remain to be answered. The experiences of winegrowers using cooler microclimates than those in which many of the Cape's superior, long-lived red wines are produced raise the issue of the relevance of the heat-summation system here. The best of the Cabernet Sauvignons of Stellenbosch and Paarl are truly superior wines; many of them come from locales that are substantially warmer, by heat-summation measures, than those of Bordeaux and Napa-Sonoma. Can the system nevertheless be helpful in the identification of promising, yet-unexploited microclimates?

The map of heat-summation regions suggests that this may indeed be the case (Fig. 7.7). The distribution of the Cape's coolest regions (I and II) is determined by exposure to the ocean air or elevation, but only parts of the regions so delimited are suitable for viticulture. For example, the southern half of the Cape peninsula is too rugged; the southern zone of the Overberg District has sand dunes that would not sustain the vines; and substantial areas of the interior mapped as (I) and (II) are without adequate soil or water supply. Despite all these limitations, however, there is no doubt that certain of the cooler regions could be used for quality viticulture, as the Hamilton-Russell wine farm in western Overberg is proving. The hinterland of the town of Ceres, east of the Tulbagh District (and not even part of any officially designated wine region or district) is a locale that may hold promise for the future.

The impediment to vineyard expansion in such potentially significant areas for quality wine production lies less in the natural environment than in the structure and policies governing the South African wine industry. Winegrowing in experimental zones of this kind is not prohibited, but it is severely limited by the existing controls over cultivation and production. These restrictions stem from the time when overproduction nearly destroyed the industry; the K.W.V. exists in part to ensure that this never happens again. Thus the allocation of "quotas" of production to winegrowers, a system that has the effect of sustaining a pattern which, essentially, confines viticulture to the established districts. Few growers could risk assigning part of their allotted quotas to experiment in the frontier regions, however promising they might be. Worse, the quota allocation system does not differentiate between wine destined for the brandy distillery and premium wines to be marketed behind

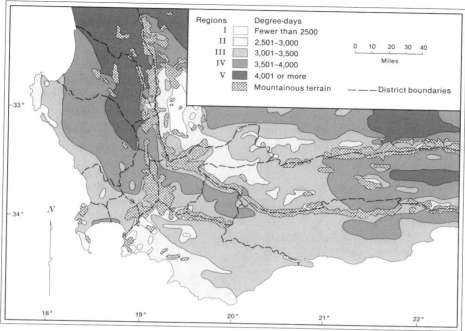

Figure 7.7. Heat summation regions at South Africa's Cape, with officially designated wine districts superimposed on the pattern. From a Master's thesis by E. le Roux, Klimaatstreek Indeling van die Suidwes Kaaplandse Wynbougebiede, *University of Stellenbosch, 1974.*

"Superior" labels. Since the volume of ordinary wines is so much greater, quality is sacrificed under the long-existing quota system.

As the Hamilton-Russell venture at Walker Bay proves, these obstacles are on occasion overcome, though at great risk and disadvantage. Thus Hamilton-Russell's wines must be marketed behind labels that cannot identify vintages or even varietals, in order to avoid conflict with quota stipulations. But the fact remains that

> cultivars (which include the Rhine or Weisser Riesling, Gewürztraminer among whites and the fussy Pinot Noir among reds) give their best in climates cooler than many of our traditional viticultural districts offer. Elgin, Ceres, Walker Bay—these are among areas that might provide prospects for improved performances of such vines. But production there is restricted. . . . if the frontiers of quality are to be pushed forward, it becomes obvious a fresh look is justified to see where it could be possible to support— not financially, but by the relaxation of some artificial restrictions—those willing to undertake new ventures in new areas. . . . In any case it is time to differentiate, in quota allocations, between brandy producers and winegrowers.[5]

Indeed, the heat-summation map (see Fig. 7.7) should be viewed in context of South Africa's premium-wine cultivars. The Hamilton-Russell venture proved (and it was confirmation of experience elsewhere in the Cape) that the Cabernet Sauvignon at the Cape no longer likes the cool environments it prefers in Europe and North America; the south-facing upland vineyard under cool Region II conditions

Over the mountains from Tulbagh District lies the Ceres area, where environmental conditions may favor viticulture but where legal restrictions inhibit experimentation.

was found to be too cold for these vines. But other varieties, including the Pinot Noir and Chardonnay, were well suited to these cool conditions. Given the potential evident from the heat-summation map, the Pinot Noir may well become one of South Africa's major premium-wine cultivars, once self-inhibiting restrictions just described are lifted. The Chardonnay, too, may take its rightful place. In the early 1980s there were barely more than 10,000 vines of the Chardonnay in South Africa, well below 0.01 percent of the national total—still less than the Pinot Noir, with under 80,000 vines and 0.02 percent.[6]

As noted earlier (Chapter 2) South Africa's specialty cultivars are the Pinotage and the Steen, and of these the Steen, with more than one-quarter of the total national acreage, leads by far; it may be said to constitute the cornerstone of the South African wine industry. The next-ranking variety, in terms of acreage (17 percent) is the Palomino, once the most popular cultivar but used principally for distilling and now overtaken by the Steen. And the leading red variety is neither the Pinotage nor the Cabernet Sauvignon, but the Cinsaut (15 percent), the grape long called the Hermitage in South Africa and one of the ancestors of the famous Pinotage.

The Steen not only leads in terms of total acreage; it also is the most widely distributed variety in South Africa. Even in Stellenbosch District, famed for its premium reds, the Steen is the most widely grown cultivar. Much of the harvest is used in the production of "jug" wines, but the grape is capable of yielding delicate, dry, honey-sweet, late-harvest, Sherry-style, white Port-style, and sparkling wines; it also is distilled into brandy. By contrast, the Palomino, its acreage now declining, has been the workhorse of the fortified-wine and brandy industry; this variety remains the prime Sherry producer in Spain but has lost this position to the Steen at the Cape. Still, the dependable, prolific, low-acid Palomino covers large acreages in Swartland, Olifants River, Robertson, Worcester, and the Little Karroo, its juice mostly used for distillation or bulk-wine production. It is evidence of both the natural environment of the Cape and the old traditions of the wine industry that the Muscat d'Alexandrie—the Hanepoot—remains the third-ranking white cultivar, used for some table-wine production but mainly for fortified-wine purposes as well as for grape juice, table grapes, and raisins.

Hence the more interesting white varieties, such as the White Riesling, Chardonnay, Sauvignon Blanc, and Gewürztraminer, occupy far smaller, even minuscule (as in the case of the Chardonnay and Sauvignon Blanc) acreages. The Colombard, Clairette Blanche, and Sémillon all represent 3 to 4 percent of the total acreage with some regional concentration evident: the Sémillon prevails in Paarl, the Clairette Blanche in Stellenbosch, and the Colombard in the northern and interior districts. Only a small part of the vintage from these cultivars is bottled as varietal wine; most of it is used in blending. The estate varieties prove what can be done with these cultivars at the Cape: Le Bonheur Estate's Sauvignon Blanc is regarded as the Cape's best; its Chardonnay, still privately held, is promising, and the Colombards from Uiterwyk and Spier can be noteworthy wines in some years. This lends all the more interest to the production of premium white wines from the small vineyards of such cultivars, with which remarkable achievements already have been made.

No red cultivar can match the domination of the Steen, but the rise of the heavy-bearing, easily managed Steen, in context of the history of Cape viticulture, is rather recent. In 1960 a red cultivar, the Cinsaut (then still called the Hermitage), still was the most widely planted variety in South Africa, accounting for 27 percent of the total acreage. Since then it has declined to barely half this figure, still a substantial total but no match for the white Steen. In part, this reflects changing domestic preferences (South African consumers prefer white wines), and in part it relates to the rise of the "glamor" red cultivars, the Cabernet Sauvignon and the Pinotage. In addition, a declining interest in fortified wines and brandy, compared to dry red and white table wines, has contributed to the Cinsaut's relative reduction. Nevertheless, this is a versatile variety, and it continues to figure importantly in Cape viticulture. It has yielded notable Ports and Jeropigos (a South African specialty, a very sweet fortified wine, high in alcohol and sugar), interesting rosés in the cooler areas of the Cape, and in especially favored areas can be vinted into good varietal table wines in light as well as fuller-bodied styles. The Cinsauts of Landskroon Estate and of Audacia Estate have long been among the best of these. The Cinsaut is used as a blend in premium red wines as well, and not surprisingly its distribution shows a concentration in the coastal districts, especially Stellenbosch and Paarl, with a major cluster also in the Worcester District.

The Cabernet Sauvignon, however, is the red grape that yields the great majority of the Cape's premium wines, its comparatively small acreage (about 3 percent of the total) notwithstanding. Most of the Cabernet vines stand in Stellenbosch and Paarl, with smaller acreages in Constantia; but quality-conscious winegrowers in every district have small vineyards of this cultivar, seeking to make use of

The Southern Hemisphere's wine industries are not monopolies of the large, populous countries. The wines of Madagascar are represented by these labels. The Lazan'i Betsileo is described by oenophile H. Wright as "the best rouge in Madagascar: Bordeaux-like, but lighter-bodied." The Reserve d'Ambalavao Soavita is noted as being "dry and not especially full-bodied, but well structured and pleasant drinking."

microclimates deemed suitable for its late-ripening grape. This is the cultivar of the estate, of the experimenters among winemakers in South Africa. Almost all Cabernet Sauvignon grown at the Cape is destined for varietal or Cabernet-dominated blended wines, and among these wines are the region's most complex and long-lived. The names of some estates have been built on their superior Cabernet Sauvignons, such as Kanonkop, Meerlust, Alto, Montagne, Muratie, Rust-en-Vrede, Rustenberg, and Vergenoegd in Stellenbosch District and De Zoete Inval, Welgemeend (in a Merlot blend), and Backsberg, Boschendal, and Nederburg (the S.F.W. wine farm) in Paarl, among others. In addition, there are superb blended wines, many of them more remarkable than the varietal alone, in which the Cabernet Sauvignon is combined with Cinsaut, Merlot, Cabernet Franc, Shiraz, and other red grapes to produce complex, interesting wines. Paarl's Landskroon Estate is known for such blended wines, which have gained the strong acceptance on the South African market they merit.

Among the noble cultivars the Cabernet Sauvignon dominates, but other varieties show much promise. Of course South Africa's "own" red grape is the Pinotage (see Chapter 2) which, sadly, has somewhat fallen from favor in recent years. Like the Zinfandel, the Pinotage has a distinctive flavor, and local consumers during the 1970s began to prefer a lighter style of Pinotage. This had the effect of reducing the output of the darker, more complex, longer-lived Pinotages of yesteryear. Still the Pinotage today accounts for somewhat less than 3 percent of the total grape acreage, about double the quantity of a decade ago, and the wine always will have its adherents. Estates such as Kanonkop, Jacobsdal, Middelvlei, and Overgaauw in Stellenbosch and Landskroon, Fairview, and Backsberg in Paarl are noted particularly for their superior Pinotages.

As in the case of the white varieties, some of the most fascinating experiments in winegrowing are taking place with comparatively tiny stands of estate-grown cultivars. The Shiraz (with which Australian winegrowers have had the greatest success in the Southern Hemisphere) is grown extensively in Stellenbosch and Paarl, and is made as a varietal and used as a blending wine. Of special interest is the Tinta Barocca, first developed especially for "Port" production under Cape conditions, but later used in the creation of an interesting, characteristic varietal red, again in Stellenbosch and Paarl but also in Swartland. Exciting possibilities exist for the Pinot Noir, still a very small acreage divided among mainly Stellenbosch estates, but also spreading in Paarl and Tulbagh. And several Cape estates are cultivating California's Zinfandel, including Blaauwklippen, Montagne, and Kanonkop; Bertrams, a respected producer-wholesaler, has marketed a Zinfandel for some years from Stellenbosch vineyards.

The presence of other red cultivars (Alicante Bouschet, Carignan, Gamay Noir, Malbec, Pontac, Souzao) confirms the Cape's capacity to support virtually the entire range of *vinifera*; it is to be hoped that industrial economics, national politics, and temporal realities will permit the full flowering of one of the world's most colorful wine industries.[7]

8

AUSTRALIA:
DIONYSUS DOWNUNDER

Austalia is a country and a continent, region and realm, fabled frontier. Its name evokes images of pleasant climes and sunny skies, scenic shores and open plains, vast livestock ranches and modern cities. Tropical winds waft its northern peninsulas, while Antarctic cold chills the waters off its southern coasts. The western interior is hot and desert-dry; the highlands of Tasmania are cool and soaked by a hundred inches of rain in some years. Australia may not be known as a region of extremes, but its geography is not without stark contrasts. Australia's wine regions are similarly diverse and different. Unlike South Africa's Cape, with its clustered wine districts, or the latitudinally dispersed vineyards of Chile and Argentina, the wine regions of Australia lie scattered from east to west, and from the dry interior to moist Tasmania. There are vineyards in the hinterlands of every major city, from Sydney to Perth. Vines are cultivated in every one of Australia's seven large political subdivisions, and under widely varying climatic conditions.

And yet, for all its continental size and environmental potentials, Australia produces less wine annually than South Africa or Chile. The total vineyard area in 1984 still was under 200,000 acres, about the same as Brazil and substantially less than Chile (270,000) and South Africa (250,000). Several factors lie behind this situation, and history undoubtedly is one of these. Winegrowing in Australia began less than two centuries ago, and except for New Zealand, it is the Southern Hemisphere's youngest wine industry. Domestic consumption is another factor. Australia's population is not large (15 million) and per-capita wine consumption is about 5 gallons—more than the United States but much less than Argentina or Chile. Commercial practices constitute still further reason for Australia's comparatively modest wine production. Australian wine today is seen on foreign markets in increasing volume, but this is a recent phenomenon. For many decades few Australian wines reached overseas consumers, in part because of a widespread misunderstanding that Australian wines would not "travel well."

Today the Australian wine industry is changing rapidly, and before long it may stand in second, not fourth, place (by volume) in the Southern Hemisphere. New regions are being opened to viticulture; technological improvements have transformed the industry; collaboration with Californian, French and German winegrowers is increasing; new wineries are started. There was a time when winemaking in Australia was principally a hot-climate proposition, and fortified wines dominated. In the past three decades there has been a qualitative as well as quantitative revolution, and consumer preferences also have changed. Australian table wines on international markets and in European and American competitions have proven the vinicultural potential of the island continent downunder.

New South Wales, where Captain Phillip and his colleagues planted Australia's first vines, briefly held first place among Australia's wine regions. Today, cooler South Australia holds the lead, with well over 60 percent of all wine production; New South Wales is now a distant second with 23 percent, still a substantial volume nevertheless. Victoria ranks third (13 percent), and Western Australia now produces about 2 percent of Australia's wines. There is some wine production in Tasmania, where prospects for quality wines are bright, and wine also is made in small quantity in Queensland near the towns of Stanthorpe and Roma. Grapes are even grown near Alice Springs in the desert interior of the Northern Territory.[1] This wide dispersal of the vine in Australia only hints at the viticulture possibilities yet to be exploited. Climates range from warm tropical to cool mesothermal (see Figure 1.7), and within this range there are Brazil-like conditions in the east, Argentina-like regimes in the irrigated desert, New Zealand-like climes in Tasmania, and true Mediterranean seasons in the south and southwest. It is something of an irony that nearly half of Australia's grape harvest is destined for raisin production (table-grape production is relatively small), when the opportunities for winegrowing are so varied and promising.

The geography of Australian viticulture displays a clustering of wine regions in the southeastern corner of the continent, south of a line extending approximately from the vicinity of Muswellbrook in the Upper Hunter Valley region of New South Wales to the northern tip of Spencer Gulf west of Adelaide in South Australia (Fig. 8.1). More than 90 percent of Australia's wine is produced in the triangular region so delimited, most of it in the southeastern sector of South Australia. Here the climatic pattern is quite intricate: B (dry) conditions develop westward, Csb (dry-cool summer) conditions around Adelaide yield to Csa (dry-warm summer) regimes toward the interior, and the dry-summer regime fades into Cfb (humid temperate, cool, moist summer) in Victoria. Australia's southeast is quite cool; heat summations in Coonawarra, South Australia, are below those of Burgundy. In this area southeastern Australia exhibits one of the rare zones of transition from dry-summer Mediterranean to moist-summer mesothermal climate which, wherever it occurs in the world, can yield the greatest of wines.

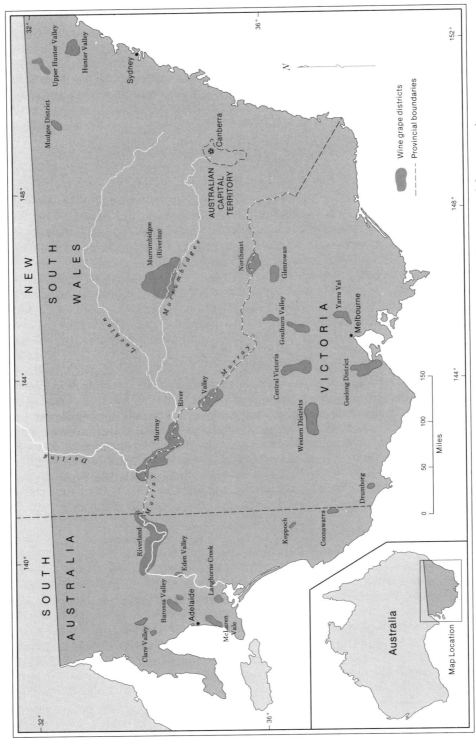

Figure 8.1. The roughly triangular region of Australia within which 90 percent of the country's vineyards are located.

The generalized map of Australian wine regions also should be viewed in the context of the country's dimensions. The southeastern corner defined by that line of viticultural delimitation covers approximately 300,000 square miles, or about twice the area of California. The southeastern sector of South Australia, where some of the country's leading wine regions lie, looks small on the map, but from the tip of Spencer Gulf to the shore of Discovery Bay is a distance of more than 400 miles. Thus, Australia's wine regions in many instances lie widely separated, making geographic regionalization difficult. This reality also has had an impact on attempts to create an Australian appellation system. While "there are areas that by sheer isolation fall into natural appellation designations," as one observer wrote, others lie closer together but display contrasting cultural traditions and wine styles.[2] The strongest link between vineyard regions is created by the great Murray River, the Mississippi of Australia, and its tributary, the Murrumbidgee. Fed by melting snows on the Australian Alps and Blue Mountains of the Great Dividing Range, the Murray River is the source of irrigation waters for tens of thousands of acres of vineyards. From Rutherglen to Riverland and beyond, the Murray is the lifeblood of winegrowing.

The dispersal of Australia's wine regions may be a prime reason why the names of these districts are so little known in the outside world. European consumers who have become familiar with California, Mendoza, and the Cape as regional identities may know of Australian wines, but not their regional sources. The Hunter Valley, Barossa Valley, the Clare Valley, and Coonawarra remain obscure places on the mental maps of many Americans and Europeans who appreciate quality wines. In truth, Australian labeling practices have also contributed to the obfuscation. While some Australian labels are models of detail, geographic as well as varietal, others hark back to a time long past in other countries. As recently as 1983 a protest from France induced a Hunter Valley winemaker to change the name of a wine he had intended to label "White Bordeaux" to "Hunter Valley White Bordeaux"![3]

Nevertheless, Australian wines at their best exhibit strong regional character and, as will be noted below, individual districts are often known for particular styles. In 1983, 57 percent of the country's production consisted of table wines, and 16 percent represented dessert wines (25 years ago fortified wines exceeded table wines by a margin of three to one), and regions such as the Hunter, Coonawarra, and McLaren Vale are associated with particularly successful cultivars and styles. Individual winegrowers, too, are recognized for their special achievements. As would be expected on the changing Australian wine scene, new wineries appear while other fade and fail; but among the approximately 330 registered wineries (1983) are names that have been associated with quality and style for generations. Like wine industries everywhere, Australian winegrowing has its characters, winemakers who not only produce noteworthy wines but who also are spokesmen for the industry. Murray Tyrrell, the man who has been called the "Mouth of the Hunter" (and the reference was *not* geographic) exemplifies this cadre of growers who champion their regions, and who prove by example what those regions can produce. Tyrrell's red wines from his Hunter Valley vineyards are respected in Australia and recognized internationally. As winemaker and as publicist, Tyrrell has done much to put the Hunter Valley on oenophiles' mental maps.

In some respects the Australian winegrowing industry resembles California's,

From this modest winery of Tyrrell's in Australia's Hunter Valley come some of Australia's finest wines.

its producers ranging from huge companies to tiny "boutique" wineries. There are established, estate-type wineries whose premium wines are made from their own vineyards, large cooperatives owned by hundreds of growers, and major corporate producers. Among these largest companies are the most familiar names in Australian winemaking: Lindeman, Penfold, Wynn, Seppelt, Orlando, McWilliam, Yalumba, Hardy. The majority of the larger companies have a headquarter-facility in a major city (usually Sydney or Adelaide), with wineries and vineyards in other states' wine regions as well.

Lindeman is a good example. The firm was founded in 1843 by a surgeon named Lindeman, who had a practice in the Hunter Valley area and started a vineyard there. With his three sons he expanded the family holdings, and through the marriage of his daughter acquired the famed Kirkton vineyard first developed by James Busby. As additional land came under the Lindeman name a central facility was established in Sydney where, around 1900, the firm claimed to have constructed the largest wine cellar in the Southern Hemisphere. Although (again as in the United States) Lindeman was bought by a larger corporation, the Philip Morris Tobacco Company, the Lindeman name continues, and its wines are highly regarded. Another leading name is Penfold, a firm that owns nearly twenty vineyards and estates throughout the Australian viticulture zone. Established in 1848 by a Dr. Penfold at Magill, about four miles east of Adelaide, the firm changed ownership repeatedly but retained its original name. It is noted especially for two of its claret-style wines, Grange Hermitage and St. Henri, regarded by many as among Australia's finest premium wines. Still another prominent company is Seppelt, founded in 1851 and headquartered at Tanunda in the Barossa Valley. This has remained a family firm, and its holdings include large vineyards in Barossa, in the Murray Valley region, and elsewhere. Also famous is McWilliam, a family firm dating from the late 1870s with major holdings in the Murrumbidgee district, Robinvale in the Murray Valley, and prestigious Mount Pleasant in the Hunter Valley. McWilliam also played an important role in the development of winegrowing in New Zealand.

These major wine companies in some ways are unlike their overseas counterparts in that they present a rather more complete line of wines, not only in terms of style but, more important, in terms of quality. True premium wines are produced under the labels of Penfold, Lindeman, and other corporate firms; some of Australia's most respected winemakers work for these companies. Lindeman's Ben Ean winery in the Hunter Valley, acquired in 1912, has remained a discrete entity, its label a mark of quality wines quite distinct from the large range of more ordinary Lindeman's wines. Penfold's Grange Hermitage, one of Australia's truly classic wines, was developed by winemaker Max Schubert as a blend of Shiraz with 5 to 15 percent Cabernet Sauvignon. It stands apart from the regular line of Penfold's wines, made from grapes of its numerous vineyards, combined to ensure year-to-year uniformity. Seppelt's sparkling wines from its Great Western Vineyards are another example of specialization in a larger corporation (Seppelt also produces noted Sherry- and Port-style wines at its Seppeltsfield winery in the Barossa Valley).

The large corporate wineries contributed crucially to the modern transformation of Australian winegrowing, and not only by producing premium table wines. These were the organizations that had the resources to invest in research and equipment when the time came. The Orlando winery at Rowland Flat in the Barossa Valley became a leader in Australian viniculture during the 1950s, when the firm founded by Johann Gramp in 1847 (and still carrying the family name) introduced controlled pressure fermentation of white wines. Not long afterward, cold fermenation also was begun, and the change from fortified wines to dry, crisp table wines was under way. Gramp's 1953 Barossa Riesling, the first product of the new technology, still is acknowledged as a turning point in Australian winemaking. But another innovation was to come: Colin Gramp, technical director for the winery, during a 1954 visit to Germany saw the popularity there of sparkling wine made by the Charmat method, the *perlwein*. Gramp appointed a German winemaker to produce a similar wine in Australia, and in 1956 the first bottle of Barossa Pearl was marketed. The appearance of Barossa Pearl, which eventually sold more than 40 million bottles, has been described as the "single most significant advance in Australian winemaking and marketing. [It] launched many Australians into wine drinking."[4]

Such was the reward of Gramp's investments and innovations that demand increased beyond expectation—and beyond the family's willingness to meet it. The Gramps decided to sell the winery, and in 1970 it changed hands. It now became known simply as the Orlando Winery, but it remained one of Australia's major wineries. Further technological improvements were made, and the line of Orlando wines was expanded by the addition of delicate, sweeter wines (notably from the Riesling and Gewürztraminer) and interesting reds under the Jacob's Creek label, blends of Shiraz, Cabernet Sauvignon, and Malbec. The grapes for Orlando's wines come from several sources, including the company's own vineyards in the Keppoch District (about 40 miles north of Coonawarra), contract growers in Coonawarra,

Hardy is among Australia's major wine companies. Hardy's Nottage Hill Claret is one of the company's most respected lines.

the Barossa Valley itself, the nearby Eden Valley, and the Riverland. Orlando's wines are known for their consistent quality, and they usually rank high in Australian wine competitions. Gramp's Orlando showed the way, and the winery remains in the forefront of winemaking today.

Other major Australian wine companies include Thomas Hardy and Sons, a family firm that has remained so; it is based in Reynella, although grapes come not only from Tintara, but also from McLaren, Coonawarra, and even the Hunter; and Wynn and Sons, famous for its Coonawarra Estate Cabernet Sauvignon but with vineyards in the Murrumbidgee Irrigation Area as well. This represents the dominant spatial pattern: the larger wine companies, with the exception only of their place-specific wineries such as Lindeman's Ben Ean, make their wines from grapes grown in many districts. They do not, therefore, reflect the geographic individuality of

1975
AUSTRALIAN
CABERNET SAUVIGNON
RED TABLE WINE

VINTAGED AND BOTTLED BY
KAISER STUHL WINE DISTRIBUTORS PTY. LTD.
NURIOOTPA, BAROSSA VALLEY, SOUTH AUSTRALIA

PRODUCE OF AUSTRALIA
CONTENTS 750 ml (25.4 fl oz) ALCOHOL 13.0% BY VOLUME

Kaiser Stuhl, long among Australia's leading cooperative wineries, was for decades an anchor for Barossa Valley grapegrowers. Its wines were marketed under labels such as that shown here. Recently the winery was purchased by Penfold, and a new era has begun here.

Australia's wine regions, in the sense that their wines are combinations of harvests from various locales.

Australia's cooperative wineries come somewhat closer to regional-geographic identity, because the growers tend to be clustered in particular areas. Thus the Barossa Co-operative Winery, whose wines were for many years marketed under the Kaiser Stuhl label, was owned by more than 500 winegrowers in and near the Barossa Valley. This organization was founded in 1931, when a group of local growers sought a way to counter the effects of the Great Depression. The first cooperative cellar was completed in 1933, and the grand name Kaiser Stuhl, derived from the geographic name of a prominent mesa overlooking the valley, was adopted in 1958. In the same year the winery began offering wines from individual vineyards especially suited to the production of particular styles, an innovation that proved very successful. One of the first individual-vineyard wines was Wyncroft, a late-harvest white from

The main cellars of Renmano at Renmark in the Murray River region. Renmark has long been one of Australia's leading cooperative wineries. The company recently was merged with the Berri firm, creating a new corporation, Berri-Renmano.

an Eden Valley vineyard. Like the large corporate firms, therefore, Kaiser Stuhl also has its premium line along with its well-known standard blends. Recently the winery was purchased by one of the large companies, Penfold.

Several cooperative wineries emerged in the Murray River regions where soldiers-settlers had been awarded farmland (see Chapter 3). The oldest of these, Renmano, also is among the largest grape–crushing cooperatives in Australia today. Founded in 1916 and based at Renmark, Renmano at first produced mainly brandy and fortifying spirits, turned to Sherry- and Port-style wines in 1930s, and increased its table-wine production after World War II. Today it has well over 400 members. Renmano is best known for its large crush of table-wine grapes, and one of the cooperative's most popular wines has been its Renmano Muscat, a popular, light, dessert wine. Renmano recently was amalgamated with the Berri Cooperative to form the Berri-Renmano firm.

The Berri Cooperative was established after World War I to handle the harvests of about 600 member-growers in the Berri and Barmera irrigation areas. By volume, Berri is Australia's largest cooperative winery, but most of its huge harvest is vinted for sale to other wineries; some table wines are marketed under the Mine Host label. Waikerie Co-operative has long had its wine bottled by the Kaiser Stuhl facility in the Barossa Valley, and is now owned by Penfold as well. Loxton Co-operative is of more recent vintage, and was established during the soldier-settler era after World War II. Among Australia's cooperative wineries, however, Kaiser Stuhl (to use the Barossa Co-operative's more familiar name) had the strongest regional qualities, as reflected not only by the distribution of its growers but also by the character of its wines. Not all observers regard this as an asset: in an evaluation of the cooperative's wines, a reviewer recently suggested that perhaps

> the final answer for Kaiser Stuhl lies in the production of styles which blend the characteristics of regions like Coonawarra with the naturally rich fruit flavours available in the Barossa Valley. [Thus] Kaiser Stuhl may . . . shed forever its regional image.[5]

Geographer-oenophiles might view such a prospect differently.

The great majority of Australia's wineries are comparatively small and based on local, intraregional vineyards, and these reflect more faithfully than the large corporations or cooperatives the special qualities of their respective regions. True, some of the smaller boutique wineries may not have the capital to invest in new oak every year, or to keep up with the latest in technological developments. But the established small wineries—the Tyrrells, the Redmans, the Tahbilks, the Balgownies, the Moss Woods—whether venerable or youthful, are the wineries that produce wine as the "summation of their region," in geographic parlance. The flavor of history, of southern cold, of western frontier is captured in the wine, to be experienced as proof of the regional diversity of Australian wine environments.

Custom and Cultivar

Nowhere is the transformation of Australian winegrowing more evident than in the vineyards themselves. If the 1960s and 1970s were the decades of the winemakers and the wineries, the 1980s and 1990s may be the decades of the viticulturists and the vineyards. The wineries now match the most advanced in the world, the technology is second to none, and in the cellars Australian winemakers have proven their innovative capacities. Now the focus of attention is on the grapes. The composition of the vineyards is changing as dramatically as the wineries did.

The recency of this change is remarkable in light of the situation in the early 1970s. Perhaps the one pattern that was established early, prevailed then, and continues to hold is the prevalence of Australia's first premium red grape, the Shiraz. Even in the early 1970s there were as many as 20,000 acres of Shiraz in Australia. For many decades it was the only red grape grown in the Hunter Valley, where it yielded the lighter-style, soft reds for which the region became famous. It also was planted extensively in South Australia where, in the Barossa Valley and neighboring districts, its wines were full-bodied and quite assertive. The Shiraz was Australia's prime regional association: a grape of limited (though noted) success in France's Rhône Valley had found a more productive home in the Southern Hemisphere. Blended with small amounts of Cabernet Sauvignon, it created Australia's most famous wines.

A sign of the changes to come lies in the two red grapes which, in the early 1970s, ranked behind the Shiraz in total acreage. The Grenache, with more than 15,000 acres, was the only other extensively planted red cultivar, popular because of its high productivity and grown throughout the irrigated areas. Today the

Grenache is on the decline, and with the Mataro (most of its 4000 acres in 1970 were in South Australia) it may be a mere remnant by century's end. The Grenache, for jug reds, and the Mataro, sometimes blended with Shiraz and also used in the making of Port-style wines, have lost their attractiveness in the new vinicultural era.

In 1970 the Cabernet Sauvignon was just beginning to become reestablished, and the story of its rise to prominence reflects the revolution in the Australian vineyard. Cabernet Sauvignon vines had been brought to Australia by the nineteenth-century pioneers who opened the viticultural frontier, but most of these vines withered away. The Cabernet Sauvignon does not yield abundantly, and it did not suit the prevailing tastes for fortified wines. In the 1960s its resurgence began, but in the early 1970s there still were only some 4300 acres in all of Australia, most of it in South Australia but about 700 acres in the Hunter. A few noted varietal Cabernets had been made (the 1954 from Wynn is remembered with admiration), but most of the Cabernet's wine became part of a blend.

Then the new era began. A number of growers in various regions planted substantial acreages of Cabernet, and experimented in their wineries. Max Lake aged his Cabernets in small oak barrels and produced some of the Hunter Valley's most noted wines. So enthusiastic was he about his venture with this noble grape that he wrote a book extolling the Cabernet's virtues, predicting in effect that this would become Australia's premier red cultivar.[6] That prediction may well come true. By the time Lake's book was printed, the number of Hunter Valley wineries growing Cabernet had increased to thirty; in five years production of Cabernet Sauvignon wine rose twelvefold. Developments elsewhere were even more spectacular. In the late 1970s more than one hundred wineries in Australia marketed Cabernet varietal wines, and acreage exceeded 10,000. Harry Tulloch, at the Viticultural Research Station in the Barossa Valley, contributed crucially to this success through his research into clones of the Cabernet, developing two stocks especially suited to Australian environments. And although the Australian market as a whole exhibits a preference for white wines, premium reds always are in demand, and the best in short supply. Thus the expansion of Cabernet Sauvignon continues, as does the debate over the comparative merits of Shiraz-based and Cabernet-dominated blends.

In the blends (not only Shiraz-Cabernet, but also Cabernet-Merlot, Cabernet-Malbec, etc.) lies the future. Several of Australia's best Cabernet Sauvignons come from the cooler regions of South Australia, where the prospects for the traditional blending cultivars are very good; as vineyards under Merlot and Cabernet Franc mature, the greatest of Australian red wines yet made will evolve. But good Cabernet comes not only from the established premium-wine regions. The quality of Cabernet Sauvignon from the irrigated districts also is most satisfactory. And so the heyday of the Cabernet continues.

Given such radical changes, it is not surprising that Australian oenologists have tried to predict what the future may hold. During a 1983 seminar conducted at Roseworthy Agricultural College in South Australia, it was suggested that, by the end of the century, Cabernet Sauvignon would be the most widely planted red cultivar in Australia; Shiraz would be in second place.[7] No other red cultivar would even come close, but the third-ranking variety was a surprise: the Pinot Noir, which as recently as 1970 covered just 60 acres. Only the Grenache and the Mataro also appeared on the projected list.

As in South Africa, numerous other red cultivars, ranging from the Cinsaut and Carignan to the Muscat de Frontignan and the Alicante Bouschet, are grown on comparatively small acreages in various districts of Australia. The big two, however, dominate the wine scene, exceeding by far the total acreage and production of all the others combined.

It is important to note that all the foregoing refers to Australia's red varieties. Far greater acreage is (and has long been) devoted to white grapes, and among these the all-purpose Sultana (California's Thompson's Seedless) reigned supreme in the early 1970s, its 50,000 acres constituting a larger area than all other white varieties together.[8] Locally called the "Murray Valley Pinot," the Sultana produced a wide range of dry and sweet table wines, sparkling wines, and Sherry-type wines, and was used for distilling purposes as well. Those uses still continue, but a variety that stood in distant second place, the Muscat d'Alexandrie (Muscat Gordo Blanco, or simply "Gordo" in Australian parlance) has overtaken it. In the early 1970s there were 10,000 acres under the Gordo, mainly in the Murray Valley regions, in Murrumbidgee, and in the far west in the Swan Valley. Much of the vineyard expansion of the 1970s was devoted to this Muscat, and Australian projections suggest that it will maintain its lead.

If the predictions made at Roseworthy are to be believed, the Sultana will decline to third, and possibly even to fourth place. This is because of the rise of the Rhine Riesling ("Rhine" to distinguish it as a real Riesling from the so-called Hunter Valley Riesling, which is actually a Sémillon) over the past twenty years. Few vineyard changes in Australia mirror more acutely the winegrowing transformation of the past decades than the emergence of this noble variety at the expense of the "Murray Valley Pinot." Around 1970 the Riesling covered small acreages, mainly in South Australia; today it is grown in virtually every wine district, producing excellent wines especially in the cooler areas of the south. Much more Riesling is now blended into Australia's well-made jug whites since the modernization of technology warranted the use of better grapes.

Australia's other "Riesling," the Sémillon, is the other white grape to challenge the supremacy of the Thompson's Seedless. It, too, has expanded significantly from its vineyards of 1970, when there were approximately 5000 acres, of which 3300 stood in New South Wales. Much Sémillon has been sold misnamed as Hunter Valley Riesling, but such misappellation was not necessary: the wine was regarded as "the most distinctive and readily distinguished regional wine style in Australia."[9] Indeed, the Sémillon produces interesting Australian white wine, and not only from the Hunter; it grows extensively in South Australia and in the Murray River's irrigated areas as well. It is vinted and sold as a varietal and blended with other whites, including the Trebbiano, and reaches the consumer under an almost endless variety of labels ranging from the specific (such as the St. Leonards 1981 Sémillon) through the erroneous (Wyndham Estate Hunter River Riesling) to the "White Burgundy" versions.

Since far more white wine is made in Australia than red, the lower-ranking white cultivars assume considerably more importance as part of the total crush than do the lesser reds. Among widely planted whites, the Trebbiano also is gaining, its juice put to various uses, including some small varietal bottling. The Palomino and Pedro Ximenez, Australia's Sherry-wine grapes, continue to contribute significantly, although they were more prominent during the fortified-wine era. The Doradillo,

RHINE RIESLING

VINTAGE:	1977
BIN:	231
VARIETY:	Rhine Riesling
BOTTLED:	May, 1977
GROWING AREA:	Coonawarra and Eden Valley

CHIEF WINEMAKERS COMMENTS:
A premium Australian Rhine Riesling showing a fresh, flowery bouquet and crisp, full flavour.
The grapes were grown at Coonawarra and Eden Valley, two of the cooler wine growing areas of Australia, renowned for producing wines of great varietal character. The combination of growing areas and the grape type used has produced a wine with a delightful Rhine Riesling character.

PENFOLDS WINES PTY. LTD.
SYDNEY & ADELAIDE
PRODUCE OF AUSTRALIA

F/10068   **750 ml**

This Penfold label provides information concerning a varietal wine that has gained in popularity in Australia. Especially in the cooler areas, the Rhine Riesling has done well, and its acreage has expanded considerably.

the prolific vine of the irrigated areas that yields mainly distilling wine for brandy making, also has recorded a proportional decline, but it remains among the top ten whites.

Again the emergence of a noble white cultivar exemplifies the modern era, just as Cabernet Sauvignon has among the reds. Around 1970 only a few Chardonnay vines were in Australia, and some of these were not even recognized as such until ampelographic research proved their ancestry. In the late 1960s Max Lake and Murray Tyrrell, two leaders of the Hunter Valley region, planted these newly identified Chardonnays in their vineyards. As was the case with the Cabernet, this experiment was closely watched and widely emulated. Soon the suitability of the Chardonnay under a variety of Australian environments was confirmed, and today the range of this noble grape extends from New South Wales to the Margaret River district of Western Australia and from the Upper Hunter Valley to Tasmania. Its wines already rank among Australian winemakers' most noteworthy achievements, although a variety of styles is produced that range from Burgundy-like, oaked, and bottle-aged wines to early drinking, fresh types that have not been aged in wood at all; sparkling,

Champagne-style wines and even some sweet Chardonnays also have appeared on the market. The more delicate Chardonnays are made from grapes grown in the cooler districts, but even in the irrigated, warmer regions the grape yields good wines. From the Murrumbidgee Irrigated Area (where about one-quarter of the total Chardonnay acreage stood in the early 1980s) the Orlando winery produces low-priced, very good Chardonnay varietals that have put this premium wine within reach of many consumers for whom the premium, cool-region wines would be too expensive. Nor has the Hunter Valley lost its pride of place: Tyrrell's Chardonnays have outranked noted Burgundies and California Chardonnays at international tastings. The Chardonnay is on its way to primacy among Australia's quality white wines.

The success of—and preoccupation with—the Chardonnay has perhaps obscured the potentials of other noble white grapes. Remarkable success also has been achieved with the Chenin Blanc, especially in Western Australia; with the Gewürztraminer (nearly 30 percent of which stand, notably, in the warm-climate Murrumbidgee Irrigated Area); and with the Sauvignon Blanc in South Australia, among other less common white varieties. The technology exists, the viticultural possibilities are now being exploited, and the potentials are virtually limitless.

Regions and Areas

In South Africa, Chile, and even in Argentina and Brazil an environmental thread links the wine districts, and it is possible to summarize a regional geography of the winelands. Such generalization is impractical in continental Australia. Such is the patchwork of clustered and far-flung wine regions downunder that even the regional nomenclature presents problems, especially for the outsider but even in Australia itself. A cursory comparison of the maps in popular wine guides will emphasize the point: no two are exactly the same. In part this is another reflection of the changing Australian wine scene: districts that appear on a map of 1985 may not show on a 1970 map—because they did not exist fifteen years ago. But the fundamental problem is not just a matter of time and flux. Considering the enormous asset of strong regional name identity for the wine industries of France, California, and South Africa (among others), the absence of a tight *appellation d'origine* system, even in tentative form, will constitute a major disadvantage to Australia's wine industry and its products on the world market in decades hence.

Certainly there is regional identity and specialization in Australian winegrowing, and in Mudgee (New South Wales), Margaret River and Mount Barker (Western Australia) lie Australia's first appellations. Several Australian wine regions are historic and time-honored; others are marked by particular natural environments, cultural traditions and landscapes, or viticultural adaptation, or some combination of these. The Hunter Valley and the Barossa Valley are undoubtedly the best-known Australian wine regions, based on these factors and of course the wines they have long produced. But the Barossa Valley is in comparative decline (if not apparently "headed for oblivion," as suggested by an Australian specialist); and the Hunter Valley is now mapped as the *Lower* Hunter Valley, following the emergence of winegrowing in the Upper Hunter Valley.[10] Even the established regions are not immune to the forces of change. What follows, therefore, is an assessment of the situation in the mid-1980s, in the context of continued variation in time and place.

The political geography of Australia begins with the familiar map that divides the country, mainly by geometric boundaries, into eight units of which six, including Tasmania, are states and two are federal territories (one for the capital, Canberra). Only one boundary is mainly physiographic or natural: that between New South Wales and Victoria, defined by the Murray River. Since vineyards lie on both sides of the river in its extensive basin, the political boundary here cuts across a viticultural region of substantial uniformity. Thus, there is far more difference between viticultural environments of southern Victoria and northern Victoria than there is between northern Victoria and southern New South Wales in the Murray Valley. The districts of the Murray Valley may be said to form part of a viticultural region that not only extends into New South Wales and Victoria, but westward into South Australia as well. The Berri and Barmera areas' irrigated vineyards sustain the pattern that, in fact, continues until after the Murray turns southward near Cadell.

Neither does the boundary between South Australia and Victoria form a satisfactory viticultural delimitation. It is true, as Figure 1.7 indicates, that a climatic transition occurs in this general area; the dry-summer Mediterranean pattern of the Adelaide hinterland (Csa / b) gives way to the more continuous moisture of the Melbourne area (Cfb). In very general terms this is the type of transition that also marks the California-Oregon wine regions. The orientation of the approximate climatic transition zone differs, of course, from the north-south (or, as in the case of California-Oregon, east-west) straight-line boundary. Victoria's westernmost vineyards of importance, at Drumborg, display microclimatic conditions similar to those prevailing in South Australia, although total rainfall (32 inches) is somewhat higher and the summer-dry regime less pronounced or dependable.

Any attempt to establish a regional framework for Australia's wine regions is likely to involve drawbacks, which is why discussions of Australian wine regions and their wines tend to consist of area-by-area enumerations, sometimes by state, occasionally simply alphabetically. In the following discussion, the wine areas are grouped on the basis of environment, viticulture practice, and proximity into Southeast South Australia, Eastern New South Wales, the Murray Basin, Victoria, Western Australia, Tasmania, and Queensland. This scheme retains some reference to the familiar political map while accommodating the salient environmental realities. (Fig. 8.2).

Southeast South Australia

South Australia is the country's leading wine state. More wine is made in South Australia than in all other wine regions combined, and the state also leads in terms of quality. Excellent premium wines are made elsewhere also, but not in South Australia's range and quantity. As the map (Figure 8.2) reveals, the major wine districts of the state are concentrated in the wedge-shaped area that constitutes its southeastern corner. Here the coastline turns south-southeast, creating a zone of cool-weather Mediterranean climate. Here, too, the Murray River enters South Australia near Renmark, its waters diverted through irrigation canals through

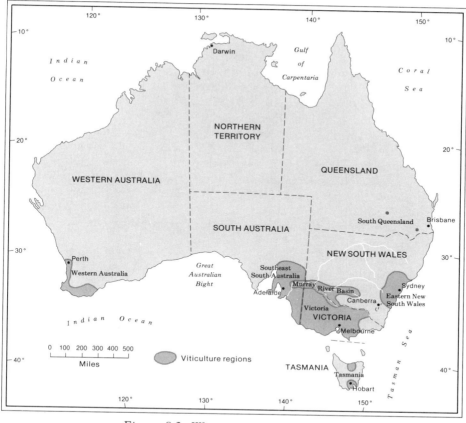

Figure 8.2. Wine regions of Australia.

thousands of acres of vineyards. The high yields obtained in these irrigated areas contribute importantly to South Australia's voluminous harvest.

The regional geography of southeast South Australia incorporates some of the country's most famous wine districts (the term "district" is here used in the informal sense and not, as in South Africa, as a legal designation). Vines were planted in what is today North Adelaide as early as 1837, and the city's environs have constituted a wine district ever since. Not long afterward the Barossa Valley was opened up, and the Barossa became one of the country's most famous names. The modern table-wine era has witnessed the emergence of other South Australian districts, several of them old and venerable but rejuvenated by modern technology and changing preferences. The Southern Vales south of Adelaide is one of these, as are the Clare Valley and nearby Watervale (often grouped as a single district) north of the Barossa, and the Coonawarra and Keppoch districts in the far south. Although the Murray River vineyards (the Upper Murray district, as it is called in South Australia) lie in the state as well, they will be discussed as part of the Murray Basin region.

THE ADELAIDE HINTERLAND

Winegrowing in the Adelaide area has been a story of success but also of stress and strain. It is an Australian version of sequence of events played out near many a city: older vineyards and wineries whose names are etched in the history of the region are engulfed by urban growth. Near Adelaide, C. R. Penfold, R. Hamilton, and J. Reynell planted their first vines; from the Magill vineyards came grapes that went into the first famed Grange Hermitage wines. The old Grange cottage, near the original Penfold winery, was built in the 1840s and gave its name to the wine. In 1982 it and what remained of the Magill property became the focus of a battle between developers and conservationists. The issue attracted much attention, but many other similar disputes already had been decided in favor of the former. Among major cities of the world only Vienna has more urban vineyards than Adelaide, but Adelaide has been less able to stem the tide of suburbanization. By 1984, most of the Grange vineyard had been pulled out.

Such events notwithstanding, winegrowing survives in the Adelaide hinterland, from the very margins of the city to the west-facing slopes of the mountains (Lofty and Barker and their foothills) that separate the Adelaide area from the lower Murray Valley. Indeed, the oft-relocated wineries and vineyards have begun to form a district extending from Angle Vale in the north to Marion in the south. More than a dozen wineries stand in the urban shadow, some of them branches of firms with larger establishments elsewhere. Others, such as Stonyfell and Hamilton, were headquartered here before their takeover by larger companies. Stonyfell long has exported to England the wines for which the Adelaide area was best known, Port- and Sherry-styles. Today the district also yields very good dry white and red table wines, sparkling whites, and rosés. Thus, while the Adelaide Plains (as the general area is sometimes called) is not one of South Australia's leading wine districts, it has a rich history and holds much interest for those concerned with the dynamic relationship between city and vineyard on the urban fringe.

THE BAROSSA VALLEY

The name Barossa is legendary in Australian winegrowing. For more than a century the Barossa Valley was the focus of viniculture, beacon of the industry, epitome of success. The Barossa Valley was more than a wine district: it became a national treasure, a pocket of German-Australian culture and tradition graced by a unique landscape and atmosphere. Even today the Barossa Valley, its towns and wineries, foodways and festivals, vineyards and wines reflect a history of pioneering and determination. A leading Australian oenologist recently praised "the cleanliness and order of the valley . . . a lesson to the rest [of Australia]."[11]

The Barossa Valley's primacy endured for many years, and the great names of the Barossa were the great names of Australian winegrowing (Fig. 8.3). Johann Gramp planted the first vines in 1847; Joseph Seppelt founded a winery in the valley in the early 1850s. Others followed, strengthening the Silesian connection and creating a cultural landscape steeped in German tradition. The spires of Lutheran churches rose above the villages, the wineries were images of home, and the names

The Barossa Valley is one of Australia's best-known wine districts, and perhaps still the leading name overseas. Viticulture dominates the economic landscape. Competition, conservatism, and changing preferences now threaten the Barossa's future among leading viticulture districts.

on the wine map, from Siegersdorf to Bernkastel and from Kaiser Stuhl to Seppeltsfield, gave the geography of the Barossa a special flavor. And the valley's wines were much admired, first its brandies and fortifieds (including some notable Port-styles) and later its table wines. With the Hunter Valley, the Barossa Valley was the most famous wine region of Australia; these two districts were Australia's Bordeaux and Burgundy, its Napa and Sonoma, its Stellenbosch and Paarl.

But times have changed, and the Barossa has lost its lead. It is not that the valley no longer produces premium wines: the best of the Barossa still are noteworthy achievements. Several of South Australia's other wine districts, however, have emerged as competitors for Barossa's winegrowers, and now Coonawarra, Clare-Watervale, the Southern Vales, Keppoch-Padthaway, and other names are associated with the quality-wine field once dominated by the Barossa. Such are the potentials for these districts that dire predictions are being made for the Barossa's ultimate decline. A recent projection holds that the valley's 20,000 acres of vines (1983) will dwindle to a mere 3500 by the year 2001, a decline to be matched by expansion in the neighboring Eden Valley, the Clare district, the area from Padthaway to Coonawarra, and several districts in the adjacent state of Victoria.[12]

These forecasts may be premature (the Hunter Valley, too, has gone through periods that seemed sure to signal its demise), but there can be no doubt that the Barossa's hegemony is over. To some degree the very conservatism etched in the valley's landscape is to blame for this, because Barossa growers were reluctant to replace dependable, productive cultivars with newer and nobler varieties when the

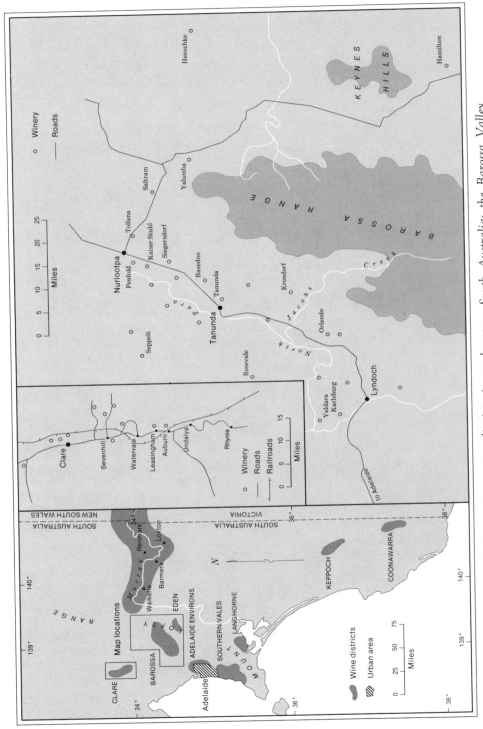

Figure 8.3. *Two winegrowing districts in southeastern South Australia: the Barossa Valley (right) and the Clare-Watervale District.*

The historic Seppelt Winery, dating from the 1850s, lies in the heart of the Barossa Valley.

modernization of the 1950s gained momentum. But the fundamental reason lies in the physical geography of the South Australian wine triangle. Other districts proved to possess more extensive areas of the desired microclimates than did the Barossa, and in combination these began to overshadow the old heartland of South Australian viticulture. In the meantime, the Barossa's regional identity faded in the crush of thousands of tons of grapes imported from other regions.

Yet the Barossa Valley in the 1980s remains a notable and interesting wine district, and not for historic reasons alone. More so than the Hunter Valley, the Barossa over large areas displays a true monoculture, the vineyards carpeting the valley and resting against the surrounding slopes. The valley proper is not large, varying in width from about two to seven miles and extending inland for some twenty miles, flanked by the Barossa Mountains. The main stream in the district is the North Para River, which flows southeast through the valley to elbow westward near Rowland Flat (Fig. 8.3). The Barossa lies about thirty miles northeast of Adelaide, and about the same distance inland from the Gulf of St. Vincent; the Yorke Peninsula across the Gulf further separates the valley from the open sea. Thus the Barossa and the Clare Valley to the north contrast with Coonawarra and environs to the south, a situation that is expressed by the comparative heat summations. Nuriootpa's total is 2838°F.; Clare to the north records 3231, and Coonawarra in the Southern triangle averages 2175, evincing a cool ripening season indeed. Coonawarra's reading reflects not only its higher and therefore cooler latitude, but also its greater exposure to maritime influences.

Certainly the Barossa's microclimates are moderate, ranging from high region II to low region III, readings familiar to winegrowers in California's Napa Valley.

A SOUVENIR OF THE BAROSSA VALLEY

The Semillon and Rhine Riesling grapes which produce
this wine make it a pleasant, slightly sweet table wine that
is young, fresh and crisp.

The 1974 vintage wine is suitable for consumption with
any food or for pleasant drinking anytime.

PENFOLDS WINES PTY. LTD. ADELAIDE
WINE MADE IN AUSTRALIA
750ml

F/10068

*Tourism has come to play a major role in the economy
of the Barossa Valley. The response has been to cater
to the stream of visitors in various ways, including the
production of "souvenir" wines under labels of which
this is an example.*

But the district's relative decline has more to do with entrenched tradition and rising competition than with environmental limitations. A pattern of grape importing developed when company wineries found local growers reluctant to replant their vineyards, so that "Barossa" wine very often was bottled in, but not grown by, Barossa winemakers. In time the district's distinctive traditions became a substitute: tourism now is a pervasive industry in the valley, and not just the wines but also the food, music, dress, and feasts attract the visitors. Catering to this influx has become an alternative to premium winegrowing for many a winery faced with market challenges from South Australia's "upstart" quality regions. The larger company wineries do include fine wines among those sold on their premises, but these may not all be Barossa Valley wines. Orlando, Penfold, and Seppelt have large establishments in the district, but what remains of the Barossa's regional identity is best revealed by the small and exclusively Barossa-vineyard wineries.

Today the Barossa's familiar names—Krondorf, Yalumba, Hardy's Siegersdorf, Hoffmanns, Bernkastel—produce an astounding array of wines, including "Champagnes," "Rhine Rieslings," "Spätleses," "Moselles," "Sauternes," "Clarets," "Sherries," "Ports," and "Burgundies," along with tourist-appeal "Passionwein" and, in ultimate imitation, a *Schillerwein*. Many of these "Barossa" wines come from grapes grown in vineyards far from the famous valley proper, and in such profusion of labels and styles the identity of the Barossa is lost.

Several smaller wine districts lie east of the Barossa Valley, including the Eden Valley, often characterized as merely a part of the Barossa when in fact it is not. Several noteworthy wineries lie in this eastern arc of smaller vineyard areas, including Wolf Blass northeast of Nuriootpa, and Henschke and Mount Adam in the Eden Valley on the east side of the Barossa Range (see Fig. 8.3). Henschke proves with Shiraz, Cabernet Sauvignon, and Riesling what can be achieved in this area, and Mount Adam is now making some of Australia's finest (and most expensive) table wines.

THE CLARE VALLEY

About fifty miles north-northwest of the Barossa Valley lies the Clare Valley, farther inland than the Barossa, warmer, and yet recognized increasingly for its capacity to yield premium wines. The vineyard area extends from the vicinity of the town of Clare southward beyond Watervale, so that the district often is referred to as Clare-Watervale (see Figure 8.3). This is a hilly area, with elevations of 1000 to 1500 feet, producing some microclimates with lower heat summations than that of Clare itself. The climatic regime is Mediterranean with an average of about 25 inches of rain annually. Viticulture here is old (the first vines were planted in the 1840s), and several of the district's wineries, notably Sevenhills and Quelltaler, have long histories. Clare's rise to prominence is more recent. In the past, winegrowers sold most of their harvests to large corporate wineries, but when Australian preferences changed, the district's potential for premium wines brought a new era. The number of wineries increased, and as the Clare's wines gained national recognition, the district came to be called the "Hunter of the South," in appreciation of its long-lived reds and fine whites. Like the Hunter Valley, the acreage of Cabernet Sauvignon has expanded, proportionally at the expense of the Shiraz; but unlike the Hunter, the Clare's Rieslings are true Rhine Riesling wines, not Sémillons.

As elsewhere in South Australia, and indeed in Australia generally, the pattern of winemaking in the Clare District continues to change. In the mid-1970s there were just a half dozen wineries, but today that number has tripled; smaller wineries have been absorbed by larger companies, while new ventures have achieved remarkable success in a short time. The Stanley Wine Company, for example, maker of noted wines, was taken over by the huge Heinz corporation. This led one of the winemakers at Stanley to establish his own small winery, Enterprise, which is known already for its deep, fruity reds and highly individual, interesting whites. The latter, including an oak-aged Sauvignon Blanc and a pleasantly spicy Gewürztraminer, prove the capacities of the Clare Valley.

Long-range predictions for the Clare District suggest that vineyard expansion

CABERNET SHIRAZ
1975 VINTAGE

This wine, an equal blend of Cabernet Sauvignon & Shiraz, was made from selected Clare Valley grapes and aged for 12 months in new American Oak puncheons before bottling in October 1976. We recommend 4-5 years cellaring to realize its full potential.

GOLD MEDAL   CLARET CLASS   ADELAIDE 1975
SILVER MEDAL   CLARET CLASS   CANBERRA 1975

CLARE VALLEY WINE
PRODUCED & CELLARED BY ENTERPRISE WINES 2 PIONEER AVENUE CLARE SOUTH AUSTRALIA

Enterprise Wines proves what the Clare Valley is capable of producing. The winery's reds as well as whites have been awarded numerous medals. Its Cabernet-Shiraz blend, an Australian specialty, is a fine example of the style.

will continue, perhaps to double the acreage by the end of the century (perhaps to as much as 10,000 acres), and that the number of wineries also will continue to grow. Already, there are wineries as far south of Clare as Auburn (so that the district might well be called Clare-Auburn rather than Clare-Watervale). The hills and valleys of this favored area, with its equable climate and valued calcareous subsoil, are among South Australia's finest settings for premium winegrowing, although declining rainfall with increasing distance from Clare does constitute a problem.

THE SOUTHERN VALES

South of the Adelaide area lies McLaren Vale and the adjacent McLaren Flat, a district that (with its surroundings) also is called the Southern Vales or, simply, the Southern District (Fig. 8.4). The topography of this area does not resemble the

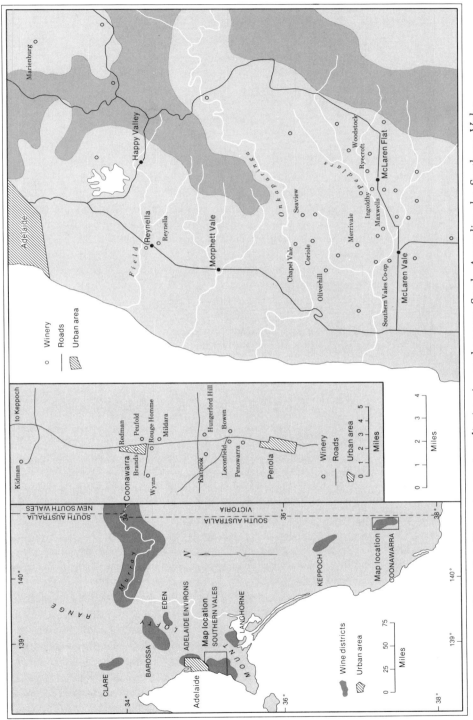

Figure 8.4. Two winegrowing districts in southeastern South Australia: the Southern Vales (right) and the Coonawarra District.

well-defined valley of the Barossa; rather, the countryside is gently rolling in the basins of several streams, among which Pedlar's Creek and its tributaries are the most important. The Southern Vales lie about sixty miles south of the Barossa Valley, and thus their location relative to the bay-indented coastline is rather different; the Mediterranean climatic regime prevails, and heat summations in this district vary, on an average, rather widely around 3400°F.

Again unlike the Barossa and its German-Silesian imprint, the McLaren District is of mainly English heritage. The vintage is celebrated during an annual "bushing" ceremony highlighted by Elizabethan feasts, and among names on the map are those of Maxwells, Woodstock, Chapel Vale, and Oliverhill. Undoubtedly the most famous historic name associated with this district is John Reynell, who planted vines he had acquired at Cape Town on his farm in 1838 and vinted his first wines in 1843. Development has been almost uninterrupted since, but the district really came into its own during the past decade as its wines gained recognition and (so important on the Australian scene) prizes at official tastings. In the process the district also has expanded geographically, extending today from north of the village of Happy Valley near Reynella to well south of the town of McLaren Vale. Its northern margins now lie barely ten miles south of Adelaide (and several McLaren winegrowers are escapees from urban encroachment), and the viticultural pattern has undergone quite radical change in recent years. Urbanization continues to erode the vineyards nearer Adelaide. In the early 1960s there were perhaps a dozen wine establishments in the district, including two large companies (Hardy and Reynella) and a handful of small family wineries. By the mid-1970s that number had grown to forty, including the only cooperative in the district, Southern Vales Co-operative Winery at McLaren Vale, established in 1965 by 185 grapegrowers in the Southern Vales and now a proprietary winery. In the mid-1980s there were well over 100 wineries and vineyard operations in the district, testimony to the market in Australia (and overseas) for good red wine.

Indeed it is premium red table wine for which the Southern District has become well known, but other quality wines are produced here as well. Good Rhine Rieslings, including late-harvest styles of note, Chardonnays, and Sauvignon Blancs are made by wineries, some of which are more appreciated for their Cabernet Sauvignons, Shiraz, and blends. Once known for bulk-export production and fortified wines, the Southern Vales still can produce some noteworthy Port- and Sherry-style wines, among which the vintage "Ports" form Hardy and Reynella rank high.

But the most interesting of the McLaren Vale's wines are those from the small wineries that maximize and thus reflect the district's viticultural potentials. The Cabernet and Shiraz varietals from Coriole, Daringa, Ingoldby, Osborn, Ryecroft, Seaview (an early, larger producer of McLaren reds that attracted national attention), Settlement, Bleasdale, Woodstock, and Coolawin are among these rich, fruity, often ink-dark wines of great balance and longevity that will, as cellar investments, enhance the reputation of the Southern Vales for decades to come.

COONAWARRA

The name Coonawarra symbolizes the new era of Australian winegrowing. Here, deep in the southeastern "wedge" of South Australia and very near the border with

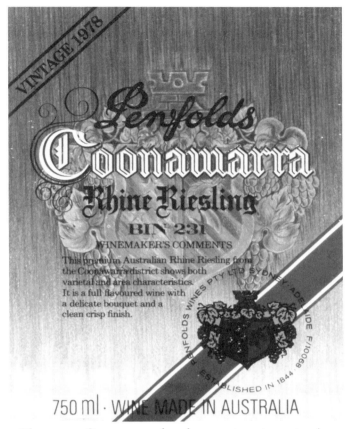

The name Coonawarra has become prominent in Australian winegrowing. The district's cool conditions and the delicacy of its wines have attracted winegrowers and consumers alike.

Victoria, lies a minuscule wine district of maximal interest and importance. Just one mile wide and a mere eight miles in length, and extending approximately north-south, centered on the village of Coonawarra, this district is as well defined as any in Australia (see Figure 8.4). A clearly circumscribed patch of red soil, underlain by a calcareous substratum and vitalized by a permanently accessible water table, has transformed this strip of gray-brown, Eucalyptus-studded countryside into a verdant oasis of vines. With its lowest of heat summations (a Burgundy-like 2175°F. at Coonawarra), this district is unique in Australian viticulture.

Vineyards were established quite early in the vicinity of the district. John Riddoch, a pioneer-farmer, established a winery near the town of Penola in the 1890s, and by several vintages before the turn of the century proved what was possible there. But the market for quality table wines was too small, and Riddoch's inventories kept growing, so upon his death in 1901, much excellent table wine was sold for distillation into brandy! Yet, in a sense, Riddoch left a legacy, because one of the workers in his winery, William Redman, shared his vision of a wine district at Coonawarra and persevered when other winegrowers abandoned the vine and turned to fruit and vegetable growing. Redman bought a parcel of Riddoch's estate and, convinced that Coonawarra would some day achieve the recognition it deserved, persisted in growing grapes, selling part of the harvest to distillers and marketing his wines through distributors, the only recognizably Coonawarra wine to be sold commercially. Redman lived to see his dream come true. After the end of World War II, in 1947, a Redman Claret won first prize in Adelaide, and from then on his name—and that of Coonawarra—were bywords in Australian wine circles and gained fame around the world. In the year of William Redman's retirement, the *Rouge Homme* label was introduced, and in 1965 the winery and its now-famous label were sold to the large Lindeman firm.

Today Coonawarra is the scene of competition among wineries large and small. All the large corporate wineries wanted a Coonawarra holding or connection (which is why Lindeman bought *Rouge Homme*), and the map resembles a Who's Who of Australian winemaking. Not only Lindeman, but also Seppelt, Hardy, Wynn, Penfold, and Mildara have their stakes in the district. But the invasion of the giants did not eliminate the smaller growers. William Redman's son Owen established his own Redman Winery after the Lindeman takeover, and his wines, a Cabernet Sauvignon and a Shiraz "Claret," exemplify the magnificent reds of Coonawarra.

Coonawarra's cool summers and long ripening seasons make for great wines in the best vintage years, when the Mediterranean regime keeps its promise and the summers are long and moderate. Here in the far south, however, the climatic risks do increase, principally late-season rain and early-season frost. In the best years, the grapes develop a combination of high acid, sugar, and tannins that yields truly classic reds to endure and improve for decades.

It is something of an irony that a substantial part of the Coonawarra harvest is taken, as grapes or as juice, out of the district to the wineries of McLaren Vale, Barossa, and elsewhere for vinting, blending, and/or bottling. Modern technology makes it possible, but there is something contradictory about it. Hence the journey to Coonawarra reaps rewards especially in the small wineries. Bowen Estate and Leconfield, positioned opposite each other just north of Penola, both produce not only memorable Cabernets but also interesting, generous Rhine Rieslings; Laira markets respected Cabernet and Shiraz; Katnook Estate is noted for its Riesling, Chardonnay, Gewürztraminer, and Sauvignon Blanc; and northerly-located Kidman produces an unusual "Great Red Wine of Coonawarra," a Cabernet-Shiraz blend that has attracted some attention.

Such are the environmental advantages of the Coonawarra District that the greatest threat to quality lies not in nature, but in viticulture practice. Coonawarra has been afflicted by what is called the "riverland mentality"—overproduction at the expense of quality. Soil, slope, climate, and above all the available subsurface water enable Coonawarra's vines to yield huge harvests. Only careful pruning will control the yield and sustain the intensity for which Coonawarra grapes are known at their best. The heyday of the 1960s and the inflation of Coonawarra values led some winegrowers to harvest excessive per-acre quantities of grapes, and this, during the 1970s, caused a decline in wine quality and damaged Coonawarra's reputation. Not until the 1980s did the district emerge from these years of disappointing vintages, and a new boom period has commenced as a result.

Coonawarra's small wineries hold special interest, but several larger company wineries have had much to do with the district's success. Lindeman's acquisition of *Rouge Homme* was a major event; it has been known for some years that Penfold's famous St. Henri Claret has been made substantially from Coonawarra Cabernet Sauvignon. But perhaps the most intimately associated company name is that of Wynn. Coonawarra's rise to prominence was due in substantial measure to the advocacy of David Wynn, who after World War II began a campaign to bring the district and its potential to the attention of Australian wine consumers. Then Wynn made a major investment in Coonawarra, an action by the powerful, Melbourne-based firm that gave substance to all the earlier claims. Since then, Wynn has itself been taken over by the Toohey Corporation, but the company's name continues in the wine field; Wynn's Coonawarra Estate wines are marketed extensively overseas. Wynn and Coonawarra constitute an historic and effective association.

On the wine map of South Australia, Coonawarra no longer lies alone in the state's southeastern wedge. About 40 miles north of the district, near the towns of Padthaway and Keppoch, lies a smaller but developing viticulture district bearing some environmental similarities to Coonawarra. Here several major wine companies also have established vineyards, the grapes (Cabernet Sauvignon, Shiraz, Riesling, some Sylvaner, Gewürztraminer, and Pinot Noir) transported for fermentation to other districts. Already there are several thousand acres of plantings in the Padthaway-Keppoch area, but it is too early to tell whether here, too, will emerge a major South Australian wine district in the complete sense.

While the great majority of South Australia's vineyards and wineries are situated in the leading districts just described, there are numerous small and comparatively isolated winegrowing locales—sometimes consisting of just a single vineyard maintained by a grower who is determined to prove its capacity. Among the larger of these is the Langhorne Creek area just north of the estuary into which the Murray River flows, Lake Alexandrina. There are just three wineries here, specializing in red table wines and Port-style wines, but producing in addition a surprisingly large range of other wines. The Langhorne Creek area is no upstart district; the Bleasdale winery has been in the same family since 1860 and Metala (under various names) since 1890. Another example is the tiny Wakefield River Estates near Balaklava, due east of the tip of the Gulf of St. Vincent, a vineyard without winery, but whose wines, fermented and bottled by an established firm, have achieved recognition. South Australia has an established wine industry, but viticultural frontiers still exist.

As a wine region, Southeast South Australia is the country's premier producer, its district wines representative of the best the country can yield. Importantly, the region never was afflicted by *phylloxera*, and with Chile it remains the only major Southern Hemisphere region so blessed. *Phylloxera* reached Australia in the 1870s; it was detected near Geelong, Victoria, in November 1877. It spread northeast, striking the Rutherglen area in 1895 in an onslaught that petered out in New South Wales. Whatever the reasons, South Australia remained untouched. Perhaps the climatic patterns, or possibly the isolation of vineyard districts, protected the region against the scourge of the century. Undoubtedly the legal restrictions against any movement of vines outside the phylloxerated area also were effective.

But at times nature seems determined to withdraw its favors. In February and March 1983, the wine districts of South Australia were subjected to terrible bushfires, followed by torrential rains and devastating floods. The bushfires threatened Coon-awarra, but did far more damage at Clare and in the hills of the Southern Vales. Many rows of vines in the Clare District were burned, and there was much smoke and heat damage where the vines themselves were not destroyed. Then the storms came, breaking the drought that had fanned the flames, attended by high winds and brutal hail and, inevitably, floods. In the Barossa Valley, the North Para River overflowed its banks in a ferocious wall of water that devastated vineyards, smashed winery equipment, contaminated stored wine, and broke thousands of bottles of wine. Mud filled the cellars; cardboard-boxed wines disintegrated and lost their labels. Hoffmanns, Tollana, and Chateau Leonay (where more than 10,000 gallons of wine were lost) suffered the most, but in the Barossa as a whole more than 250 acres of vineyard were wiped out, and the entire vintage was afflicted. Winegrowers from Clare to Coonawarra predicted that the effects of nature's 1983 assault would still be felt in the 1984 vintage. Those who lost substantial vine acreage will feel the effect much longer: the replanted vineyards will not begin to bear until the end of the decade.

Eastern New South Wales

New South Wales is the pioneer wine state of Australia, scene of the first attempts at viticulture, and site of the earliest vintages. Lessons learned in New South Wales were applied in Victoria and South Australia, and eventually the early lead was lost. But winegrowing in the old settings continues, and the Hunter Valley remains not only the premier wine district of New South Wales, but one of the prime viticulture districts in all of Australia.

The region defined as Eastern New South Wales incorporates not only the venerable Hunter Valley, but also the younger Upper Hunter Valley, where wine-growing has diffused, the Mudgee District, and a number of lesser viticulture areas scattered widely throughout the eastern part of the state. These include the Rooty Hill District, in the urban shadow of Sydney, once an area of promise but now being overtaken by urban sprawl; the area around the town of Young, near the source of the Lachlan River, a fruit-producing zone where vines in certain locales yield well; Cowra, near the middle of the state, where experimental viticulture has met with considerable success, although no local wineries have yet been established; and individual vineyards widely scattered from Cobbitty near Sydney to Forbes and beyond. Not included in this wine region are the vineyards of the Murrumbidgee and Murray areas in the south, which form part of the Murray Basin Region.

THE HUNTER VALLEY

About 100 miles north of Sydney lies the Hunter Valley, one of the country's most famous wine districts (Fig. 8.5). Far enough from the great city to be safe from urban encroachment but close enough to benefit from its large market, the Hunter always has had a close relationship with the state capital. The failure of early viticulture on the shore of Port Jackson and the banks of the Parramatta River

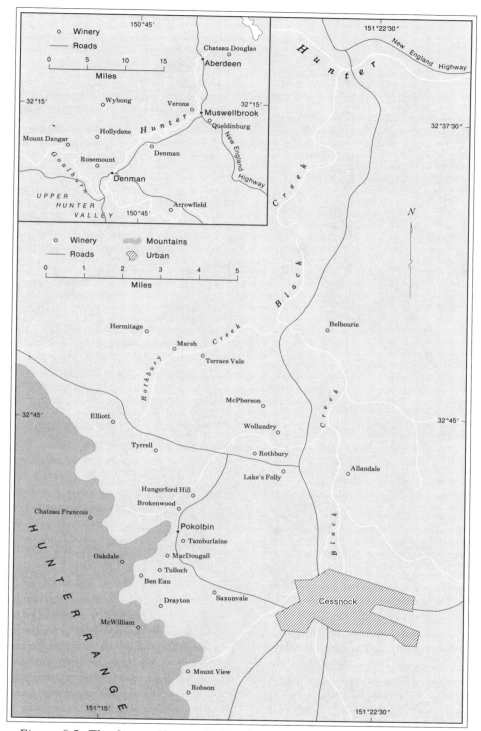

Figure 8.5. The Lower Hunter Valley (large map) and the Upper Hunter Valley, eastern New South Wales winegrowing districts.

The Lower Hunter Valley presents one of Australia's most beautiful and characterful viticultural landscapes. Eucalyptus-studded and graced by mainly modest winery establishments, the Hunter is an oasis in eastern New South Wales.

extended the search for suitable environments; the first wines were taken to Sydney by boat even as capital flowed from Sydney's banks to the Hunter. The valley's fortunes rose and fell as boom followed bust, and more than once the district seemed headed for extinction. Today, once again, the Hunter thrives—not by virtue of quantity, but because of its premium, quality wines.

The Hunter River rises on the east-facing slopes of the Great Dividing Range but actually flows southwest before elbowing eastward below its juncture with the Goulburn River. Before it reaches the ocean just north of Newcastle, the river develops a meander course in a wide basin crossed by numerous tributaries. In the southern segment of this basin, about 30 miles inland, lies the wine district that has made the Hunter Valley famous, centered on Pokolbin and Rothbury villages and served by the town of Cessnock. The Upper Hunter Valley District, around the town of Muswellbrook, lies some 50 miles farther into the interior.

The Hunter Valley (or Lower Hunter Valley, as some now call it) is situated in an unlikely place for quality viticulture, at least in context of the climatic map (see Fig. 1.7). The climate classifies as Cfa, signaling moderate annual (but warm summer) temperatures and a rainfall regime that brings moisture throughout the ripening season. Cessnock's degree-day summation is a staggering 4228°F.; at less than 100 feet above sea level, the elevation cannot contribute to cooling. Frequent and prolonged cloud cover does ameliorate the daily heat, however, and winds from the interior sometimes combat the excessive humidity that threatens damaging mildew and rot. Average annual rainfall at Cessnock is about 28 inches, of which as much as 5 inches, on average, fall during the last two months of the ripening season.

Winegrowing in the Hunter can be a hazardous venture, as numerous problem vintages of recent decades attest. But when conditions are favorable, the Hunter can produce great, memorable wines, complex reds and full-flavored whites that rank with Australia's most distinctive—and with its best. This is ensured by the Hunter's diversity of slope and soil, by its varied microclimates embedded in the dominant regime and, above all, but the magnificent work of the valley's winemakers, of whom several stand among Australia's leading vignerons.

The geography of the Hunter Valley underscores these achievements. Located on the Hunter's red soil from volcanic rock is Tyrrell's Vineyards, where the indefatigable Murray Tyrrell makes medal-winning Chadonnays and traditional, Sémillon-based Hunter Valley "Rieslings." Tyrrell has tried numerous cultivars in his vineyards, including not only Cabernet Sauvignon and Shiraz but also Merlot, Malbec, and Pinot Noir. Tyrrell's 1976 Pinot Noir made world headlines by ranking first at a Paris tasting that included the best from Burgundy itself. Not far away lies (Max) Lake's Folly, where the noted Lake's Folly Cabernet Sauvignon, and more recently an acclaimed Chardonnay of depth and character, are made. The name of Drayton also remains on the map, marking the work of a winegrowing family dating from 1860. Drayton's Bellevue Winery produces noted Shiraz (Hermitage) and old-style white wines. Other pioneer names (Elliott, Robson) continue to grace the Hunter, even when the wineries themselves are no longer owned by descendants of the founding families. Wyndham Estate, established in 1828 and the state's oldest continuing vineyard, is among these. It acquired the Wyndham name in the 1960s, after more than a half-century of Penfold ownership. The Hunter Valley winemaking center of Wyndham's is Hermitage Estate, a winery born of the boom in that decade and purchased in 1978. The energies of Brian McGuigan have led the Hermitage name to the forefront of Hunter winegrowing and commercial success.

The Hunter's geography also reflects the times: large company wineries are establishing long-range production plans, while smaller wineries create distinctive regional styles. Lindeman's Ben Ean Winery, with vineyards first planted in 1870, was acquired by the giant company in 1912 and remains an historic landmark, its identity carefully protected and its wines drawn from vineyards exclusively in the Hunter Valley. Though marketed as Lindeman's "Hunter River Burgundy" and "Hunter River Chablis," these are notable wines, very characteristic of the Hunter region. Mount Pleasant is a McWilliams prestige operation, producing a range of wines of which the "Pinot Hermitage" is perhaps the most interesting. The Rothbury Estate emerged in the late 1960s as a joint venture by a group of Sydney businessmen; its holdings of more than 1000 acres are the largest owned by a single winery in the valley. Tullochs is now owned by Gilbey's, and winemaker Harry Tulloch has established his small Mount View Winery on the southern margin of the district, west of Cessnock. Thus the pattern resembles that of South Australia, as large corporate wineries stand beside small family operations, and accommodation continues.

Not counting vineyard holdings by companies that do not have Hunter Valley wineries, there are nearly thirty operations, large and small, in the Lower Hunter Valley. Many of these were established during the 1970s, including several that have achieved recognition for their faithful regional styles. Allandale, founded in 1977, is of interest for its California-style purchase of high-quality grapes from independent Hunter growers. The vineyard sources are identified on the labels of each varietal wine, so that several different Chardonnays (for example) are released in the same

Famous names on the Hunter map: a rural intersection in the valley.

Sign of the times: the Rothbury Estate is the largest single vineyard holding in the Lower Hunter Valley, born of the boom of earlier years.

vintage year. Brokenwood (1971) is owned by a group of partners, all of whom participate in the winery's operations, and the vineyards are planted exclusively to red grapes for a very limited vintage.[13] Marsh Estate (1971), formerly known as Quentin, produces two characteristic Hunter wines, a Hermitage (from Shiraz) and a fairly representative Sémillon, and a vintage "Port" that is a reminder of old times in the valley. Among other Hunter wineries that represent the district well are Chateau François, Tamburlaine, Terrace Vale, and Wollundry, recent adherents to—and exponents of—a tradition that is more than a century old.

The Hunter Valley is one of Australia's most characterful wine districts, its cultural landscape an epitome of the industry. Modest winery buildings are situated amid meticulously tended vineyards, the ruler-straight rows of green creating a mosaic of oases amid a patchwork of pastureland and stands of Eucalyptus. The valley bluff rises to the southwest, overlooking a gently undulating countryside watered by creeks and punctuated by small dams. The atmosphere is laden with history, but glimpses of the cellars point not to the past, but to the future. The Hunter remains, in the words of one Australian observer, a national treasure.

THE UPPER HUNTER VALLEY

About 50 miles northwest of Pokolbin, as the crow flies, the Hunter River reaches Muswellbrook and, after flowing southwest past Denman, turns east (see Figure 8.5). That segment of the Hunter has become the focus for the wine district known as the Upper Hunter Valley, product of the boom of the 1960s but with a lengthy (if interrupted) viticultural history. A century ago wine was made on Rosemount Estate, and the same vicissitudes that diminished winegrowing in the Lower Hunter temporarily extinguished it in the Upper. But the vine stood near Denman before the great majority of Hunter Valley vineyards were planted.

Although separated by some 50 miles, there are geographic reasons to combine the Lower and Upper Hunter into a single wine district. Not only do they lie in the basin of the same river; the climatic regimes are essentially similar (although the Upper Hunter receives less rain); soils over much (but not all) of the two areas are comparable; and viticultural practices for many vineyards are much the same. Irrigation, the *sine qua non* in the Upper Hunter, occurs also in the Lower Hunter Valley.

But significant differences do exist. While it is true that many Lower Hunter vineyards and wineries were established in the same period that witnessed the emergence of the Upper Hunter operations, there was none of the Lower Hunter's continuity here, none of the historic momentum, and none of the regional association with particular cultivars and wines. Another major point of contrast lies in the varieties of wine produced: the Upper Hunter is basically a white wine–producing district. Here the Sémillon and Rhine Riesling dominate, the Chardonnay is planted extensively, and there is Gewürztraminer, Sauvignon Blanc, and Blanquette. In every winery but one, the white crush exceeds the red. Certainly there are acreages of red grapes, notably Shiraz and Cabernet Sauvignon, but the emphasis is on white wine.

The emphasis, also, has been on volume and on the opportunities created by the wine boom of the 1960s. Wineries sprang up in the Upper Hunter as large companies bought up vineyard land: Arrowfield, Black Hill Cellars, Chateau Douglas, Denman Estates, Hollydene, Horderns Wybong Estate, Mount Dangar, Queldinburg, Richmond Grove, Rosemount Estate, Rosemount Wybong and Verona emerged within little more than a decade. The modern architecture of *nouveau* wineries began to mark the cultural landscape of the Muswellbrook-Denman area. Penfold plunged in with a major investment in more than 600 acres of vineyard land. Mechanization would be the hallmark of this modern wine district.

The end of the boom brought reconsideration and retrenchment. Penfold withdrew, and the largest of the Upper Hunter operations, Arrowfield, seemed about to collapse under a combination of problems, not the least of which was a disastrously rainy 1975 vintage with which its mechanized equipment could not cope. The Upper Hunter learned what the Lower Hunter had experienced so many times: in the ups and downs of winegrowing, the up years are clouded by uncertainty and the down years can threaten to exterminate the whole regional industry.

Today the Upper Hunter has stabilized, although some of the original names no longer appear on the map. Arrowfield has abandoned its scattergun policy and concentrates instead on its best Sémillons and Rieslings. Rosemount Estate is noted for its fine, consistent Rhine Rieslings, after a period of uncertainty. Rosemount's varietal wines, including also Gewürztraminers and Sauvignon Blancs as well as fine Cabernet Sauvignons, have taken the winery to a position of leadership among Upper Hunter Valley wineries. The Upper Hunter is not yet a district for boutique wineries, however. Size and volume remain the keys to strength and survival. It

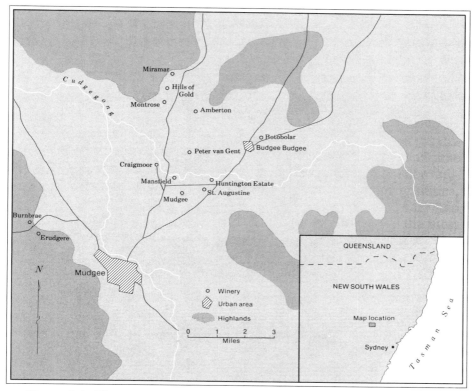

Figure 8.6. The Mudgee District in eastern New South Wales, first wine district to establish an Australian "appellation" system.

may be, as some observers have suggested, that the Upper Hunter is a district of the future, organized and ready for the coming surge in demand for white wines. The potential that generated the boom of the 1960s still exists, but while the Upper Hunter awaits its renaissance it will have time to find direction and develop character.

MUDGEE DISTRICT

The Mudgee wine district, about 135 miles northwest of Sydney (and thus due east and in the same latitude as the Hunter Valley) is one of Australia's most interesting viticulture areas (Fig. 8.6). Grapes are grown among other fruits at elevations averaging 1800 feet, sufficient to cool the subtropical environment and to lengthen the ripening season substantially. Mudgee is an aboriginal word for "nest in the hills," and indeed the area is set in a scenic highland valley. The possibilities for winegrowing here were recognized early: the first vines were planted in the 1850s, when the Roth family name became the synonym for wine in this district. Adam Roth, the first winegrower, timed his venture correctly: when gold was discovered nearby, his wine, grapes and vegetables were in great demand. From the proceeds he was able to install his sons on their own individual properties. In 1880 there were thirteen

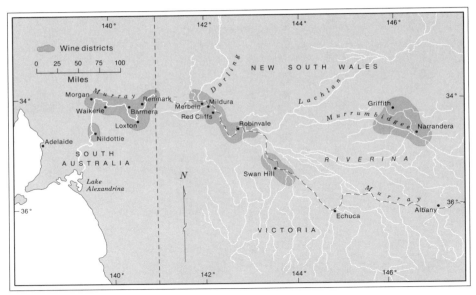

Figure 8.7. Wine districts in the Murray River Basin, Australia.

wineries in and around Mudgee, and six of them belonged to members of the Roth family. Mudgee seemed destined to become the premier wine district in the state.

The early fervor faded, however, and viticulture at Mudgee declined. Most of the Roths turned to other pursuits, as did members of the Kurz family, also pioneers at Mudgee. The anti-German sentiments of World War I, felt so strongly in South Australia, also had their impact here. Rothview, the family winery, was renamed Craigmoor; Fredericksburg, a property owned by Frederick Buckholz, acquired the name Westcourt. In the 1930s only two wineries survived in the Mudgee District.

When the 1950s and 1960s brought revival, Mudgee's viticultural strands were still intact. One especially important remnant was a remaining stand of true Chardonnay, identified in the Kurz vineyard by a visiting French ampelographer. Mudgee became a significant source for Chardonnay rootstock following this discovery; but in the late 1960s there still were only three vineyards in the Mudgee area. Then came the rush of the 1970s, when Mudgee's potentials were rediscovered and the number of wineries grew steadily. Today, a dozen wineries carry individual Mudgee labels, and the district is known especially for their collective effort to create Australia's first *Appellation Controllée* system. Formally introduced in 1978, this scheme ensures peer judgment and control over the district's wines, producing wines of guaranteed origin. It exemplifies what Australia has long needed, and Mudgee will be remembered for having been the first to introduce it.

Mudgee is not a district of giant corporate wineries and vineyard holdings. The (comparatively) small winery prevails here, and in truth the winegrowers have gone their individual ways, so that no real regional styles have come to dominate. Among Mudgee's most interesting wineries is Craigmoor, the recreation of the Roth winery founded in 1858, which produces Cabernet Sauvignon, Shiraz, and Chardonnay varietals that can hold their own with the Hunter's, a Rhine Riesling and Gewürztraminer, and fortifieds that have long kept the winery in business and continue to sell well. The Amberton winery exemplifies what is possible in Mudgee District with careful viticulture and technically up-to-date winemaking: Chardonnays, Cabernets, Shiraz, and Rieslings have won gold medals at district tastings. Huntington Estate represents the best among family ventures in the district, its Chardonnays judged to be the superior style of the appellation. Miramar, Montrose, Botobolar, Burnbrae, Mudgee, Hill of Gold, Mount Vincent Mead, Augustine, Mansfield, and Pieter van Gent all produce wines of interest. Botobolar's Marsanne, Montrose's Bemosa Sauternes, and Peter van Gent's Shiraz reflect the range of quality wines the Mudgee District can produce. Geography has contributed to Mudgee's delayed development, but the breakthrough has now occurred, and Mudgee's place among Australian wine districts is assured.

The Hunter and Mudgee Districts are the quality winegrowing areas of New South Wales, but in terms of volume they are no match for the irrigated regions of the basin of the Murray River and its tributaries. The Hunter crushes about 3 percent of the total Australian harvest. But the Hunter and Mudgee make up in quality and style for what they lack in quantity.

The Murray Basin

The Murray River is the chief artery of a great drainage system that flows essentially westward from the Great Dividing Range. As it traverses its low-relief basin, the river is joined by tributaries from the north and south, that is, from New South Wales and from Victoria, respectively, since it forms the state boundary from the Australian Alps in the east to the border with South Australia in the west. Two of New South Wales's major rivers, the Lachlan and Murrumbidgee, join to flow into the Murray above Mildura. The Goulburn River of Victoria (not to be confused with the Hunter tributary) reaches the Murray from the south. Once in South Australia, the Murray continues westward until, not far beyond Waikerie, it turns abruptly southward to its estuary in Lake Alexandrina (Fig. 8.7).

The Murray system dominates livelihoods in its vast drainage area; the appropriate name Riverina has been given to the southernmost region of New South Wales. Winegrowing is an important element in the agricultural makeup of this physiographic province, and here, from Rutherglen and Murrumbidgee in the east to Waikerie in the west, stand the high-yielding vineyards that produce the bulk of Australia's grapes and wine. Dozens of boutique wineries in the Hunter or McLaren Vale can be outproduced by one massive bloc of irrigated Riverine vineyards. In the Murray Region, Australian winegrowing takes on the aspect of California's Central Valley.

The Murray Region consists of a number of discrete areas and districts, some of them famous names in Australian winegrowing, strung in clusters along the river and its tributaries. They share a dependence on irrigation water, a prevalence of white varieties, a preponderance of high-yielding vines, and a history of fortified-wine production. But in the Murray Region, too, times have changed. Old cultivars have been replaced in response to changing market preferences and, hence, company requirements. Here, in the flatlands of the Murray River basin, the large corporate wineries harvest (or purchase) their huge volumes for mass production. Their investment decisions reflect their projections of what Australia will be drinking in the years and decades to come. Not long ago it would have been unthinkable that more than one-quarter of all Chardonnay acreage in Australia would lie in one Riverina district, the Murrumbidgee Irrigated Area (or M.I.A., as it is often abbreviated). While purists will turn to the Chardonnays of Southeast South Australia, premium cultivars can be grown purposefully in the Murray Basin settings, and thus the average consumer has access to a quality varietal at a moderate price. The Murray Region may be the region of companies and cooperatives, of mass production and bulk vinification, but its wines often are far better than their equivalents in Northern Hemisphere countries such as France and Italy. In terms of market value, they are among the world's best.

MURRUMBIDGEE IRRIGATED AREA (RIVERINA)

This rich and productive fruit district lies centered on the town of Griffith, between the Lachlan and Murrumbidgee rivers in Riverina, New South Wales. This is a district of high heat summations and low rainfall; Griffith records an average of more than 4100 degree-days and an average annual precipitation of 15 inches. Here vines can yield as strongly as any in the world; harvests for lesser varieties grown for distillation purposes can exceed 20 tons per acre. But, as was noted earlier, noble cultivars also stand in Riverina. The district is a patchwork of large-scale corporate viticulture, contract growing (many of the growers are soldier-settlers or their descendants farming their land grants), and smaller but complete winery operations. Several of Australia's giants are here, including Orlando (owners of much of the Chardonnay acreage), Wynn and, most notably, McWilliam. The McWilliam firm operates three wineries in the district, and from its own vineyards as well as a number of carefully monitored contract growers, McWilliam's winemakers secure fruit that yields remarkable wines. McWilliam's Cabernet Sauvignon from this district is well known as one of the industry's best wine values, and a range of whites displays a consistent freshness that belies the tough viticultural environment in which they originate. Among the smaller independent winegrowers who market their own wines, Italian names tend to dominate, and the rather large population of Italian descent forms an appreciative local market.

THE MIDDLE MURRAY VALLEY DISTRICT (SUNRAYSIA)

The Murray River is flanked by vineyards as far east as Rutherglen and beyond, but there, in northeastern Victoria, rainfall, sun, and soil permit unirrigated viticulture, and the grape does not survive by artificial watering alone. Downstream from Echuca the Murray Region takes on its real character, and around Swan Hill begins the pattern that is to prevail into South Australia. Annual rainfall has declined to a mere 10 inches, summers are hot, heat summations exceed 4000°F., and irrigation is no longer a supplementary luxury but, rather, an indispensable necessity.

From the Swan Hill area to below Mildura the great river is flanked by expanses of irrigated vineyards owned by corporations, members of cooperatives, contract growers, and smaller independent operations. Leading among the corporate wineries is Mildara, centered at Merbein near Mildura but with vineyards throughout the area (and a stake also in Coonawarra). Mildara for many years was known for its very good brandy, and it continues to offer fortified wines, but today its line of dry table wines, red and white, commands respect. Mildura Vineyard Wines represents the smaller Murray Region establishment (and the New South Wales side of the river as well, as it lies on the right bank), producing dry red and white table wines as well as fortified wines.

The major grape-growing areas within the Middle Murray District are clustered in the Mildura-Merbein-Red Cliffs triangle, at Robinvale, and in the Swan Hill and Lake Boga areas, but vineyards can be found almost anywhere along the river's course and within reach of its irrigation waters. The extensive system of irrigation that has turned this region green was laid out by two Canadian experts, George and William Chaffey, who were invited in 1887 by Victoria's government to organize irrigated farming. They chose the sites of Renmark and Mildura, and planned much of the region's agricultural development. It was W. Chaffey who saw the viticultural potentials and, the job completed, established his own vineyard; from this beginning grew Mildara Wines. The region remained a source of distilling wine, coarse fortified wines, and a minority of better high-alcohol styles, and its main reputation was for its enormous yields of grapes per acre. But again the technological revolution brought change and progress. The Lindeman firm in 1973 purchased a large bloc of vineyard land above Red Cliffs, and at Karadoc constructed one of Australia's largest wineries for the production of dry table wines. McWilliam's large winery at Robinvale also strengthened the corporate presence in the Middle Murray Valley. Thus the district, while not a premium winegrowing area, creates a livelihood for thousands of small grapegrowers and yields acceptable wines of many types.

THE LOWER MURRAY VALLEY DISTRICT (RIVERLAND)

When the Murray River enters South Australia, it flows in a southwestward meander pattern past the town of Renmark and the village of Berri and, after elbowing northwest near Loxton, it turns due south beyond Waikerie at the town of Morgan (see Fig. 8.7). The Lower Murray Valley District encompasses this entire course and valley, approximately to the midpoint of the southward segment. The Langhorne Creek area near the river's mouth is not part of it. So defined, the Riverland is the largest producing district (by volume) of Australia. It is the key to the state's leading position in Australian winegrowing.

The environment of the Murray River valley in South Australia differs little from that of the Middle Murray Valley District. At Berri, the annual rainfall remains below 10 inches and the heat summation hovers about the 4000 degree-day level. What is different is the sheer magnitude of grape- and winegrowing in this district. It eclipses anything seen farther east. Vast vineyard acreages, huge per-acre yields, and a veritable army of growers (many of them land-grant recipients) generate an unequaled annual harvest of grapes for fermentation within and outside the district. In some ways the Riverland is the heart of Australian viniculture.

This, however, is no area for boutique wineries or the romance of personalized winegrowing. This is the cultural landscape of efficiency and mass production, large-

The vine clothes the lowlands of the Murray River as far as the eye can see. This scene is near Mildura.

scale organization, and practicality. The largest and oldest wineries in the district are cooperatives, not family operations. To handle the enormous crush, cooperative wineries were formed at Berri (largest winery in Australia), Renmark (Renmano, oldest of the cooperatives), Waikerie (in association with Barossa's Kaiser-Stuhl), and Loxton (youngest of the four, of postwar vintage). These are the largest, but by no means the only wineries in the district. Among nearly two dozen wineries are the establishments of major companies (Hardy's Cyrilton Winery at Waikerie, Hamilton's Winery at Nildottie), vineyards of Penfold, Orlando, and Seppelt, and independent establishments such as Lubiana, Maljurna, Stamou, and Vindana. There even are some truly small wineries such as County Hamley, which produces noted red table wines blended from home-grown Shiraz and Cabernet Sauvignon, and Szabados, where Hungarian-style wines are made.

The fertility of the Murray basin's soils, the provision of water, and the availability of advanced cellar technology have enlarged the number of wine styles made in the Riverland District from the old fortifieds to an almost unlimited range. One winery boasts of marketing no fewer than forty styles, ranging from brandy to sparkling. And despite this versatility and volume, huge quantities of grapes, juice, and blended wine leave the district for crushing, fermentation, and bottling elsewhere. The Lower Murray Valley District is the dependable fountain of Australia.

Victoria

The state of Victoria ranks a distant third as a wine-producing region of Australia, and much of its harvest, as in South Australia and New South Wales, comes from its share of the extensive irrigated vineyards in the Murray River's basin. The state's

Figure 8.8. Wine districts in the state of Victoria.

comparatively small production is reflected by the map: its scattered districts are small and usually consist of a cluster of only a few wineries.

Quality viticulture in Victoria has a bright future, nevertheless. The environment has the coolness of southern South Australia, and most of the districts lie in Region II (2501 to 3000 degree-days). The precipitation regime loses its strict Mediterranean pattern in Victoria, so that rainfall during the ripening season is somewhat heavier. Most of the state's wine districts receive between 20 and 25 inches of precipitation, and since evaporation losses are low, irrigation is not normally needed in the region as defined on Figure 8.2 (and thus excluding the Murray area).

Victoria's districts are variously defined, and the same district may have more than one name. There is general agreement on several delimitations, however. Northeast Victoria centers on the Rutherglen-Glenrowan area, although some Australian maps divide the two (Fig. 8.8). The Goulburn Valley also is called Tahbilk, after its leading and oldest winery. The Yarra Valley northeast of Melbourne and the Geelong District west of Port Phillip Bay usually are identified as such, and the district around Bendigo is called Central Victoria. The vineyards in the Stawell area are variously called the Western District(s), Great Western (after the small town whose name was given to Seppelt's famous "champagnes") and also, though rarely, the Pyrenees District, since the vineyards lie on north-facing, gentle slopes of a modest range named the Pyrenees. Finally, the vineyards at Drumborg, near Portland in the southwest, do not yet constitute a district but may in time come to form the nucleus of still another Victoria wine center.

Whatever the nomenclature, the district map of Victoria inevitably excludes some noteworthy establishments. Individual wineries and their vineyards lie scattered throughout much of the state, cradled by hills, sustained by streams and aquifers, and favored by the moderate climate. Tisdall's Mount Helen, with its winery at Echuca on the Murray River but vineyards in the Strathbogie Ranges, is a good example: fine Cabernets, Chardonnays, and Pinot Noirs come from the mountain-cooled vines. As long as there are wine enthusiasts willing to take the risks, Victoria will have the opportunities aplenty.

NORTHEAST VICTORIA (UPPER MURRAY DISTRICT)

This is one of those imprecisely defined wine districts that complicate Australia's viticultural map. The largest and in many ways the most historic district of Victoria lies around Rutherglen in the northeast, where there was a true wine boom in the late nineteenth century, a heyday that ended with the *phylloxera* onslaught. Some maps also include the Glenrowan area, south of Rutherglen on the Ovens River, a tributary of the Murray River, in this district. There is more geographic justification for the inclusion of the viticulture area around Corowa, on the New South Wales side of the Murray River (see Figure 8.8). Whatever the regional definition, there is ample justification for the separation of this district from the Murray Basin vineyards downstream. The latter depend entirely on irrigation; the Northeast Victoria vineyards are substantially unirrigated, although some artificial watering does occur even here.

As a Victoria wine district, the Rutherglen area does stand alone. Heat summations here are substantially higher than elsewhere in the state and approach 3700 degree-days, compared to 3140°F. at Bendigo (Central Victoria District) and 2660°F. at Geelong in the south. Summer temperatures are high, and much of the average annual precipitation of about 25 inches comes during the winter and spring, creating the local need for supplemental watering. Part of the viticultural landscape of the Rutherglen area does take on Murray Region characteristics.

The economic geography of the Northeast, however, is unmistakably Victoria. There is no domination here by large corporate wineries. Regional identity is associated with the more modest-sized, often older wineries. For many decades this district was known for its dessert wines and other fortifieds, and some winemakers still produce quality wines of this kind. Chambers (near Rutherglen) markets noted Muscats and Sherry-style wines in addition to its dry table wines; Morris (also near Rutherglen), founded in 1859 and now part of another company, also produces some of the district's superior Muscats. Stanton & Killeen still make a fine Port-style wine, but the winery's Moodemere Shiraz and Cabernet Sauvignon are representative of the best of the district's newer wines. Chambers produces a remarkably faithful, flinty "Chablis" from Pedro Ximenez grapes, proving what can be done with a grape first introduced for very different purposes. But in the transition, Rutherglen's winemakers have not abandoned their link with the past.

One of the area's most progressive wineries is Campbells, an old winery transformed by a replanting and modernization program in the 1960s. Its "Bobbie Burns"–label Shiraz is one of the best regional examples of the style: deep, dark, durable. Campbells' "Chablis," another of those remarkable whites from the Pedro Ximenez, also has much merit. Just west of the town is Buller's Calliope Vineyard, known for its very good red wines and especially its Calliope Vintage Port, no mere holdover from the fortified-wine period but among Australia's superior Port-style wines. Modest yields from the sandy loams atop a clay base ensure quality wines here. And the name of All Saints Vineyard, fronting the Murray River at Wahgunyah, is old, venerable, and for many years was synonymous with Northeast Victoria wines. In 1984 All Saints' cellar buildings were a century old, and still today the winery produces more wine than any other in Victoria's Northeast. Its varietal Shiraz, Cabernet-Shiraz blends, and blends with the Alicante Bouschet create wines that hint at the fullness and power that were the favorites of years past; alongside these now stand the more refined, lighter reds preferred today, and "White Burgundy," and even rosés. All Saints' Sherry-style and dessert wines still are the regional standards, proof that what the Rutherglen district did best in the past, it can still do today.

The area south of Wangaratta, in the vicinity of Glenrowan, often is regarded as part of the Northeast District, although there is substantial separation—more than twenty miles—between the Rutherglen and Glenrowan clusters. There are fewer wineries around Glenrowan, where viticulture is rather more typical of Victoria in general. Each of the Glenrowan wineries is of interest: Bailey's intense Cabernet Sauvignons are derived from wines standing in iron-rich soils, which is thought to give them their intense character, and Bailey's Hermitage, a Shiraz, has been described as the best of its kind in the world. Overall the most important winery in this area is Brown Brothers in the Glenrowan area, an older family company that has much success in Victoria and has a national reputation for its varied range of quality wines. Booths and Markwood are the other Glenrowan wineries with vineyards in what is essentially the basin of the Ovens River and its tributary, the King River, which join to flow northward into the Murray.

THE GOULBURN VALLEY

This is a small but interesting district, around Seymour on the banks of the Goulburn River which, by some definitions, extends to the Shepparton area well to the north. It contains one of Victoria's most historic wine names, Tahbilk. Established in 1860, Chateau Tahbilk apparently was named after an aboriginal word for watering place, and the winery became so famous that the Goulburn District sometimes is identified, simply, as Tahbilk. Certainly this winery merits attention. As its name implies, it really is an Australian version of a chateau, with deep, well-designed cellars more than a century old beneath the winery. From a modest acreage (under 300) of Cabernet Sauvignon, Shiraz, Marsanne, Riesling, Sémillon, and small plantings of Chardonnay, Gewürztraminer, and Sauvignon Blanc the winery produces red and white table wines (no fortifieds) of consistently high quality. The whites are appreciated for their freshness and charm, but Chateau Tahbilk is most highly regarded for its reds, wines that can improve in the bottle for decades. These wines are always released under varietal labels, and never as "Burgundy" or "Chablis."

Chateau Tahbilk has a fascinating history, and it is the chief attraction of the Goulburn Valley District. But there are other wineries here, including Mitchelton, Glengariff, Osicka, and Seymour near the town of Seymour, Henke near Yarck to the east and, if the district is taken to extend to Shepparton, Excelsior and Goulburn Valley Winery. Their vineyards share the district's assets and liabilities: the assets, chiefly, a modest heat summation (just over 3000 degree-days) and adequate rainfall to sustain the grown vines (irrigation supplements this in the first years of vine growth). But summers can be excessively hot, especially late in the ripening season, and mildew is a recurrent problem. Fierce floods in the Goulburn Valley also represent a hazard. Yet Chateau Tahbilk has no monopoly over good wines. Glengariff has won Expovin medals with its Shiraz-Cabernet blend. Mitchelton, an example of modern wine technology in Australia, dates from 1969 and, though bedeviled by natural and financial misfortune, has proven its potential. Today it is one of Australia's leading wineries, producing excellent reds and delicate whites from its state-of-the-art cellars, a standard for the industry. Osicka, established by a Czechoslovakian immigrant family during the 1950s, is best known for a durable Cabernet-Shiraz blend. Other names on (and off) the map reflect the changing wine scene in Victoria as elsewhere in Australia, where every year brings new entries to (and exits from) the vinous landscape.

CENTRAL VICTORIA

The district centered on the town of Bendigo is often called Central Victoria, although it sometimes is combined with the area around Stawell and called Great Western or Western Districts. As shown in Figure 8.8, there is good reason to identify a separate Central Victoria District, even though the wineries and vineyards are quite widely scattered. The leading wineries, including Water Wheel, Balgownie, Le Amon, Virgin Hills, and Knights, approximately from north of Bendigo southward, prove the exceptional suitability of this district for the Cabernet Sauvignon cultivar, which does well almost everywhere it stands. Elevations here vary around an average of 750 feet, heat summations average slightly over 3100, and annual rainfall is about 20 inches, its monthly distribution pattern ensuring some moisture during the ripening season. The main drainage lines flow northward to the Murray, principally the Loddon River, and there is a good deal of microclimatic variety in the district.

Winegrowers who have managed to optimize the local advantages have achieved noteworthy wines. Balgownie undoubtedly is among the most famous names in Central Victoria, its Cabernets ranking at or near the top in all Australia, its Chardonnay a remarkable wine, and its small yield of Pinot Noir regarded by many as the best made in the country. Among Victoria's most talked-about wineries is Virgin Hills, also in this district. For years this winery has produced one red wine, simply labeled "Virgin Hills" with the vintage year and no further information. The wine is believed to be Cabernet-based, but Virgin Hills's vineyards also include

Great Western, in Victoria's Western Districts, has become a name synonymous with sparkling wines—Australian "champagnes." The Seppelt name also is closely associated with Australian "champagne," in which it is a leader.

acreages of Shiraz, Malbec, and Pinot Noir; the composition of the blend remains the winemaker's secret. The Water Wheel winery, north of Bendigo, also well reflects Central Victoria's capacities with its fine Cabernets, Shiraz, and a varietal Cabernet Franc.

Here, in the view of specialists, may lie the district with the greatest potential in all of Australia.

THE WESTERN DISTRICTS

The wineries and vineyards of Victoria's Western Districts lie east and south of the town of Stawell, north of the Pyrenees, the terminal spur of the Great Dividing Range, and in the headwater area of the Wimmera River. The uninitiated might assume that the "Western Districts" would appropriately refer to a wine region in the hinterland of Perth, and others might be confused by the use of "Great Western" as another name for the district. In fact, there is a village of Great Western southeast of Stawell, and one of the most famous wineries in the district is named Seppelt's Great Western—the maker of Australia's best-known sparkling wines. Western Districts is the least undesirable name for a district that incorporates considerable environmental and viticultural diversity.

The two oldest wineries, Seppelt's Great Western and Best's Concongella, both near Great Western (and both using the Great Western toponym on their labels) lie in an area that is by no means the most favored of the district. Elevation varies from about 850 feet to 1200 feet, which is enough to reduce heat summations to 2400 to 2950 degree-days, among Victoria's coolest, so that ripening is slow and acid levels in the grapes remain high. The amount and timing of the rainfall, however, impose the need for supplementary watering, and soils in this area are notoriously poor. Late frosts pose a hazard, and yields are low. But, in the words of Len Evans, "it is one of the ironies of nature that the greatest wines are often made from areas with the poorest natural conditions. And so it is at Great Western. The champagnes of the area are well known, but the rarer unblended dry whites and reds of the area are often superb."[14]

Viticulture in the Great Western area was started by the brothers Joseph and Henry Best in the 1860s. Joseph's property eventually was purchased by the Seppelt company in 1918, but the Best name remains attached to the other vineyard, owned until 1920 by Henry's son Charles. Best's Concongella has been owned by the Thomson family since then, producing a line of older-style wines longer than almost any winery in the state. The whites have an appreciative following (Chardonnay, Gewürztraminer, Chasselas, Riesling); the reds, at their best, are soft and charming. The Seppelt's winery, on the other hand, achieved its national reputation for one wine: "champagne" Australian style. This was the work of one of the country's leading winemakers, Colin Preece, who, while perhaps best remembered for his sparkling wines, also made, at Seppelt, excellent red table wines. His Chalambar Burgundy and Moyston Claret became famous labels for quality and dependability, proving effectively that the Western Districts are capable of red as well as white wine production.

The Western Districts contain a number of other noted wineries. Boroka, southwest of Stawell, uses purchased grapes for several of its wines but releases an estate-grown Shiraz of note. Mount Avoca, in the eastern fringe of the district, near the village of Avoca, is another winery specializing in the two most successful red varietals. Redbank, in the district's northeast corner, markets no less than a dozen varietal wines—all of them red and including a vintage Port-style. Warrenmang, northeast of Stawell, exemplifies the district's small-scale, premium-quality wine-growing that has done so much to establish its national reputation for excellent red wines. Nearby, Taltarni proves that the whites can be very good as well, with a line of wines that includes a Blanc de Blanc from Chardonnay (sparkling), a crisp Chenin Blanc, a Rhine Riesling, and a Sauvignon Blanc. Chateau Remy near Avoca, a company property, produces several red styles, and Montara, near Moyston in the south, is a relative newcomer in the changing wine scene in the Western Districts.

THE YARRA VALLEY

A century ago the Yarra Valley, directly northeast of Melbourne, was regarded by many as the premier table-wine–producing district in colonial Australia. But Australian tastes went toward the sweeter, high-alcohol styles that so long dominated the

The Yeringberg label is one of the oldest in Victoria; the winery, in the Yarra Valley area, has been under the same family's control since its founding.

market, and in time the economics of viticulture on the doorstep of Victoria's largest city became impractical. Today, Melbourne's proximity notwithstanding, the rising appreciation for premium table wines, their higher market values, and the environmental advantages of the valley are stimulating a revival in one of the state's historic districts.

The Yarra Valley District is one of Australia's coolest winegrowing areas, producing wines of extraordinary delicacy and subtlety. It was a group of Swiss immigrant families who found this the winegrowing environment of their choice, and in the 1850s they founded three of the district's enduring wineries: St. Hubert's, Yering (now Yarra Yering), and Yeringberg. Of these, Yeringberg still is under the ownership of descendants of the original family; St. Herbert's, after many years of dormancy, has been revived; and Yarra Yering was replanted in 1969. There now are more than twenty, mostly small, wine establishments in the district, including garden-sized vineyards owned by small investor-winemakers. Fergusson's Winery, Yarrinya, Mount Mary, and other Yarra Valley names are sought after by consumers and collectors who know how excellent and long-lived the district's great reds can be, and how small the production remains. And as the environment would suggest, white wines of premium quality also can be—and are—produced. Yarra Yering's "Dry White Wine" is a fine, Bordeaux-style wine of uncertain source (Marsanne?) but superb balance; Chardonnays from Mount Mary and St. Hubert's, as well as Fergusson's noted Chenin Blancs and Rhine Rieslings, attest to the Yarra District's suitability for white cultivars. But in truth its red wines are its greatest glory, including not only varietal Cabernets and Shiraz, but also Pinot Noirs of promise and, notably, Bordeaux-style blends of intense color, depth, and complexity. The Yarra Valley is again a treasure of Australian winegrowing, its prospects enhanced by the proximity of the large urban market of Melbourne.

THE GEELONG DISTRICT

On the western shore of Port Phillip Bay, opposite Melbourne, lies the town of Geelong. In a vineyard near this place the dreaded *phylloxera* was first discovered more than a century ago, and the destruction of much of Victoria's viticulture began. Today it stretches the definition of the term to call the vineyards in Geelong's hinterland a district, but a scattered group of vineyards and wineries does lie here. Indeed, what is happening in the Geelong area is rather similar to the Yarra revival, and for somewhat the same reasons. Geelong's hinterland has the coolness and moderate summers that can, in the best years, yield excellent vintages. And so the names on the map—Anakie, Idyll, St. Anne's, Tarcoola, Prince Albert, Mt. Duneed, and others—are of more than passing interest. Prince Albert, for example, a tiny vineyard southwest of Geelong, is planted entirely to Pinot Noir, the only wine the winery releases. Idyll Vineyard, to the northwest, is famed for its Idyll Blush, a Shiraz-based rosé of great finesse. As in the Yarra District the red varieties hold the greatest promise in the Geelong District—just as they did 120 years ago, before wholesale burning of the vineyards, ordered by the government following the *phylloxera* discovery, wiped out many of the state's finest vines. The potential is still here, and the Geelong hinterland will again take its place among the state's true wine districts.

DRUMBORG

The Drumborg area, near Portland in the far west of Victoria, is not (yet) a wine district. It is, however, an area where a combination of environmental advantages has led to rather extensive vineyard planting. In some ways this locale has a combination of the best of South Australian and Victorian conditions: the ripening season is cool, rainfall is adequate, and spring frosts are not a major risk. Grapes from hundreds of acres of Seppelt-owned vineyards are taken for fermentation to the Seppelt winery at Great Western, but the construction of a local winery is under consideration. In that event Drumborg may experience the sequence so often repeated in South Australia and Victoria, as the principle of agglomeration takes effect.

Western Australia

The vast state of Western Australia is anchored by its capital, Perth, the country's westernmost city. Here, in the southwest corner of the continent, the desert and steppe of the interior give way to moister conditions as a Mediterranean climatic regime develops. Around Perth the summers are hot and usually bone-dry, but the winter is wet, annual rainfall averaging 35 inches. As Perth grew, so did the first winegrowing in its immediate hinterland. The initial vintage was achieved in the 1830s, but it was not until the gold rushes of later years that real expansion occurred. When the time came, the Swan River Valley northwest of Perth evolved into a true winegrowing district. Yugoslavian and Italian growers contributed importantly

SEPPELT

Drumborg

1977 RHINE RIESLING GD150

Produced from Rhine Riesling grapes picked at optimum ripeness and vintaged at our Great Western winery. The wine is showing excellent bottle development which is slightly Germanic in character and has a fine balance of acid and natural sweetness. This wine has good cellaring potential for 2-3 years.

PRODUCED AND BOTTLED BY B. SEPPELT & SONS LIMITED
ADELAIDE S.A.
750 ml· WINE MADE IN AUSTRALIA   E13017

Drumborg is prominently identified on this Seppelt label. The grapes are crushed and the wine is made at Great Western, but a local cellar is under construction and the future for the Drumborg District appears bright.

to this development, and during the period when fortified wines were popular, the Swan River District had the appropriate environment.

When tastes and technologies changed, the Swan Valley, also under the pressure of urban growth from Perth, began to decline. The search commenced for alternate vineyard sites in Western Australia, and these were soon identified. About 150 miles south of the capital the Australian coastline turns westward, creating a rectangular proruption between Geographe Bay and Flinders Bay (Fig. 8.9). Surrounded on three sides by water, this area, centered on the town of Margaret River, has become Western Australia's premier wine district. And a viticultural experiment in the Mount Barker area, still farther south and nearly 200 miles east of Margaret River, also had success, resulting in the development of a third Western wine district. The moderate summer temperatures of the Margaret River and Mount Barker areas were

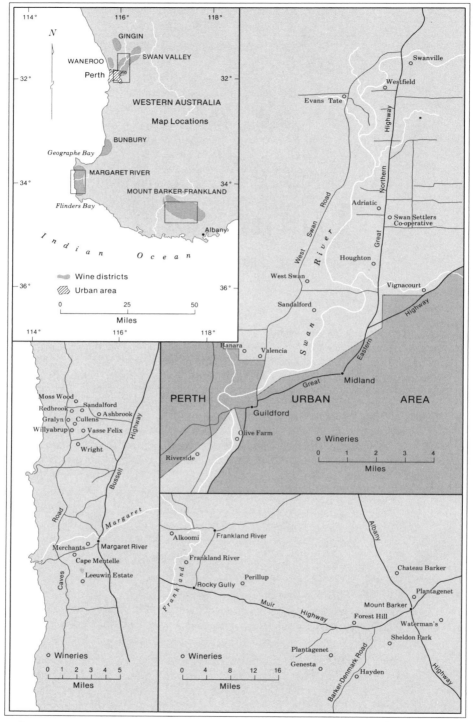

Figure 8.9. Wine districts of Western Australia: the Swan Valley adjacent to Perth (upper right), Margaret River (lower left) and Mount Barker-Frankland.

key factors in this process; heat summations at Mount Barker are as much as 1700 degree-days lower than in the Swan River Valley behind Perth.

THE SWAN RIVER VALLEY DISTRICT

Certainly the Swan River Valley is in decline as a viticulture area, but it is not extinct. Some wineries have taken the courageous decision to move south, but many others remain, and the district still produces a substantial part of Western Australia's annual harvest. The Great Northern Highway from Midland and Guildford still is flanked by modest wineries and well-tended vineyards, although urban sprawl and industrial ugliness make the Swan Valley something less than a tranquil oasis.

Winegrowing in the Swan Valley always has been a family affair, and in the 1950s there were as many as 60 wine-producing operations in the district, some employing two or even three generations of the same family. The larger, more modern establishments sometimes refer to these as "backyard" wineries, and outdated technology, overused barrels, and coarse wines do characterize some of them. But there also is fierce pride and determination here, and Yugoslav, Italian, and British growers have created a cultural landscape reflective of hard work and practicality. They have seen the outsiders come in to establish large company wineries (the Swan Valley's Big Three were Houghton's, Valencia, and Sandalford, with smaller Swanville also owned by outside interests), but they have retained their individualism and independence.

The Swan Valley's assets include a freedom from *phylloxera* and mildew, and an absence of a host of viral diseases of the vine. Its liabilities are obvious from the map: the proximity of a large and growing city, the pollution of its major river, and the excessive, desiccating heat of a summer that regularly records daytime maxima of 105°F., raising grape sugars and weakening the acid content. Heat summations in the vicinity of Guildford are well over 4300 degree-days, so ripening conditions here are comparable to those of Sicily and Spain's Sherry country. And indeed, while the taste for fortified wines prevailed the Swan River District thrived, based essentially on the local market; Sandalford's Sherry-style wines, Houghton's "Ports," Muscats, and "Tokays," and Valencia's Muscats were among the district's most appreciated wines. When preferences changed, these traditions remained, and parallel lines of dry table wines were added by those wineries able to afford the transition. The cultural heritage of the growers continues to be embodied by many of the Swan Valley wines, and the map reveals much: winery names such as Adriatic, Beor, Cobanov, Garbin, Ilich, Ozic, Zec, and Zoranic stand beside Valencia, Vino Italia, Sita, Rullo, Pinelli, and Del Sangra. The British-Irish imprint is confirmed by the Baskervilles, Glenalwyns, Houghtons, Peters, and Sandalfords of the district. In addition to Sandalford, oldest of Western Australia's wineries, Houghton, first to market wine commercially, and Valencia, now owned by Hardy, interest focuses on several smaller wineries. Gnangara produces some excellent red and white table wines from Shiraz (bottled as a varietal) and a Shiraz-Cabernet blend, aged in oak and proof that the Swan Valley can stand with the emerging southern districts. Riverside has won recognition for its Shiraz and also for its dry white wines, including a crisp Chenin Blanc. Westfield similarly represents the progressive, commercially oriented wineries that continue, relative decline notwithstanding, to grace the Swan River Valley District.

MARGARET RIVER DISTRICT

The national—and indeed international—fame achieved in a comparatively brief time by several wineries in the Margaret River area envinces the potentials of this young district. Here the environmental conditions are markedly different: heat summations at Busselton near the northern end of the district are in the 3200 degree-day range, about 1000 less than in the Swan Valley. The total decreases southward, and is below 3000 in the district's midsection. Rainfall averages about 34 inches annually, but unlike the Swan District, some summer rainfall does occur. Under such favorable circumstances (strong winds do affect the grape's setting at times) the cultivation of grapes for premium wines with cooler-climate characteristics becomes possible. Swan Valley winegrowers must use every vinicultural technique to accomplish what nature does here.

Winegrowing in the Margaret District began during the late 1960s and gathered momentum throughout the 1970s and 1980s. Prosperous professional people started small quality wineries, and soon major companies invested in the district as well. Sandalford, the Swan Valley winery, bought Margaret River property and planted Cabernet Sauvignon and Rhine Riesling, augmenting its styles. American investors took an interest in the new Western Australian ventures, and it was clear that the Margaret River District would have more than regional significance.

Among the growing number of wineries around Margaret River, several are of special importance and interest. Pioneers of the district were two physicians, and their wineries retain pride of the place. Vasse Felix, established by T. Cullity in 1967, produced its first vintage in 1972, and its Cabernets and Rieslings have been among Australia's most admired wines ever since. W. Pannell laid out Moss Wood in 1969, and during the 1970s established the winery as the district's (and the state's) leader in qualitative terms. Australian writers compare Moss Wood to Lake's Folly and Balgownie—after just a few years of production. Moss Wood Cabernet has been described in terms usually reserved for the 1961 Latours and Margaux; its Chardonnays have received similar accolades, and its Pinot Noirs are also highly regarded. But perhaps the most significant venture in Western Australia is Leeuwin Estate, with its Mondavi connection, a comparatively large operation devoted entirely to the production of premium wines. Leeuwin's 230 acres of vineyards stand under Chardonnay, Cabernet Sauvignon, Riesling, Pinot Noir, Malbec, Gewürztraminer, and Sauvignon Blanc. Its wines already rank not only among Australia's most prized, but also among the country's most highly priced, and the winery has done much to focus the market's attention upon the west and its wines.

Such is the viticultural development of the Margaret River District that virtually every winery is of special interest. Cape Mentelle, another Western winery with a California connection, markets creditable Zinfandels. Willyabrup, first planted in 1971, has won medals for its Cabernets, Rieslings, and its special Sweet Rosé. The Margaret River's promise is being fulfilled.

Leeuwin Estate in the Margaret River District has become one of Australia's most prominent wineries. Its high-priced red and white wines have been awarded numerous prizes and medals, and have helped focus attention on one of Australia's most promising wine districts.

THE MOUNT BARKER (SOUTHERN) DISTRICT

While attention focused on the Margaret River District, a viticultural experiment also was under way near the town of Mount Barker, about 40 miles inland from the southernmost coast of Western Australia (see Figure 8.9). Here, in an undulating countryside about 1000 feet above sea level, a test vineyard was planted in 1967. It was believed that the area's cool summer temperatures (heat summations of 2600 degree-days), adequate rainfall (30 inches, with slightly more summer moisture even than Margaret River), and suitable, loamy soils would support quality winegrowing. When the Mount Barker's 1975 Riesling vintage won gold medals not only in Perth but in Adelaide and Melbourne as well, the rush to the third Western Australian district was on. Farmers who already held property in the area, wealthy professional people, and (later) established companies wanting a share in the district all planted vineyards, notably in the direction of the town of Frankland. The farmer-owners of the original experimental vineyard have expanded their holdings and market their wines under the Conti Forest Hill label, although fermentation takes place elsewhere and not on the property.

The district's most successful wines undoubtedly are the Rhine Rieslings, although good Cabernet Sauvignons also are made; this is the combination produced by most of the wineries in the Mount Barker vicinity. Plantagenet is among the leaders, and Chateau Barker's Pinot Noir has become one of the district's noted wines. There now are more than twenty wineries and/or vineyards in the area, and many varietal and vinicultural experiments are in progress. Among these are Alkoomi's Malbec, Genesta's "Port" and Rosé, Pinwernying's "Sherry" and Grenache, and Waterman's Merlot. Alkoomi, in the Frankland corner of the district (where climatic conditions differ substantially from the Mount Barker area) represents the best, its limited releases of several white and red varietals and a blend of Cabernet, Shiraz, and Malbec ranking among the district's most interesting wines.

As viticulture around the original experimental locale has expanded, the dispersal of vineyards and wineries has gone far beyond the Mount Barker area. Some regard the Frankland area as a separate district; others identify the south as the Frankland–Mount Barker District. It would seem only fair to call it the Southern District; that would nicely balance Victoria's "Western" Districts. Whatever the nomenclature, it should be noted that, after Mudgee (N.S.W.), Margaret River and Mount Barker have been established as Australia's second and third appellation regions.

In Western Australia, as in the other winegrowing states, a number of wineries lie outside the districts here delimited. Around Bunbury, south of Perth and north of Margaret River, lies what is locally called the South West Coastal District, and here Capel Vale is a winery of note, a small operation producing red and white varietals. At Wanneroo, north of Perth along the coast road, cluster a half-dozen wineries, including Conteville and Hartridge. Hardy, the large firm that owns Houghton in the Swan Valley, also owns a vineyard property at Gingin, about forty miles north of Perth along the Brand Highway, where the vines are sustained by spring water and the sea breezes help moderate the summer heat. It all is further proof of Australia's hospitality to the grapevine and its enormous potential still remaining.

Tasmania

Tasmania is Australia's newest viticultural frontier, the ultimate locale to which a cool-climate–seeking industry can go. Geelong District and the Yarra Valley are near 38° south latitude, but Tasmania lies mainly between 41° and 43° south— farther south than the majority of New Zealand wine districts (Fig. 8.10). Heat summations here are as low as 1800 degree-days.

A commercial vineyard existed in Tasmania as long ago as 1823, and continued to produce until the early 1850s. This venture eventually collapsed, and there was

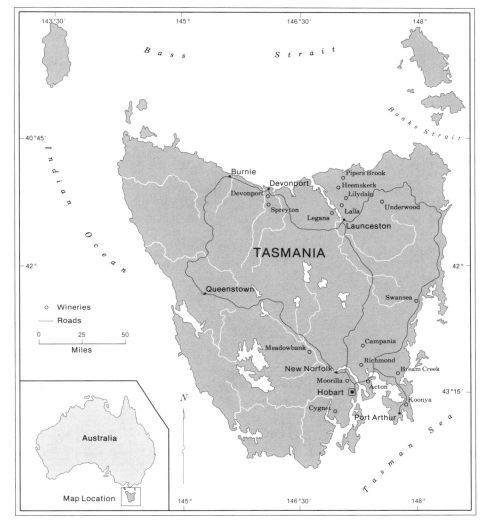

Figure 8.10. Winery concentrations in Tasmania.

no renewal of activity until a century later. In the 1950s a Frenchman, J. Miguet, planted a set of cool-climate cultivars and proved their suitability, but Miguet returned to France and this effort, too, petered out. In the early 1960s the first of a number of vineyards near Hobart, the capital, was planted by an Italian investor, C. Alcorso. His success led to imitation, and in the 1970s the area around Launceston, in the north, was opened to viticulture as well. By the early 1980s there were some twenty vineyards and/or wineries in Tasmania, and some were achieving noteworthy vintages.

Moorilla Estate, Alcorso's original vineyard at Berriedale near Hobart, continues to be a leading name in Tasmanian winegrowing. Now well established with a series of successful vintages, Moorilla is known for its light-style Cabernet Sauvignons, improving Pinot Noirs, and very fine Rieslings. Pipers Brook, north of Launceston, has more recently, and quickly, established a reputation for its excellent Cabernets and Rieslings, and its Pinot Noirs have gained much recognition. Heemskerk, also near Launceston, has a substantial vineyard of Cabernet Sauvignon (50 acres), along with smaller acreages of Chardonnay, Pinot Noir, Rhine Riesling, Gewürztraminer, and Sylvaner. Other operations are in various stages of development, and this time, it is certain, Tasmanian winegrowing is here to stay.

Queensland

If wine can be made in tropical Brazil, in Florida, and in Zimbabwe, then surely it can be made in Queensland. Indeed it is. Among winery names that are associated with Queensland are Robinson's, Angelo's and Romavilla.

The Robinson's winery lies near Ballandean, south of Stanthorpe and southwest of Brisbane, where the Great Dividing Range is in decline, elevations bring temperature aggregates down to below those of Cessnock in the Hunter Valley, moisture is adequate if not ideally distributed seasonally (too much of it comes during the summer), and soils are good. The vineyards contain Cabernet Sauvignon and Chardonnay chiefly, with smaller parcels of Pinot Noir, Riesling, and Gewürztraminer; the winery was put in operation in 1979. Under The Family label, Robinson's produces a very good Cabernet Sauvignon that is not dominated by evidence of its warm-climate origin, a fruity Shiraz, a blend of these two varietals, a Pinot Noir, and a Chardonnay.

Other wineries in the Stanthorpe area are Rumbalara Vineyards, based in Fletcher, Puglisi's Winery (whose Cabernet Sauvignon and Shiraz were the first Stanthorpe wines to receive a medal at a wine competition, in 1974 at Brisbane), Ballandean Cellars, Bungawarra Vineyards, Girrawheen Vineyards (whose 1979 Sémillon won the trophy for the best Queensland wine), Biltmore Cellars, DeLuca's Winery, Golden Grove Vineyards, and Ricca's Winery.

Romavilla is Queensland's oldest winery, having released a vintage every year since 1866. The town of Roma lies about 300 miles west of Brisbane along the Warrego Highway, and here the climate is hot, humidity is low, and rainfall averages 23 inches annually, but with the typical summer-maximum pattern of the Cfa regime. Romavilla's vintage normally is the earliest in Australia, the grapes ripening rapidly and developing the high sugar and low acid common to such environments. From a geographical viewpoint, Romavilla's is as interesting as any winegrowing venture in Australia, proving as it does the versatility and adaptability of *Vitis vinifera*.

Continuity and Change

The broad regional outlines of Australian winegrowing have, over the past century, developed a permanence that is etched on the map. The old districts—the Hunter, Rutherglen, Barossa, Swan Valley—are fixtures; the Murray-Murrumbidgee's irrigated expanses will generate the bulk volume indefinitely. The most evident geographic consequence of changing preferences is the southward relocation of premium winegrowing. From Tasmania to the far west, the redistribution of vineyards reflects the new era in Australian quality production. But when the pattern is viewed in context of quantity, it is evident that the redistribution is of minor consequence. The mass of table wines will continue to come from those vineyards which earlier yielded the grapes for fortified wines. What has changed is cellar technology, not overall viticulture. Premium winegrowing involves but a small fraction of the industry.

To the interested observer, the geographic consequences of the search for premium environments are far from insignificant. Every district where experimental vineyards are planted and winegrowing subsequently succeeds contains the promise of new and perhaps unprecedented achievements. To winegrower and consumer alike, it is an adventure occasionally rewarded with a true revelation. Winegrowing is an art as well as a science, and the probability of success is but small. But the search continues, and the map records it: from Tasmania to the Yarra Valley and from Bendigo to Mount Barker the geography of Australian viniculture is changing.

Undoubtedly the most far-reaching changes involve not only the maturing of the newer premium-wine districts, including Tasmania, but also (a) the related decline of some established but potentially disadvantaged districts, especially the Barossa Valley, and (b) the continuing shift in market preference, not only from fortified to table wines but also from red to white wines. Along with the Barossa, the Swan Valley's decline, directly related to the emergence of Margaret River and Mount Barker, will continue. (Perth's urban expansion will contribute to this as well.) The winegrowing areas in the immediate hinterland of Adelaide also will experience a decline, and even the northern sector of McLaren Vale may be so affected. Growth in Victoria's premium districts, in Clare and Coonawarra in South Australia, and in the southern districts of Western Australia will match the decreases elsewhere.

The ascent of the Cabernet Sauvignon toward premier status among red cultivars was discussed previously, but the red cultivars' share of total plantings continues to decline as consumer preference for white wines grows. This has the anomalous effect of making premium red wines ever more scarce, since they constitute the shrinking pinnacle of a declining market share. Some Australian experts predict that red grapes, by the year 2000, will occupy less than 15 percent of the total vineyard acreage. And yet the development of the new southern districts is based substantially on their suitability for red grapes, especially the Cabernet Sauvignon and, in special microclimates, the difficult Pinot Noir. Unless the domestic market reverses itself and red wines retain a stronger share, the pioneer districts of the 1970s and 1980s may have to be rationalized anew.

9

NEW ZEALAND: VINIFERA VICTORIOUS

Misconceptions about New Zealand abound. The palm trees along Victoria Drive overlooking Auckland's Waitemata harbor may surprise first-time visitors, but New Zealanders know that Auckland summers are warm, winters are mild (no snow here), and Antarctic cold is no threat. The map displays the geographic reasons: New Zealand's latitudinal position, between approximately 34° and 47° south, corresponds to a range that would, in the Northern Hemisphere, extend from Algeria to Burgundy in France. The vineyards of Germany lie at higher latitudes than any reached by South Island of New Zealand (Fig. 9.1).

New Zealand, furthermore, lies substantially east, rather than south, of Australia. The northern area of North Island, where Samuel Marsden planted the country's first grapes, lies in the same latitude as southern New South Wales and well north of Victoria. Virtually all of New Zealand's vineyards lie north of the latitude of those in Tasmania, and many lie north of Geelong and the Yarra Valley.

But Australia is of continental size, and New Zealand consists of islands. Maritime influences dominate New Zealand's climate and weather to a far greater extent than is the case in Australia, and no part of New Zealand lies protected by distance from the cooling southern airmasses that also touch the coasts of Australia. These airmasses also bring marked contrasts between moist, cloudy, windward and drier, sunnier, leeward exposures. The oceanic effect, in addition, is to make New Zealand weather rather inconsistent and at times unpredictable. Some North Island summers are comparatively dry (drought has even been an occasional east-coast

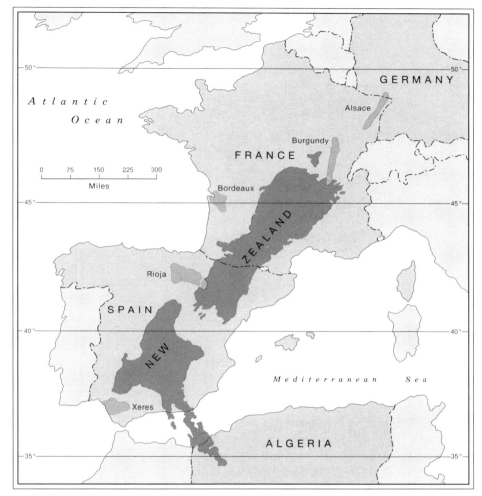

Figure 9.1. New Zealand superimposed, at equivalent latitudes, on a map of Western Europe.

problem for winegrowers), while others are gray and wet. In the best years, New Zealand's wines are among the hemisphere's finest. When the summer's promise fails to materialize, the vintage will carry the consequences. Few Southern Hemisphere wine regions record so variable a vintage sequence as does New Zealand.

Compared to the wine industries of Chile, South Africa, or Australia (let alone Argentina), New Zealand's industry is very small. But what it lacks in size, it makes up in interest. Wine districts lie scattered from northern North Island to the midsection of South Island, from interior to coast, from mountainside to valley floor. Even in comparatively sparsely populated New Zealand, the battle between city and winery proceeds as Auckland's suburbs invade the historic vineyards in their path. Here, too, boutique wineries, where the focus is on premium wines, stand beside the refinery-style establishments of corporate firms. And here, again,

Villa Maria's vineyards, among the last remaining in the city of Auckland, lie surrounded by suburbanization.

a modern transformation of taste and technology has generated a new era of experimentation and achievement. As recently as 1970, more than 73 percent of all wine sold in New Zealand was classified as dessert wine, and less than 27 percent was table wine. By 1983, about 75 percent was table wine, and dessert-style wines had declined to less than 25 percent.[1]

Viticulture in New Zealand is old, but the wine industry—in real terms—is young. Unlike South Africa or Australia, it cannot be said that the first experiments in grapegrowing gave birth to a steadily (or even haltingly) growing industry. Marsden, remembered for his pioneer plantings, and Busby, honored for his viticultural innovations, would have considered their ventures a failure a century later. Before World War II there were fewer than 200 acres of wine grapes in New Zealand, and no wine district worthy of the name.[2] It was not for want of trying: sporadic efforts did bear fruit, however limited. The Mission Vineyards, near Napier on North Island's east coast, was founded by the brothers of the French Marist religious order in 1851, and its half-acre vineyard was producing an annual wine harvest throughout the 1860s. A Spanish grower, Joseph Soler, had a small vineyard and winery near Wanganui in the 1880s. In the Auckland area there was a Yugoslavian connection, as S. Yelas, J. Vella, and later I. Yukich planted vines. A Lebanese immigrant, A. Corban, established a winery that was to become one of New Zealand's best-known firms in the early 1900s. But despite the visit of an Italian oenologist, R. Bragato, in 1895, and his favorable report on the country's potential, and notwithstanding the government's creation of a Viticultural Research Station at Te Kawhata, progress was slow and periodic at best. *Phylloxera* dealt the vineyards a severe blow during the 1890s, the Prohibition Movement of the early 1900s came

Mission Vineyards, near Napier in Hawke's Bay District, eastern North Island, proclaims itself the oldest vineyard and winery in New Zealand.

close to extinguishing what was left of the industry, and the research station was closed.

Even when revivial came, stimulated by higher import duties on imported wines, wartime and postwar growth in demand, and reformist legislation permitting bottle sales at wineries, expansion at first was slow and for many years followed the traditional lines; modernization was yet to come. Tastes still favored fortified and sweeter wines, and New Zealand's omnipresent all-purpose grape, the Müller-Thurgau, was vinted into all kinds of "styles." Back-blending, that is, the combination of fermented wine with a small volume (5 to 6 percent) of natural grape juice to produce a lower-alcohol, semi-sweet wine, was (and to a lesser extent remains) a common technique for the creation of wines much favored on the domestic market.

As recently as 1960, all of New Zealand's domestic wine came from vines grown on a vineyard area totaling just 1000 acres. Hybrid grapes, holdovers from the post-*phylloxera* period, occupied about 60 percent of this acreage. But research and experimentation were in progress, and a new era was dawning. By 1980 there were well over 12,000 acres of vines, 90 percent vinifera.[3] The range of New Zealand's viticultural environments, and the opportunities it presents, were increasingly recognized. The country had produced fortified wines and white wines in overwhelming quantity, but now there were those who saw the possibilities for reds—the Pinot Noir, the Pinotage of South Africa, the Cabernet Sauvignon, the Gamay. Winegrowers established themselves on the premise that premium red wines could be made; the Nobilo family name, for example, became synonymous with quality red wine from New Zealand. And the pattern of white cultivars, too, changed. The Müller-Thurgau continued to outproduce all others, and the Palomino remained

Corban was a pioneer in New Zealand winegrowing. The winery near Auckland, recently sold, continues to carry the Corban name.

strong, but the Chardonnay, Rhine Riesling, Gewürztraminer, Chenin Blanc, and Sauvignon Blanc made their appearance. Acreages of the newcomers remain comparatively small, but their contribution to the range of varietals and to the evidence for the country's productive capacity is large. The premium cultivars, red and white, also display affinities for particular New Zealand microclimates, so that regional specialization is becoming evident in the maturing industry.

Today New Zealand has about 14,000 acres under vines, and expansion has slowed after a period that saw the addition of an average of 1200 acres per year to viticulture. Most of the country's wine districts continue to concentrate on North Island, but the largest single bloc of vines lies at the northern end of South Island, in the hinterland of Blenheim. Thus the regional geography of New Zealand winegrowing now reflects the exploitation of potentials foreseen by Bragato a century ago, and perhaps by Busby a half-century before him.

Producers and Labels

New Zealand's wine is made and marketed by about 150 winemakers, large and small. The large companies dominate quantitatively, but although much of the premium wine is made by smaller winegrowers, these do not have a monopoly over quality. As in Australia, the larger firms also maintain quality lines. Montana, largest of all New Zealand winemakers with a 40 percent market share, also is known for some excellent finer wines.

The most widely known companies among New Zealand winemakers include several names with Australian connections (present or past). These firms carry a customary (N.Z.) following the winery name, as in McWilliam (N.Z.) and Penfold (N.Z.). Cooks (N.Z.) is a different case, a company founded by a group of Auckland entrepreneurs but with a strong export orientation, and properly known as Cooks New Zealand Wine Company. Corbans, still carrying the family name but now owned by Rothmans, Vidal-Villa Maria, two family companies now combined under single ownership, and Glenvale, also a family firm, likewise rank among larger producers. During the 1970s Vidal was owned by Seppelt of Australia, but that association ended when Villa Maria's owner purchased Vidal.

As elsewhere, wineries of all sizes continue to be bought and sold, and corporate relationships change. Forty percent of Montana's stock is owned by Seagrams; half of McWilliam's (N.Z.) shares belong to Lion Breweries, and Lion Breweries is in position to acquire control of Penfold's (N.Z.) interests. These adjustments (and many other transactions involving smaller wineries) reflect the changed position of the emerging wine industry in the national economy.

Special interest focuses on the boutique wineries, where many of New Zealand's superior wines are made, and on certain other wineries of modest dimensions that have chosen to produce quality wines. These have grown in number, but not all have succeeded. Among those that have become established are names now associated with some of the country's finest wines. Te Mata Estate near Havelock North and Napier (on North Island's east coast) is noted for its exceptional red wines, especially a remarkable Cabernet-Merlot blend of great promise. Babich, not far from Auckland, has been among the leaders with its Pinot Noirs. Eskdale, deRedcliffe, Collard, and Matua Valley are among other quality-oriented, smaller wineries making the best of New Zealand's microclimates.

Labeling has been an elusive issue in New Zealand, but the early 1980s brought new legislation and some semblance of order. From the 1983 vintage on, varietal wines must have 100 percent grape juice, of which 75 percent must derive from the cultivar identified on the label. A blend must state the dominant variety first (as in Cabernet Sauvignon-Merlot). Generic wines are required to be made from 100 80 percent grape juice. In New Zealand there is a customary difference between bottle- and jug-marketed generic wine. Generics such as Beaujolais, Burgundy, or Claret usually are made from a single grape variety, normally a vinifera. Jug (or flagon, cask) wines are likely to be blends, and still may contain juice derived from hybrid grapes. Brand (proprietary) labels tend to represent a consistent style. These normally are blended wines, and the label is likely (but not required) to reveal their varietal composition. Montana's Blenheimer, a popular white from its South Island vineyards, Cook's Chasseur and Clairmont, Corban's Liebestraum, and McWilliam's Bakano Claret are among better-known brand labels. One advantage of the brand labels, from a geographic viewpoint, is that the proprietary name often relates to the vineyard or locale where the grapes were grown. The Blenheim in Blenheimer is the name of the South Island town in whose hinterland Montana's vineyards lie. The practice of vineyard identification is increasing, a positive development in the absence of an appellation system.

The label reveals little as yet to assist the consumer in the assessment of quality. In New Zealand as in Australia, terms such as "Private Bin" or "Bin No."—

once a sign of exclusivity—now are so common as to have little utility. The term "Estate" does not reflect what it does in South Africa, nor has it a legal foundation. Wineries routinely announce on bottle labels the medals won by their wines at wine competitions. This can be useful if precise, but the information sometimes is general and not relevant to the variety and vintage in the bottle.

These continuing developments in industry and legislation reflect the sustained evolution and coming of age of New Zealand's winegrowing. The position of the industry in the country (social as well as economic) still is undergoing adjustment, and changes are yet to come—for example, when customs and tariff barriers between Australia and New Zealand are progressively lowered during the 1980s, and the free flow of wine alters market competition. But the 1970s set the new pattern and established New Zealand as a country able to produce not merely coarse fortified and sweet wines, but fine table wines of merit. The response of the domestic market was strong: in 1970, annual per-capita wine consumption was a mere 1.3 gallons, and before the end of the decade it had doubled. In the early 1980s consumption averaged 3.3 gallons, still the lowest in the hemisphere except Brazil, but reflecting strong growth for New Zealand.

Such figures underscore, nevertheless, the limitations and small dimensions of the domestic industry. With a population of just 3 million, local demand for wine is the smallest by far of all Southern Hemisphere wine-producing countries. With its quality wines just gaining international recognition, New Zealand does not have an established position on overseas markets, although the export picture has brightened in recent years. The long-range future remains clouded, recent achievements notwithstanding.

Regional Geography: The Districts

Wine grapes are grown from the Northland Peninsula of North Island to the Canterbury Plain of South Island, from the vicinity of Whangarei to the hinterland of Christchurch. The majority of the vines—about 80 percent—stand in North Island vineyards, but what is significant about this statistic is that fully one-fifth of the vineyard acreage now lies on South Island. In 1980 there were nearly 2700 acres of vines on South Island, against just 10 in 1970.

Other changes appear on the map of New Zealand viticulture (Fig. 9.2). Among major wine districts, only one showed a decline in vineyard acreage during the expansion of the 1970s: the Auckland area, oldest true wine district in the country. In 1975, when the Auckland hinterland had 1850 acres of vineyards, this was the leading district, with 32 percent of the national total. By 1981 there were fewer than 1400 vineyard acres here, constituting just 10 percent of all winegrowing.[4] Dispersal of winegrowing also marks the map as scattered vineyards and wineries, remote from the established districts, succeed in particular microclimates.

New Zealand today has five major wine districts and a half-dozen locales where winegrowing occurs but no real districts have yet developed. These smaller locales are not insignificant, because here lie some of the wineries that produce noted premium wines. Near Christchurch and Nelson on South Island, in Northland and

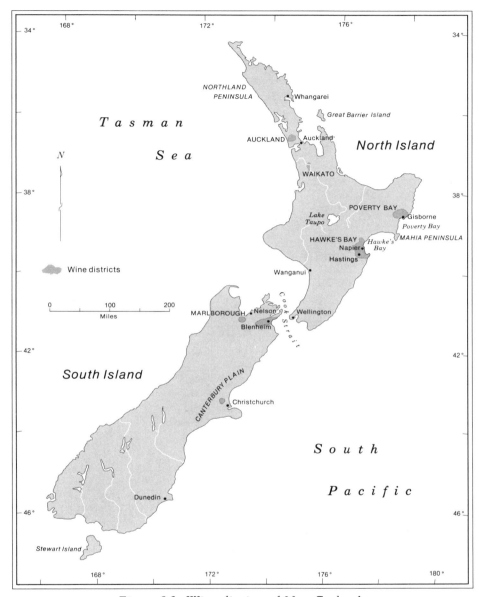

Figure 9.2. Wine districts of New Zealand.

scattered in various other North Island locations elsewhere, winegrowers have found microclimates that provide opportunities for specialized viticulture. But the major districts generate the bulk of the harvest *and* some excellent premium wines as well: the Auckland District, historic and durable, two east coast districts, where some quality wineries have been established, the Te Kawhata area, scene of early experimentation, and the Marlborough vineyards, newest of the big five.

The Corban family name has been associated with Auckland-area winemaking for most of the present century. Corban's wines are among New Zealand wines sold on foreign markets. This Sylvaner Riesling, a popular New Zealand style, is seen in American wine stores.

NORTH ISLAND: THE AUCKLAND DISTRICT

As in Australia, wine districts in New Zealand sometimes have more than one name. The Auckland District is the broadest possible appellation for a cluster of vineyards that survive within the city and suburbs, plus a viticulture area located mainly northwest of Auckland. The district is variously called the Henderson Valley, the Kumeu-Huapai District, and the Henderson-Kumeu District (Fig. 9.3).

Whatever its geographic designation, this is one of New Zealand's historic wine districts. Grapes have stood here from the turn of the century and, stimulated by the growth of the nearby urban market, viticulture thrived. While consumers preferred fortified wines, disease-resistant hybrids yielded adequate juice, and the climate, often moist and cloudy (rainfall averages more than 60 inches annually) was not a serious drawback. When preferences turned to table wines, several larger wine companies relocated to the drier east coast districts. But there were winegrowers who knew that the Auckland District has microclimates and soil zones capable of supporting premium grapes. As the hybrids disappeared and vineyard acreage declined under the pressure of urban growth, specialized viticulture of Cabernet Sauvignon, Pinotage, Pinot Noir, Sauvignon Blanc, and Sémillon (among other vinifera) emerged

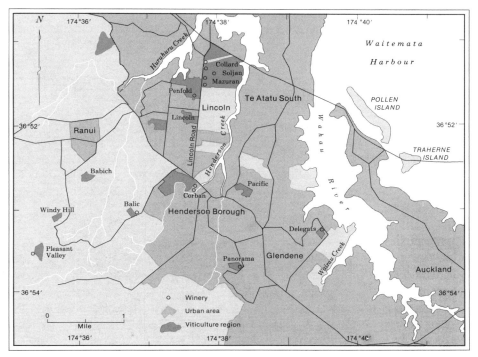

Figure 9.3. Interdigitation of urban sprawl and viticulture in the Auckland District, North Island, New Zealand.

in carefully selected locales. From these vineyards now come some of New Zealand's most respected wines.

The Auckland District is an area of mostly modest winery establishments, with dispersed, prudently placed vineyards often adjoined now by homes and businesses in the Henderson area but more rural toward Huapai, a rolling countryside, pleasantly green pastures, stands of trees, and an overall atmosphere of prosperity. Several of the wineries face Henderson's Lincoln Road, where it is difficult to envisage that this once was isolated farm country. Some vineyards survive even in Auckland itself. Passengers landing at Auckland's International Airport can see, from the runway approach, the vines of Villa Maria Wines; the winery stands surrounded by suburbia near the foot of Mangere Hill. Many of the wineries in the Henderson-Kumeu area are of special interest. Babich has attracted attention with medal-winning Cabernet and Pinot Noir; Collard Brothers is one of the Lincoln Road wineries, now with supplemental vineyards in the east; Corban remains an historic establishment; Delegats, a family winery dating from 1947, produces very good white and red table wines; Penfold (N.Z.) has an establishment designed to accommodate tourists on the Henderson wine route; Matua Valley is one of the younger (1974) wineries dedicated to quality, premium-wine production; Nobilo is recognized internationally for its superb red wines; Coopers Creek began production in the 1980s; San Marino has won top honors with its Riesling-Sylvaner and releases other superior white as well as red table wines; Selaks has been producing wine at its

Nobilo Vintners is recognized internationally as one of New Zealand's leading wineries. The winery concentrates on premium red wines (the 1976 Cabernet Sauvignon was one of the best wines ever made in New Zealand), but it also markets some whites. The estate and its main vineyards lie in the Auckland District.

Kumeu winery for more than fifty years.[5] Few of these wineries concentrate exclusively on dry table wines; most continue to release Port- and Sherry-style wines, and some still make old-style fortified wines. But the pride of the district lies in its red table wines, especially its Cabernets, some of which, in good vintage years (such as Nobilo's 1976) develop into excellent, complex wines of depth and durability. The Auckland District may have lost its quantitative lead, but its quality wines rank second to none.

THE HAWKE'S BAY DISTRICT

The east coast of North Island is indented by two adjacent bays, of which the southernmost, Hawke's Bay, is the largest (Fig. 9.4). North of the Mahia Peninsula lies Poverty Bay. The two largest New Zealand wine districts lie near the shores of these bays.

The Hawke's Bay District lies in the hinterland of the major coastal town, Napier, and Hastings and Havelock are part of this region. The Hawke's Bay area, with about 33 inches of average annual precipitation, is the drier of the two east coast districts, and summers here are long and very warm. Heat summations, nevertheless, are not high, averaging 2500 degree-days (lower than the Barossa Valley

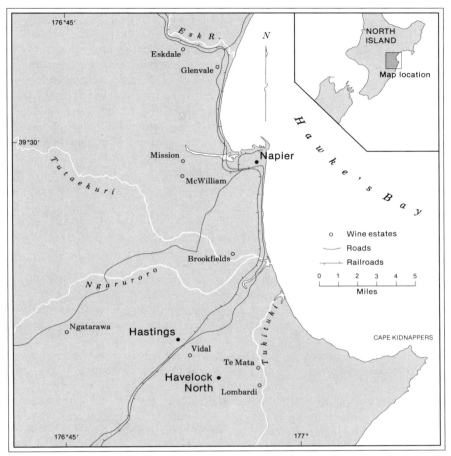

Figure 9.4. The two districts on the east coast of North Island, New Zealand: Hawke's Bay and Poverty Bay.

but substantially higher than Coonawarra). After the Auckland District, this un-doubtedly is the most interesting New Zealand wine region. Extensive vineyards of McWilliam and Penfold and the parcels of contract growers are interspersed with historic local operations and modern boutique wineries exploiting the area's varied microclimates and soils. Years ago the Müller-Thurgau dominated the viticultural landscape here, and hybrids covered large acreages as well. Today there are stands of Cabernet Sauvignon, Merlot, Pinot Noir, Chardonnay, Chenin Blanc, and other premium cultivars that thrive in the district's favorable environments.

Mission Vineyards is the successor to the original Marist Brothers winery of the 1850s, relocated several times but laying claim to being the oldest surviving New Zealand winery. The establishment sustained severe damage during the 1931 Napier earthquake, but a new cellar was built and the winery, now modernized, has shared in the industry's progress and expansion. Among other noted wineries is Te Mata Estate, another older winery revived in the late 1970s, its north-facing slopes planted with premium varieties, and its wines among the country's finest, especially its Cabernet-Merlot blend. Eskdale Winegrowers, a small winery in a valley north of Napier on the road to Taupo and Auckland, also releases premium table wines in limited quantity. Other wineries present different perspectives. Vidal Wine Producers has a winery and, on the premises, a large tourist facility, all in suburban Hastings; this establishment reflects the growth of wine-related tourism as it anchors the official Hawke's Bay Wine Trail. Ngatarawa, well inland from Hastings, has a member of the Corban family as winemaker. One of the larger wineries, Glenview, as well as Lombardi and Brookfield are older wineries that long produced mainly fortifieds and have successfully extended their lines. All of this is set in the verdant matrix created by the holdings of the large corporations and their growers. Picturesque and viticulturally diversified, the Hawke's Bay District is a microcosm of New Zealand viticulture at its best.

POVERTY BAY DISTRICT

The Poverty Bay District is another district known by more than one name. Also called the Gisborne District, after its major urban center on the bay, this is the country's largest viticulture region areally, its vineyards owned substantially by (and its individual contract growers connected to) several of the country's major companies. Montana's huge, refinerylike winery stands in Gisborne in sight of Poverty Bay and adjacent to Penfold's equally modern facility. Montana's Ormond winery (formerly the family-owned Waihirere Winery) lies in Gisborne's hinterland at the base of the Raukumara foothills. The emphasis here is on volume and quantity, although smaller family wineries do survive, for example Matawhero, where good white table wines have been added to an older line of fortifieds. Several Auckland wineries own vineyards or buy grapes from contract growers here: Corban has a holding, Nobilo's whites are made from Gisborne-grown fruit, and San Marino buys Müller-Thurgau here to supplement its Auckland District harvests.

The Poverty Bay District's warm summers and fairly moist environment (annual precipitation averages 40 inches), along with its fertile soils, always have favored quantity grapegrowing. Some parcels of hybrids still stand here, a memory of old times. Another memory became a sudden reality again in the early 1980s, when *phylloxera* appeared in Gisborne's vineyards. Ugly patches of yellowed vine leaves and shriveled grapes expanded yearly and threatened the heart of the district's vineyards. The battle was joined, but *phylloxera*, once it has established a beachhead, is not easily contained. The verdict remains in the balance.

THE WAIKATO DISTRICT

The only other North Island wine district with more than 200 acres of vines is Waikato, less a contiguous district than a set of dispersed grapegrowing parcels. At its heart lies Te Kawhata, about fifty miles south of Auckland, site of the government's Viticultural Research Station and its adjacent experimental vineyards. The main facility and vineyards of one of New Zealand's leading firms, Cooks, lies just to the

Montana's large and modern facility in Gisborne (Poverty Bay District) symbolizes the winery's dominant position in the New Zealand wine industry. (Courtesy of Montana.)

DeRedcliffe Estates produces one of New Zealand's most interesting red wines (and a fine white as well). Several smaller wineries, including TeMata in the Hawke's Bay District, have succeeded admirably with Bordeaux-style Cabernet-Merlot blends.

north. Established in 1969, Cooks concentrates on premium red and white wine production, and in the early 1980s routinely marketed all its Cabernet Sauvignon overseas. East coast grapes supplement Cooks' local production, and a line of ordinary wines is made for the domestic market. To the northeast, at Thames, is Totara Vineyards, dating from 1925 and operated since 1950 by a Chinese family who have a holding in the Auckland District and buy grapes in Gisborne as well. An especially interesting vineyard is deRedcliffe Estates, set in a valley east of Pokeno (about halfway between Te Kawhata and Auckland), where only three cultivars, for two premium wines, are grown: Cabernet, Merlot, and Chardonnay.

Waikato's scattered vineyards have expanded somewhat during the decade of growth, but proportionately less than other wine districts. In 1975 the district had slightly more than 600 acres of vineyards, and this constituted more than 10 percent of the national total. In 1982 there were some 850 vineyard acres, but these

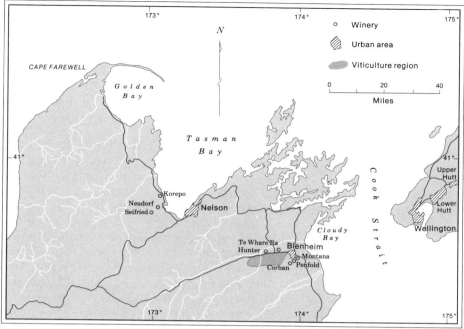

Figure 9.5. The Marlborough District at the northern end of South Island, New Zealand.

represented just 6 percent. Environments in the district to some extent resemble those of the Auckland District, and the emergence of Hawke's Bay and Poverty Bay have contributed to its relative decline. Cooks, for example, is in the process of establishing a Hawke's Bay winery.

No other wine district has developed on North Island, although scattered vineyards exist from Northland (where Continental is the country's northernmost winery) and the Bay of Plenty to the hinterland of Wellington near Waikanae (where Pierre Wines has 25-year-old vineyards) in the south. Limitations other than the environmental inhibit the exploitation of microclimates recognized long ago by Bragato as highly promising. Given greater demand and proximate markets, New Zealand would truly come into its own.

SOUTH ISLAND: THE MARLBOROUGH DISTRICT

The Marlborough District, in the hinterland of Blenheim on South Island's northeast coast, developed over a period of less than a decade into New Zealand's third-largest viticulture region (Fig. 9.5). It was one of the country's most closely watched winegrowing experiments, and its success has been part of the revolution.

The environment here is not what might be expected of South Island: summers are long and sunny, and precipitation is moderate, averaging 30 inches annually. Montana, New Zealand's giant, invested heavily in the district during the mid-1970s, planting hundreds of acres of Müller-Thurgau, Riesling, and Sauvignon Blanc, and building a winery at Blenheim. Penfold and Corban soon followed, and contract growing expanded as well. Smaller wineries were established to produce the district's best, including Te Whare Ra and Hunter's Wines. This is an environment of great potential for Chardonnay and Pinot Noir, along with other red (Cabernet Sauvignon and Merlot) and white (Gewürztraminer, Sauvignon Blanc) varieties. The district's wines are favored by consumers and admired by specialists: Montana's (white) Blenheimer is a popular brand, and its Marlborough Cabernet Sauvignon has a lighter style that improves annually as the vines mature.[6]

The Marlborough District (also known as the Blenheim District) is the only real viticulture district on South Island, but winegrowing at nearby Nelson, and near Christchurch farther south, also has noteworthy results. The Nelson area in 1985 had just 100 acres of vineyards, virtually all owned by family wineries (Korepo, Neudorf, Seifried), and yielding premium wines. Noted among these are Korepo's Gamay Beaujolais and Neudorf's Cabernet Sauvignon, as well as Seifried's Rhine Riesling. Near Christchurch lie New Zealand's southernmost producing commercial vineyards of St. Helena Wine Estate, whose Pinot Noir has won awards. Lincoln College, a constituent agricultural college of the University of Canterbury (Christchurch), also has produced wine from experimental vineyards, but still this does not represent the full range of viticulture. Vines stand even in the hinterland of Dunedin, in Otago, and in time wine may be produced even here. This would mean that winegrowing would extend across the full latitudinal range of both islands, confirming potentials suggested by the map.

Among the countries of the Southern Hemisphere, New Zealand stands apart: it has neither Mediterranean nor steppe/desert climes, and it lies remote even from its nearest foreign market (North Island lies about as far from New South Wales as France does from Greece). But New Zealand has the *sine qua non*: growers whose skill and determination have unlocked its viticultural potential. Today New Zealand is conquering the hemisphere's last frontier, its winegrowers recording the final chapter in a saga of global diffusion that began with the first transatlantic voyages and the initial transequatorial plantings in Peru.

NOTES

Chapter 1

1. Population data and area figures in this book are based on statistics in *The Hammond Almanac* (Maplewood, N.J.: Hammond, 1983).

2. Among several cartographic representations of the globe's climates, the most successful has been the system devised by Vladimir Köppen in 1900 (revised by Rudolf Geiger in 1927). The terminology used here is based on this scheme.

Chapter 2

1. E. Hyams, *Dionysus: A Social History of the Wine Vine* (New York: Macmillan Co., 1965), p. 294.

2. Ibid., p. 296.

3. C. L. Leipoldt, *300 Years of Cape Wine* (Cape Town: Tafelberg, 1974), p. 5.

4. Ibid., p. 18.

5. F. de Jongh, *Encyclopaedia of South African Wine* (Durban: Butterworth, 1981), p. 31.

6. H. Fransen, *Groot Constantia* (Cape Town: The S. A. Cultural History Museum, 1978), p. 10.

7. G. Knox, *Estate Wines of South Africa* (Cape Town: David Philip, 1976), p. 24.

8. L. Evans, *Australian Complete Book of Wine* (Sydney: Paul Hamlyn, 1977), p. 15.

9. P. Saunders, *A Guide to New Zealand Wine* (Auckland: Wineglass Publishing, 1982), p. 7.

Chapter 3

1. *Tax and the Wine Grape Industries.* Report by the Senate Standing Committee on Trade and Commerce (Canberra, 1977), p. 194.

2. P. Saunders, "C.E.R. Leaves Opportunity with New Zealand Wine," *The New Zealand Wineglass* 20 (1982): p. 7.

Chapter 4

1. Asociacion de Exportadores y Embotelladores de Vinos, *Decreto de Subregiones de Origen* (Santiago: Ministerio de Agricultura, 1980), pp. 1–2.

2. Asociacion de Exportadores y Embotelladores de Vinos, *El Vino de Chile: Su Industria, Su Mercado* (Santiago, 1983), pp. 2, 3.

3. D. Jackson and D. Schuster, *Grape Growing and Wine Making* (Martinborough: Alister Taylor, 1981), p. 39.

4. Asociacion de Exportadores y Embotelladores de Vinos, *El Vino de Chile*, p. 7.

5. Hyams, *Dionysus: A Social History of the Wine Vine*, p. 301.

Chapter 5

1. C. Churchill, "Argentine Wines," *The Friends of Wine* 19, no. 2 (1982): 67.

2. Ibid., p. 69.

3. Instituto Nacional de Vitivinicultura, *Wine Growing in Argentina* (Mendoza, 1983), p. 11.

4. H. J. de Blij, *Wine: A Geographic Appreciation* (Totowa, N. J.: Rowman & Allanheld, 1983), p. 198.

5. E. Queyrat, *Guia de los Vinos Finos Argentinos* (Buenos Aires: Hachette, 1982), p. 46.

6. E. Queyrat, *Los Buenos Vinos Argentinos* (Buenos Aires: Hachette, 1983), p. 78.

Chapter 6

1. S. Sutcliffe, *André Simon's Wines of the World* (New York: McGraw-Hill, 1981), p. 554.

2. I. Falcade, *Influencia da Insolacao Sobre a Qualidade da Uva* (Porto Alegre: Universidade Federal do Rio Grande do Sul, Departamento de Geografia, 1981), p. 18.

3. J. Dickenson, "A Lot of Awful Wine in Brazil?" *Decanter* 4, no. 11 (1979): 82.

4. J. Osvaldo Albano do Amarante, *Vinhos do Brasil e do Mundo* (São Paulo: Summus, 1983), p. 140

5. Sutcliffe, *André Simon's Wines*, p. 555.

6. V. Trex, *Vinho: Um Santo Remedio* (Porto Alegre: Estado do Rio Grande do Sul, Assembleia Legislativa, n.d.), p. 19.

Chapter 7

1. C. W. Gregory, "Winegrowing in Zimbabwe," *Wines and Vines* 63, no. 9 (1982): 68–69.

2. J. D. Burger, *South Africa Viti-viniculture* (Stellenbosch: Viticultural and Oenological Research Institute, 1983), p. 10.

3. Data from a table in G. Knox, *Estate Wines of South Africa*, 2nd. ed. (Cape Town: David Philip, 1982), p. 28.

4. For details see C. J. Orffer, *Wine Grape Cultivars in South Africa* (Cape Town: Human and Rousseau, 1979), p. 96.

5. D. Hughes, "Foreword" in J. Platter, *New Book of South African Wines* (Delaire: John and Erica Platter, 1983), p. 5.

6. Orffer, *Wine Grape Cultivars*, pp. 30 and 76.

7. J. Kench, P. Hands, and D. Hughes, *The Complete Book of South African Wine* (Cape Town: Struik, 1983).

Chapter 8

1. L. Evans, "The Wines of Australia," in Sutcliffe, *André Simon's Wines*, p. 561.

2. A. Young, "Wine in Australia," *Chronicle* of the Society of Wine Educators, Summer 1982, p. 14.

3. F. Doherty, "Let's Get Our Labels Straight," *Wine and Spirit Buying Guide*, September 1983, p. 57.

4. M. Muschamp, *Wine and Winemakers of Australia* (Melbourne: Hill of Content, 1977), p. 50.

5. J. Parkinson, "Kaiser Stuhl: Their Late Picked Whites," *Wine and Spirit Buying Guide*, October 1981, p. 26.

6. M. Lake, *Cabernet: Notes of an Australian Wineman* (Adelaide: Rigby, 1977).

7. J. Halliday, "A Look Toward the Year 2000," *Wine and Spirit Buying Guide*, August 1983, p. 12. The predictions were made by Peter Dry.

8. Figures for the early 1970s are from L. Evans, *Australian Complete Book of Wine* (Sydney: Paul Hamlyn, 1977).

9. Ibid., p. 182.

10. J. Halliday, "Another Look Toward the Year 2000," *Wine and Spirit Buying Guide*, September 1983, p. 15.

11. Evans, *Wines of Australia*, p. 587.

12. Halliday, "Another Look Toward the Year 2000."

13. One of the partners, J. Halliday, is author of *The Wines and History of the Hunter Valley* (Sydney: McGraw-Hill, 1979).

14. Evans, *Australian Complete Book of Wine*, p. 81.

Chapter 9

1. Wine Institute of New Zealand, *Seventh Annual Report For Year Ending 30 June 1982* (Auckland, 1982), p. 46.

2. Saunders, *Guide to New Zealand Wine*, p. 7.

3. T. Frewen, *New Zealand Wine Annual 1983* (Auckland: Burnham, 1983), p. 3.

4. Ibid.

5. J. C. Graham, *Know Your New Zealand Wines* (Auckland: Collins, 1980), p. 73.

6. R. Small, "The Wines of New Zealand," in S. Sutcliffe, *André Simon's Wines*," p. 601.

INDEX